AF575513

# MY LIFE UNDER DEADLINE

*This book is dedicated to all the outstanding women music writers out there.*
*May you continue to put your heart and soul into your work.*

*We write to taste life twice: in the moment and in retrospection.*
—Anaïs Nin

# MY LIFE UNDER DEADLINE

*Frontline Dispatches from a Trailblazing Woman Music Writer*

**Cree McCree**

**Foreword by Rickie Lee Jones**

RARE BIRD
LOS ANGELES, CALIF.

THIS IS A GENUINE RARE BIRD BOOK

Rare Bird Books
6044 North Figueroa Street
Los Angeles, California 90042
rarebirdbooks.com



FIRST HARDCOVER EDITION



For more information, address:
Rare Bird Books Subsidiary Rights Department
6044 North Figueroa Street
Los Angeles, California 90042

Set in Minion Pro
Printed in the United States

10 9 8 7 6 5 4 3 2 1

Library of Congress Cataloging-in-Publication Data available upon request

# Contents


*Foreword* by Rickie Lee Jones 7
*Introduction—Music That Gives Me Magic and Why* 9

**I.**

*At the Crossroads: Deep Blues* 13
*Delta Force: The Blues According to John Campbell* 17
*John Campbell: One Believer* 22
*Have You Seen Mick Taylor, Baby, Standing in the Shadow?* 26
*Delta Blues* 30
*Son Thomas Makes a Ladyhead* 34
*Raiders of the Lost Spark* 37
*The Genre-Busting Brilliance of Clarence "Gatemouth" Brown* 41
*BB King: The King of the Blues on the State of the Blues* 44
*John Lee Hooker: The King of the Boogie* 46
*Obituary: Chris Whitley (1960–2005)* 54
*Memphissippi Sounds: Blues at a 21st Century Crossroads* 56
*The Many Lives of Little Freddie King, New Orleans Blues Royalty* 59

**II.**

*Soul Sisters...* 62
*Blazing Away with Marianne Faithfull* 70
High Times *Greats: Janis Joplin* 83
*Jessie Mae Hemphill: Hangin' with 'The She-Wolf of Como"* 94
*Seven Deadly Sins: Lust—Pamela Des Barres* 104
*Malevitus Celebrates While We Incinerate* 109
*Divine: Laughter and Lust in the Dust* 112
*PJ Harvey: Is This Desire? (Island Records)* 125
*Lucinda Williams: Live Show Review, Jazz Fest 2007* 127
*Rickie Lee Jones Puts Down Roots in New Orleans* 129
*Rickie Lee Jones: The Duchess of Coolsville is Back* 138
*Rickie Lee Jones: Of Intimacy and American Standards* 152

**III.**

*Sweet Home Louisiana* 157
*Loup Garou: The Godfathers of New York Zydeco* 161
*Francis X. Pavy: Zydeco Picasso* 166
*Dr. John Ain't for Turistas* 170

*Jam Today: Boozoo Chavis* 173
*Bas Clas* 177
*Dr. John Mined Spiritual Connections* 179
*Dancing on Sacred Ground* 181
*Smith Diaries: Back in New Orleans* 183
*The Chance Music of New Orleans' Kidd Jordan* 185
*Shuttered SideBar in New Orleans Continues...* 188
*All You Need is Roux: A Personal Jazz Fest Retrospective* 191
*Wendell Brunious Named First Musical Director...* 194
*Harrison's "Passion" Mixes Hard Swing, Trap Hip-Hop* 197
*New Orleans Jazz & Heritage Festival: A Bounteous Banquet* 200

**IV.**
*Droppin' Some NYC: The '90s Jam Band Scene* 202
*Blues Traveler: Blues for the Road* 207
*It's OK to Be Happy* 209
*Jam Today: And the Lord Said Reclaim Rock 'n' Roll...* 215
*Jam Today* 219
*Jam Today: My First Dead Show* 222
*The Iliad and the Mosh Pit* 226
*Rolling with the Spin Doctors* 231
*Live Rounds: Jono Manson Band, Nightingale, New York City* 237
*In the Limelight: The Visual Ecstasy of New York City...* 239

**V.**
*Declaration of Independents—Introduction...* 250
*Bill Hicks: Comedy for the Head* 253
*The Eye of Texas: Roky Erickson* 257
*The Gospel According to Blind Joe Death: John Fahey...* 264
*Nick Cave: Murder Ballads (Mute)* 276
*Native Son: Tom Bee* 279
*Link Wray: Shim Sham Club, New Orleans* 282
*X: Shim Sham Club, New Orleans* 284
*Sonic Youth/Descension/Prolapse* 286
*Kelley Deal 6000: Deal Stories of the Highway Patrol* 289
*Golden Palominos: They Shoot Horses, Don't They?* 292

*Afterword* 295
*Acknowledgements* 297

# Foreword

*By Rickie Lee Jones*

THERE ARE TWO KINDS of journalists in rock 'n' roll. The first, usually male but not exclusively, sits in his room and writes about records, about the songs he has heard, and about the kind of people he pursues when he ventures out of his room and into the streets. He might be a skinny ok lookin' guy with no particular personality, or he might be as charismatic as the men in the bands he wishes he could join. Not likely but maybe. He lives, like all of us, through the music and then, as the music takes second place to the men who make the music, through them. Their sexual conquests, their absolute unaccountability seems ideal to the adolescent boy. Just rollin' through life with no particular empathy, just the drum and the bass and an occasional chorus. This kind of writer can usually get a job writing about music on a monthly basis. But the disconnect between reality and his pen grows ever wider. His life follows his work.

The other kind of journalist is the one whose work follows their lifestyle. They jump into the van with the band. They rent a car and follow the music from town to town, as Cree did. They learn about the music, the spirit, the reason this stuff exists. They immerse themselves in the life of musicians to be the bullhorn of rock 'n' roll. They are holy. Rare and equally as worn and wise as the musicians they write about.

I met Cree McCree in New Orleans through my friend Lexie Montgomery, one of those individuals whom almost everyone in my circle knows, or knows of, and we are curated by her happenstance. We are like-minded. We are a lifestyle. In fact, I can pick two people I know and promise they most likely know, or know of, everyone I have ever known, no matter what country or decade. Cree knew Lexie and Lexie said, "Cree is Good." So, I agreed to meet with Cree for an interview.

Cree is from the old days, the beginning of "punk" and the wilds of jambands. She is one of the early rock journalists whose confidence grew as her integrity solidified and she helped us understand the music and the musicians whose work was revelatory to her. She threw herself into the work. She became rock 'n' roll. She followed the bands; she lived their lives.

The stories she publishes here show this diversity. A life chosen, a song revealed. How absolutely authentic Cree is to rock.

Back in 1982, I spent every day of my life in New Orleans hanging with a couple of black singers, following them home or meeting them at the club, quietly studying. One was an old black man who sang at a bar, I don't even remember his name. The other, a young guy who played piano for a few bucks in the French Quarter. That was James Booker. He's famous now but he wasn't then. I followed the footsteps I knew to be inspirational. So did Cree. We are devoted to the craft, not just the writing, not just the singing of the melody, but the life, the living that creates the sticky substance of music.

I am proud of Cree and introduce her work—and her—to you here, not as a relic of the great days of rock 'n' roll, but as a living study of womanhood. It is not for fame we come, but to say we were a part of that great machine, the music of our time that ripples today into so many money-making machines. Cree McCree has been devoted to getting the word out about those acts unheard by the larger world, and to making sure those of whom she speaks are rightly understood. I am grateful for her insistence that music editors pay attention to my later work.

Cree McCree, as much the story as the storyteller. A woman of her time, devoted to the pursuit of rock 'n' blues and rolling with the punches. The Great American Song.

Rickie Lee Jones
New Orleans, 2024

# Introduction

## *Music That Gives Me Magic and Why*

### *New York City, June 1991*

Several eons ago, back in the spring of '89, I decided I was outta here. Oh-so-cool New York, with its velvet-roped prisons posing as palaces and its sad pseudo scene of jerk-off "art rock" and jackhammer noise bands, was clearly no place for a hot boogie queen whose spirit was withering from the lack of Real Music. So I said screw this town, I'm moving to New Orleans.

Then two things happened, almost simultaneously, that not only changed my mind, but fundamentally changed my life.

The first was named John Campbell, and the wholly unholy holy spirits he was raising on his 1934 National Steel guitar, over in the corner of a little Vietnamese restaurant called Monsoon, revealed the deepest, most secret recesses of the blues to my own body and soul.

The second was a young jam band called Blues Traveler, who rocked me so far out and rolled me so far in—over at this funky little dive called Nightingale where they played like there was no tomorrow—that I was bathed in an aura of radiant light.

John Campbell taught me that a blues song is a victory. Blues Traveler taught me to trust in trust. And lo and behold, miracles began to happen in New York City.

Just this week, in the span of a single day, I toasted John Campbell's publishing deal while the final mixes from his Elektra debut album raised the hair on my neck; listened to rough cuts from Blues Traveler's second A&M disc, *Travelers and Thieves*, which is a monster in the making; got word that, starting this Monday, Joe Flood's fabulous "Miss Fabulous"—the unofficial anthem of the whole bar-band scene—goes national as HBO's summer-season theme; and watched the Dreyer Brothers resurrect the spirit of the old Lonestar Cafe.

So here's to all the true believers, the Real Music people of New York City, those who came before and those who followed. You know who you are.

—"Jam Today," *Downtown*, June 12, 1991

*New Orleans, LA, July 1, 2024*

My, what heady times those were! And I was right in the middle of it all, scrawling notes in the little mini-composition books I carried in my vest pocket and pulled out whenever an epiphany hit me, as it often did back then, almost invariably on the dance floor. I tried to capture the magic pulsing through my groin, which animated every part of my body and fired up all my synapses, which was like catching fireflies in a jar, but worked surprisingly well most of the time. Though my half-drunken scrawls were often illegible, the very act of writing them down seared the memories into my brain so I could conjure them for readers. This was definitely *not* the usual m.o. for my fellow music writers, mostly male, who generally stood in the back of clubs diligently scribbling down set lists.

At the time I wrote the 1991 excerpt that opens this intro, I was riding high. After several years as a freelance writer for TV magazines and celebrity slicks, I'd just been given my own no-holds-barred music column in *Downtown*, an alternative weekly, which I dubbed "Jam Today." Defying the Red Queen's dictum in *Alice Through the Looking Glass*—"jam yesterday, jam tomorrow but never jam today"—I embraced the popular Britspeak term for my own m.o.: living for the moment. And *My Life Under Deadline,* when I was filing multiple stories weekly, proceeded at a breakneck pace. I had another weekly music column in *Downtown Express*, and was also on the rise at *Details* magazine, where founding editor Annie Flanders gave me carte blanche to write about my heart's desire: music that gives me magic and why.

*Details* enabled me to introduce both Blues Traveler and John Campbell to a national audience, and helped me score some genuine scoops. I was the first journalist to interview Marianne Faithfull after she got fully sober and staged a grand personal comeback at St. Ann's church in Brooklyn. And after years of stonewalling the press, longtime Rolling Stones guitarist Mick Taylor finally told his side of the story about leaving the "World's Greatest Rock & Roll Band" to me for an interview in *Details* shortly after he moved to New York City.

During the 1990s, I also became a longtime contributing editor at *High Times*, where I got to get stoned with bands I loved and scored some plum assignments: a cover story on Janis Joplin that breathed new life into her legend; and the first-ever comeback "interview" with 13th Floor Elevators founder and resident genius Roky Erickson, who was only beginning to emerge from his pot-bust incarceration at Rusk State Hospital. I even managed to persuade *Spin* magazine, the alterna-rock bible, to bankroll a trip to the Delta and Mississippi hill country, where

I took a deep dive into the living blues of little-known but foundational artists for a big spread in *Spin*.

So as a working music writer, I was on as much of a roll as many of the musicians I was documenting. And though it didn't last, I fully embraced a time when anything seemed possible, and sometimes even the completely improbable came to pass.

Most improbable of all? This self-proclaimed "hot boogie queen," who wrote so disdainfully in "Jam Today" about New York's "sad pseudo scene of "art rock" and jackhammer noise bands," ended up meeting (and later marrying) Donald Miller, the founding guitarist of the kamikaze snuff-jazz trio Borbetomagus. Which would have made me eat my dismissive words if Donald hadn't been even more disdainful of the "art rock" poseurs and self-styled noise meisters in his own milieu. And, perhaps not surprisingly, that fateful odd-couple conjunction in a dive bar on Second Avenue on Thanksgiving night in 1992 opened my ears to a far wider range of music that gives me magic.

My infamous jackhammer jibe aside, I'm proud of the fact that, thirty or forty years later, every word I wrote rings as true to me today as it did at the time I wrote them, and conjures up exactly what it was like to "be here now" then.

Whether I was covering the wild melee that ensued during a Prolapse/Descension/Sonic Youth show in London, hangin' with drone-blues legend Jessie Mae Hemphill, the She-Wolf of Como, or giving a bone-close listen to Nick Cave's eviscerating *Murder Ballads*, the stories I spun under deadline have aged as well as my favorite songs.

I'm also thrilled to report that *My Life Under Deadline*—which had a literal double meaning when I'd been invaded by a mega-aggressive Stage IV cancer and was told to "get your papers in order"—isn't running out the clock just yet. I got an 11th hour reprieve when my latest scans showed "no evidence of cancer." And while I'll need to be on guard against recurrences, I'm making the most of my current get-out-of-jail-free card, and continue to soldier on as a music writer well into my late '70s. It's also given me the luxury to dig even deeper into my archives and unearth a few hidden gems dating back to my heyday on the cusp of the '90s.

My 1983 how-to book *Flea Market America: A Guide to Flea Enterprise* (now in its second printing) helped me jumpstart my forty-year side gig as a freelance writer who filed countless articles under deadline. But I had nothing to show for it but bulging files of old clips until I decided to turn them into a book of stories. And in the process of compiling my best music writing, I realized it was every bit as compelling as a good fiction writer's collection of short stories. Even if you don't know who John Campbell or

Son Thomas or Boozoo Chavis was, or who Kelley Deal or Bas Clas or Francis X. Pavy is, they are all compelling characters. And who they were at the moment in time I wrote about them comes vividly to life in these pages.

Which is the most any writer can ask of her work.

—Cree McCree, New Orleans, LA, July 1st, 2024

# I.

## At the Crossroads: Deep Blues

### *Introduction: My Long, Circuitous Journey to the Roots of the Blues*

MICK JAGGER TAUGHT ME how to dance, as anyone who's seen me strut my stuff on the dancefloor can attest. Like many other smalltown Yankees in the early '60s, I was first introduced to the blues by the Rolling Stones, who mined the motherlode of music by black artists from the deep south and its northern outpost in Chicago by listening to "race records" far more available in England than in Jim Crow America.

The Stones dug deeper into the blues than most of their fellow British invaders, pitting their bad-boy cockiness against The Beatles' teeny-bopper appeal and recording tracks by real-deal heavyweights like Willy Dixon, Rufus Thomas, Chuck Berry, Bo Diddley and Muddy Waters (who wrote the song that gave the band its name). And though it wasn't until years later, after I moved to New Orleans that I heard soul queen Irma Thomas sing her original R&B chart-topping version of "Time Is On My Side," I vividly recall blasting the Stones' cover of "Time" to ease my pain after a high school crush dumped me, and wailing "time, time, time is on my side" while I preened and postured like Mick.

My long, circuitous journey to the roots of the blues eventually led to close encounters with Stones' lodestars like John Lee Hooker and BB King when I was living in New York City, where I also bonded with Mick Taylor two decades after I watched him play his first gig with the Stones at their free Hyde Park concert honoring the late Brian Jones. But it was my much-older first husband, the flamenco, blues and folk guitarist Rolf Cahn, who helped me bushwack my path to the deep-blues crossroads, which he discovered only after making several migrations himself.

A Jewish refugee from Hitler's Germany, Rolf fled with his parents to Detroit and went back to wreak revenge behind enemy lines in the OSS (the Office of Strategic Services, a precursor to the CIA), following a detour to study Chinese in Berkeley, where he met his K'ang Ju Fu master and first picked up the guitar. After the war, he traveled to Spain to study flamenco in Andalucia, a gypsy enclave steeped in Moorish and Jewish music from a long Arab occupation, and bought a custom-made nylon string guitar from the revered luthier Esteso in Madrid. Later made famous by the flamenco maestro Paco de Lucia, the Esteso became Rolf's unlikely passport to acoustic American blues, primarily a steel string domain.

One of the early instigators of the blues and folk revival of the late '50s and early '60s, Rolf was a regular at Club 47 in Cambridge, one of the first northern venues to feature black musicians from the US South. He was also a major force in the revival's West Coast enclave. Rolf played the legendary Ash Grove in LA and co-founded the Cabale in Berkeley, which hosted a firmament of ascended blues masters like Mississippi John Hurt, Jesse Fuller and Elizabeth Cotten and Lightnin' Hopkins.

Lightnin' never played the Bay Area while Rolf and I lived there; the Cabale closed nearly a decade before we met. But Rolf introduced me to the genius of Lightnin' Hopkins, the man he called King of the Blues, and tapped the primal source of his power in "The Time The King Anointed J.C," a blues fable he told to introduce a Lightnin' performance on KPFA radio in 1963:

*"What was the blues? The deepest, darkest forces the man of the blues has confronted are not depravity, and not degeneracy, and not indignity, and not brutality and not barbarism. The deepest, darkest force of them all was the Boss, Death itself. And so a man looked at Death and returned from that terrible journey and gave Death his final, despairing defiance. The blues was the strength to look at Death, knowing you are of Death, and then turn back to Life and say, yeah! Here I am! Alive! The Adalucians of flamenco spoke magnificently of the same journey."*

Many years later, in New York, John Campbell, another Lightnin' devotee, summed it up more succinctly: "The blues song is a victory." And that victory was profoundly personal. As a young Texas/Louisiana bluesman, Campbell was gifted with Lightnin's old National steel resonator—which he almost relinquished (twice!)–as you'll learn in the opening piece of the blues section, which almost by chance has Lightnin' as a throughline even though I never saw him play.

Rolf did introduce me to other Cabale alumni like Sonny Terry and Brownie Magee, who made magic together on stage but hated each other with such a vengeance they had separate dressing rooms written into their contracts as a rider, and we had to pay our respects to them individually backstage. We even had the Chambers Brothers over for dinner shortly after Rolf's oldest son Jesse stopped playing drums with the Brothers, who traditionally used young white drummers. (Jesse's mom, Barbara Dane, was a formidable artist in her own right who played with the Chambers and other blues cats like Willy Dixon and Memphis Slim.) Visiting eminencias from Spain also passed through our house, and introduced me to various forms of flamenco, including the deepest of them all: Soleares, the wrenching cry from the heart of duende (a heightened state of emotion, expression, and authenticity, often described as a powerful, almost supernatural force that a performer can access) at the crossroads of life and death.

Though I never mastered the high art of flamenco footwork, during my years with Rolf, I became an avid improvisational blues dancer. But it was only long after we split up, and I hit New York City on the cusp of the second great blues revival of the late '80 and early '90s, that I took a deep dive into the source and traveled south to Mississippi and began writing about everything everywhere all at once, to borrow a phrase from the recent hit movie.

My *Everything Everywhere All At Once* whirlwind started very close to home, when I moved into a house in the West Village directly across the street from Monsoon, a Vietnamese restaurant on the corner of Sullivan and Houston, which morphed into Crossroads after John Campbell blew into town, threw down the gauntlet with his National steel, and began attracting devotees to midnight masses. It felt like the center of the universe in a burgeoning New York City blues community that encompassed both the old and new Tramps, Dan Lynch, the Under Acme, Rodeo Bar and both the uptown and downtown Lonestar Cafe, among others. It was also an after-hours hotspot where sooner or later you met everyone you needed to meet.

Crossroads was where I first crossed paths with John Allison, son of blues and jazz piano great Mose Allison, whose weekly live gigs at Fat Tuesday's we caught several times. Still a dear friend, John became my ambassador to his native Mississippi while he was shooting the documentary *It Hurts Me Too,* and introduced me to many of the first-generation blues artists I profiled for *Spin* and other magazines.

Among them: Jessie Mae Hemphill, the "She-Wolf of Como," who shared her bed with me and a menagerie of poodles in her trailer in Como, Mississippi, and was a fiercely independent blues woman. ("My songs come just like somebody was writin' 'em on the wall, and I got a whole lot of power that I ain't even used yet.") And James "Son" Thomas, whose blues cut as close to the bone as the hollow-eyed skulls he sculpted from hill country clay harvested by his grave-digger son. ("You don't just tum into a skull all at once. You lies in the ground a good while before you get to be that skull.")

The Crossroads era came to a screeching halt with the untimely death of John Campbell in 1993, when his star was rising and the future seemed so bright you had to wear sunglasses, like John always did. But my journey continued, most memorably in 1995, when Donald and I spent our honeymoon in North Carolina with Tim and Denise Duffy, whose Music Maker Relief Foundation resurrected the long-dormant careers of Piedmont blues royalty like Guitar Gabriel and snake-handling diva Willa Mae Butler, the Wild Enchantress of the all-black tent show circuit of the 1930s. To celebrate our wedding, the Duffys broke out mason jars of top shelf apple moonshine and took us to rowdy way-off-the-grid drink houses you won't find in any guidebooks to white blues-buff meccas like Mississippi's juke-joints.

In the stories that follow, you'll meet these and many other ascended masters of what came to be known as "The Blues" in this country: Artists who, like the flamenco gypsies of Andalucia, have looked Death in the face, sometimes cavorted with him and even caressed him like a lover, then returned to take a victory lap with Life before they, too, give up the ghost and join the mighty spirits who came before them. Given the chance to ask the almost-mythical Robert Johnson just one question before he passed to the other side, John Campbell responded to this writer without hesitation:

*"Will you take me with you when you go?"*

# Delta Force: The Blues According to John Campbell

***Details*, April 1990**

STRANGE AND MYSTERIOUS THINGS happen when John Campbell plays the blues. Even before his thumb pick flies across the room, when the strings of his 1952 Gibson are not yet stained with blood and the battered old National steel is still nestled in its case with a mojo of John the Conqueror root, when he's still feeling the crowd with his fingers like he was easing a woman into bed, the air tingles with icy heat. Then, one by one, the packed house at New York's CrossRoads begins riding his roadhouse revival train, stoking the engine with whistles, moans, hoots, shudders and the rattle of dancing bones. By the time Campbell tunes up the National and slips the bottleneck slide over his ring finger, we're ready for deep penetration.

Storming the gates of heaven and hell, his guitar takes on a life of its own, and graves crack open. Lightnin' flashes in the brilliance of a single note that hovers in space then bends time backwards; the Wolf howls between the lines of a phrase that twists a caress into sudden ferocity; and Robert Johnson comes to call as Campbell turns his own soul inside out, transforming his demons on the angel wings of song. And we who bear witness are participants in this magic, this shared celebration of ritual, possession and the triumph of the life force over the condition of living.

"The blues songs is a victory," Campbell says, when we sit down to address such questions. A long, tall Texan with Louisiana roots, a riverboat gambler's points-and-pompadour style and translucent skin that seems to glow in the dark, he could have stepped intact out of a whole other era. "It's like grabbin' that thing by the throat, wrestlin' with it, lookin' it square in the eye, throwin' it down on the ground and stompin' on it till it turns into dancin'. If we get ahold of that feelin', man, I'm gonna ride it just as long as I can. I want us to hit that place of church. If you can't get that, you might as well stay home."

I'm fortunate enough to live across the street from Campbell's church, and over the past year I've watched the congregation swell from a few true believers to a cathedral-size crowd; dozens of supplicants are turned away at the door because there's simply no space. "Johnny's shaped this place, and we've pretty much molded it to fit around his music," says Jonathan Bass, who owned what was then a Vietnamese restaurant called Monsoon when Campbell first began playing here, and who's now the temple guard at the newly-named CrossRoads. "We were both going for that vibe, that magic, and I always had the sensation that I was a part of his music. But this is his room. He built it, and he's responsible for its success."

In 1989, Campbell's success began to embrace the wider world as well. Already acclaimed in Europe, he played solo acoustic for 10,000 people at Belgium's Peer Festival during his last tour, and was the only performer to receive two encores on a bill that included BB King and Otis Clay; his first album, *A Man and His Blues*, produced by blues guitar great Ronnie Earl for West Germany's Crosscut Records, hit number seven on the German pop charts last summer, beating out Paul McCartney and Stevie Ray Vaughan; and here in the US he was nominated for a W. C. Handy award (the blues world's Grammys) as "Best Traditional Male Blues Artist of the Year" alongside such old masters as John Lee Hooker. Now he stands on the crossroads of stardom, trying to divine his path from a myriad of tour and record offers: "If it feels right, and it means something, then I'll do it."

It's a critical juncture for this Texas country boy who both lost and found himself in New York City, and his story has never been told. He tells it to me—in a marathon series of interviews at the bar, in his Greenwich Village sublet and during an after-hours session in which the Great Campbello is revealed—precisely because I'm not a disinterested observer. His music is etched in my bones, and when I dance, I become what he calls his "hell-raiser"—the person who, in the blues counterpart of flamenco, helps conjure the spirits in both the musician and the audience.

Music is essentially notes within time," Campbell says after a CrossRoads gig. Today is his birthday—a date he shares with the legendary Leadbelly, along with his birthplace of Shreveport, Louisiana—and he's primed to hog-tie this thought while we cab it over to a friend's apartment for some predawn pool shooting.

"What makes a Lightnin' Hopkins or a Robert Petey Williams is what they choose to do with those notes. There's a process that occurs between the fingers and the mind and the heart, and that's what makes the clock on the wall stop or turn backwards. The stuff that's drug behind you gives a note its meaning—those crusty layers of history that led you to the point of making that decision. Let me put it this way: It ain't my first night out."

A hairline scar bisects Campbell's brow—which is higher than the heels of his lizard-flame cowboy boots—and curves into a crescent under his right eye, which has the inner-directed focus of near blindness. Robert Johnson, the almost mythic Thirties blues prophet, had a similar affliction in the same eye. Though Johnson's scars were the result of a knife fight instead of a head-on car crash, each had his face split open, and the mask and what it veiled were never quite the same.

"When the accident happened, I met the blues," says Campbell, who was contemplating a parallel career as a pool hustler until his vision was shattered at the age of fifteen. "I'd been playin' guitar since I was three, playin' professionally since thirteen, and I was into the blues because I liked the way the guitar sounded. But when I lost my eye, the kiddin' around was over. Suddenly those notes, and those songs, meant somethin' they didn't mean before. Shortly after that I ended up quittin' school."

Early on in his "couch-circuit" era, Campbell holed up behind a record store, where promo copies of the latest releases from Shreveport's Jewel Records were fifty cents a pop: Lightnin', John Lee Hooker, Muddy Waters, Howlin' Wolf. "I'd put on ten records and play with them all fuckin' night till my fingers bled. Sold blood to buy guitar strings. The blues spoke to me, and I didn't have any choice about it." During the Day-Glo psychedelia of the sixties, he was living in the sepia tones of the forties, crisscrossing the cusp of Texas and Louisiana. "I'd take a Greyhound down to an under-the-tunnel gig, then go to an after-hours house party where they'd give me a pack of Kools, a half-pint of tequila and five-bucks, then hop another bus and go play the kind of roadhouse where you buy two beers: one to drink and one to throw. I did lots of field parties, where we'd sit on the back of a pickup with the barbecue smokin'. I always looked at myself as 'the guitar player' in a very tribal sense."

Devotees will hear tributes to many artists fused into his blues, from the late Elmore James to Gatemouth Brown, who taught him about dynamics: "He said, 'Boy, you play real good, but you're makin' that thing holler all the time. If you don't make it whisper, no one's gonna pay attention to you.'" Now, listening to him whisper in the firelight, hearing the butterfly flutter of his fingers suddenly snap like the pool balls echoing from the back-room game, watching every note play directly on his face, which twists with pain, then smiles at a private joke between him and his guitar, I remember what he said about his true spiritual mentor, Lightnin' Hopkins: "Everything he was playin' was happenin' at that moment. Whatever came into his mind, whatever he felt, was a conversation between him and his instrument, and whoever was there with him."

The song of this particular moment is "Hidden Charms," and it sets the stage for the Great Campbello, who's about to perform some after-hours magic with a pool cue. But first he tingles my spine with the final chapter of a yet-unfinished tale. Campbell's soul mate is his "trash can with strings"—his 1934 National steel guitar—and the saga of their relationship is the heart of his story.

This much I already know. In 1982, shortly after Lightnin' died, Campbell went to see a fortune-teller. He'd been saving to buy a handmade guitar, and he asked her if it was really his instrument. The cards said no; you won't get that guitar. But you will get a legacy. Next day, he hightails it to the Rockin' Robin in Houston, and plays a lot of different Nationals. He lingers awhile on a trashed-out relic, but finally opts for a loud, shiny mint one. "Next morning, I call the guy and say I made a mistake. I want that real old beat-up one. I drove 180 miles in my white Cadillac Coupe DeVille, with my German Shepherd dog, stopped at a Dairy Queen to buy her an ice cream. I go in to swap guitars, and the guy says, 'Now that it's a done deal, I'm gonna tell you the story. Lightin' played that guitar, and 'Amazing Grace' was played on it at his funeral. It's not for sale, but I heard you play it and you can have it.'"

Now he tells me what happened several years later, when he followed his heart to New York, only to split up with the woman who drew him here. "My spirit was dampened, and suddenly here I am in the most high-tech city in the world, playin' acoustic blues guitar. I felt like my music got totally swallowed. I'm kinda ashamed to say this, but I lost myself. I felt like it had come and gone for me." He sighs so deeply I can feel the shards of his pain in my own lungs. "I just went crazy, man. I took my guitars to a music store and traded them in for a fancy modern Fender.

"I immediately realized I'd made a mistake. I went rushin' back, and then man said I still have the Gibson but the National's gone. I felt like I had sold my soul, that I'd done an injustice to those who'd gone before me. I'd lost my talismans. I ended up sellin' the Gibson, and for nine months, I didn't even have a guitar." Campbell took a day job at Matt Umanov's guitar shop, a gathering place in the Village for acoustic and electric aficionados. There he developed a friendship with a colleague of Umanov's Steve Uhrik. Over a couple of beers, he told him the whole Lightnin' guitar story. Turns out Uhrik was the guy who bought that guitar.

"Time goes by, and I start kinda findin' myself again. Once a day Steve walks in and says, you know, I think it's time for you to have that National back. Same day, I got a call from a friend who found a 1952 Gibson in Louisiana made the month and year I was born, and he shipped it up to me. Same night, I got a call from Germany and got a record contract. Steve fine-tuned both guitars, he tapped them with the bones and touched them with the water, and I ain't strayed since. And I never will. I walked to the edge of the abyss, hung one foot over, and I got a second chance."

It's one chance only in the pool room, where Campbell's step takes on a swagger and his voice transforms into the honey-dipped tones of the Great

Campbello. As he sets up a Willie Mosconi triple-bank trick shot, shuffling the balls in the rack till the rhythm of numbers and colors feels just right, divining the rack's precise placement by moving it back and forth like the table was a Ouija board, he sets us up too. "I ain't played pool ten times in the last twenty years, and I ain't even gonna bank it one time to get in the mood. I can't stand rehearsin'."

I'm reminded that he's never rehearsed with bass player Gordon Wands and drummer David Hansen, who meld seamlessly into the Saturday-night sessions when he electrifies the acoustic and lets his mood take the music where it will. As Wands puts it earlier tonight, "I'm not playin' the fuckin' songs. I'm playin' him." Now, after balancing the rack on top of the one ball, Campbell gives us the bottom line: "For me to make this shot, there has to be somethin' at risk. It has to mean somethin'. And it's Wands, his "personal spiritual advisor," who raises the stakes, "If you don't make this shot, we're gonna steal your boots."

The room is as tense as an unresolved chord as he leans over the table and shoots. The cue ball glides into the triangular arc of the triple-bank, then kisses the one ball aside and slips under the rack to nestle inside, exactly the way he called it. It's a whisper shot, quietly elegant, and for a moment time is suspended in silence until the chord resolves in spontaneous applause. Then the Great Campbello disappears inside the shadows of his personal history, as John Campbell ponders his deepest roots.

We're discussing the elusive Robert Johnson, who in a brief life span of twenty-seven years left his mark on every blues-influenced artist to follow, from his '30s peers to Eric Clapton and the Rolling Stones. Defying the existing cultural mores, Johnson affirmed his personal power, and his "Crossroad Blues" is as much a pact with God as it is with the Devil. His life remains shrouded in mystery, so I ask Campbell for illumination: If he could ask Robert Johnson just one question, what would it be?

He deliberates awhile, leaning back in his chair, fingering the talisman of his thunderbird bolo tie. "Well, if I'd been there, and I could have asked him a question," he says at last, speaking in a near-whisper, "it would have been: Will you take me with you when you go?"

## John Campbell: One Believer

### *OffBeat*, November 1991

Shadows dance in liquid pools of light spilled by candles, dozens of them, burning steadily into this midsummer night. Ancient skulls stare down at us with hollow-eyed serenity. And though we're hundreds of miles from Bayou St. John and the nearest body of water is the East River bordering Manhattan, the air is as thickly ghosted as an Anne Rice novel.

A haze of frankincense wraps smoky tendrils around the wrought-iron balcony, then drifts its lazy canopy across the high-ceilinged living room below, where John Campbell has summoned a few "one believers" to unveil cuts from his Elektra debut album, *One Believer*.

Among those who have answered the call of "The Count"—lean as a shadow with a face cut as close to the bone as the demons he conjures on his 1934 National steel guitar—is a fellow Louisianian, Jazz Fest honcho Quint Davis. An early believer who bequeathed Campbell a vicious pair of python cowboy boots along the blues man's winding, sometimes tortuous path to the mountaintop, Davis has, as always, come bearing gifts: final mixes from Aaron Neville's then-unreleased *Warm Your Heart*, produced by Linda Ronstadt.

So, it's Aaron who provides the prelude to tonight's program, which is somehow fitting. For though Campbell—a Shreveport native who crisscrossed the cusp of Texas and Louisiana during his roadhouse years—has long cast a tall shadow as a Texas bluesman, on *One Believer*, he also walks the voodoo edge. Soon, the swamp gas of such Campbell tracks as the wickedly serpentine "Wild Streak" and the midnight-hour mojos of the "Voodoo Edge" itself will be rising around us. But now, as the moon glances off the street lights of Second Avenue, the stage is still being set.

Davis plays one last Neville cut, "Angola Bound," which features Dr. John on keyboards as well as an ominously clanking chain Mac literally wrenched from a parking lot guard rail. And this, too, is fitting, for the good Doctor not only lent his considerable presence to the bayou invocations of "Broken Spell," Campbell's European-single release, but mentored the entire project throughout its gestation. "Angola Bound" also foreshadows Campbell's own relentless takes on the underbelly of the American

Dream: the moody, elegiac "World of Trouble," where "the busses don't run on the wrong side of paradise"; and the chill-your-heart "Tiny Coffin," which refuses to flinch from the daily news nightmare of innocents slaughtered in crack-war crossfire.

But all of this is still to be revealed. Now, as we move into the witching hour, it's The Count's turn to show-and-tell. He pops "Devil in My Closet" into the tape deck, with an anticipatory gleam in his eye as he shoots a sidelong glance at Davis, who's heard none of this new material before.

Davis' face lights up as the rhythm section—bassist Richard Cousins and Lee "The Reptile" Spath on skins—kicks in with the implacable charge of Joe Louis entering the ring. He glows even brighter when Campbell's guitar pounced on a minor-four that comes out of nowhere, then slithers around Jimmy Pugh's snaky Hammond organ lines. And when Campbell's growling-in-tongues vocals crescendo on the final chorus—"I'VE GOT THE DEVIL IN MY CLOSET AND THE WOLF IS AT MY DOOR"—he breaks into an incredulous grin.

"That voice," Davis murmurs. "You can't tell if it's black or white, old or young, or if it's even from this planet—where the hell's that *voice* coming from?"

Campbell just beams enigmatically, and segues the tape into the almost excruciatingly slow, steel slide of "Take Me Down," which bends time backwards before letting out the "suicide clutch" to careen across East Texas. Accelerating toward oblivion, the guitar drives mercilessly into its own abyss, taking no prisoners en route.

Davis does a double take, then lets out a whoop. "Pistols at dawn! Goddam! It's those pistols at dawn!"

And both he and Campbell dissolve into déjà vu laughter.

"The first time I ever saw John play," Davis explains after he catches his breath, "was at a blues festival at a golf-driving range in New Orleans, on a small stage, up against a fence near a bayou where they have real alligators. He was sitting in a chair, cross-legged, with his old Gibson acoustic guitar going through this beat-up Fender amplifier. I was stopped dead in my tracks; I had never heard such a sound. I said to him, 'Shit, that guitar through that amp sounds like pistols at dawn!'"

"That meant a lot to me, comin' from Quint," adds Campbell, who was soon thereafter hired by Davis as artistic director for the newly-created Benson & Hedges blues festivals (whose stages he continues to levitate in performance). "Quint gave me a shot when him and ten other people knew who John Campbell was. And I'll tell you what, there was a time when the only place I had to sleep was a hotel room that he bought me."

Times have changed, and those pistols-at-dawn are rapidly becoming the shot heard 'round the world. From its initial review in Billboard, which aptly dubbed *One Believer* "the first great blues album of the '90s," the magnetic forcefield generated by both the album and the sadly-inspired, tent show-revivalism of Campbell's live performance has grown exponentially. (His current touring band includes bassist Jimmy Pettit and drummer Davis McClarty, two Joe Ely vets who kicked serious butt on several of the album tracks, and electric guitarist Zonder Kennedy, who co-wrote some of the cuts.)

And though Campbell—a lone-wolf itinerant for most of his twenty-five-year career—remains the magnetic core of that forcefield, an entire constellation of "one believers" helped fire up the booster rockets that launched him into orbit. As he puts it, "I'm real proud of this album, but I ain't braggin' on me. I'm braggin' on the work all these people did."

People like BB King, his personal manager/guardian angel, who heretofore had served solely Dr. John; Elektra's Peter Lubin, who was so compelled by his music that he not only signed him put co-produced the album; song-writing partner and producer Dennis Walker, who, like Lubin, helped launch Robert Cray's career and remains Cray's longtime collaborator; and—along with all the other musicians and mentors like Quint Davis and Dr. John—his family of true believers at New York's Crossroads, the little corner bar he transformed into a temple where the magic took root.

"This may sound corny," observes Campbell, thirty-nine, "but my life really passed before my eyes in the process of recording this album."

It had, until recently, been a quintessential old-time blues man's life, replete with near-fatal accidents (both physical and psychic), years of pocket-change-and-whiskey gigs at field parties and honkytonks on the Greyhound circuit, faith lost and found on New York City mean streets—and throughout it all, a Zen monk's devotion to both his instrument and its enlightened masters. (It's no coincidence that his National steel guitar once belonged to Lightnin' Hopkins, or that the album's sole cover song, "Person to Person," is his homage to Elmore James.)

As *Billboard*'s Thom Duffy writes, *One Believer* has "both the freshness of a debut act and the emotional authority of a blues survivor." Peter Lubin puts it even more succinctly: "John's so old he's new."

Campbell's newborn voice as a singer/songwriter, nurtured by partner-in-crime Dennis Walker, is part of the freshness. The demon guitar player who once sang only "in self-defense" has opened his heart to read words that were always written there. And the voice speaks not only of darkness but of light, to the "prayer inside his head" he invokes in *One Believer*'s exquisite title track, a blues meditation of visionary redemption. Campbell's also expanded the textural boundaries of the blues, allowing the bayous of his boyhood to seep back into his music.

"I was such a student of the Texas style of guitar," observes Campbell, who staked out an absolute claim on that territory with his first album, *A Man and His Blues*, released on Germany's Crosscut label. "But I started playin' guitar in Louisiana when I was four years old, and now I feel like I kinda went back to my roots."

In the process, he literally let down his hair: his carefully-coiffed Texas pompadour, a longtime trademark, is now a leonine mane that frames the grinning skull dangling from his ear, and he no longer hides his mojos in his guitar case.

"I was my own worst enemy for a while in allowing myself to grow," he reflects, then laughs.

*"I may have grown into a monster!"*

# Have You Seen Mick Taylor, Baby, Standing in the Shadow?

***Details*, June/July 1990**

It's been a long time coming, but Mick Taylor has found his own voice and he's got something to say. Tonight, he's saying it at New York's LoneStar Roadhouse with a pickup blues band, an ensemble so seamless that the drunk in the corner stops slobbering out requests for "Honky Tonk Women."

"You may be high, you may be low," Taylor sings, caressing the syllables with the kind of well-worn comfort of his scruffy tennis shoes, and sliding down to the Delta on his old Les Paul. "You may be rich, child, you may be poor...but when the Lord gets ready, you got to move."

Taylor's heard this call before, most significantly in 1975, when he bid the Rolling Stones good-bye. "I'm a much better guitar player now than I ever was with the Stones," he says later over a draft of Harp ale at the West 4th Street Saloon, just around the corner from his modest Greenwich Village apartment, where the only evidence of his six-years with the world's greatest rock band is the statuette from his induction into the Rock and Roll Hall of Fame. "One of the reasons I left was to make a successful career for myself as a contemporary blues guitarist. There were lots of years afterwards when I didn't do that. But sometimes you lose your way, and have to go through all kinds of things to find yourself again."

I witnessed Taylor's Hyde Park debut with the Stones in 1969, when he vanquished the ghost of Brian Jones with guitar solos that soared as high as the white butterflies released into the London skies that day; and I have vivid memories of his remarkable synchronicity with Keith Richards during the gold era of concerts that began with the *Let It Bleed* tour. I hadn't seen him in seventeen years. Now I became hungry to hear the untold story of his personal pilgrimage, which resonates with the collective impact of the London blues bridge to America. On the eve of his first record release in over a decade—a live album compiled from a 1989 European tour by a new indie label called Maze—he agreed to a series of interviews.

"I'm glad this first album is a live album," Taylor says, after I've had time to digest the rough mix. "Because it's a very accurate statement of where

I'm at right now: a straightforward blues album." Well, mostly. The title track is a lusty original called "Stranger in This Town," which loops back to the basement-tape feel of *Exile on Main Street* and is driven by a Stonesy guitar riff. "Oh, it is, it is," he agrees. "I could always play solos, but one of the most valuable things I learned from Keith was how to create riffs." And a key "Stranger" lyric line—"don't waste your time looking back, gotta take that burden off your back"—is only the most obvious of several subliminal subtexts that begin to surface, including Taylor's decision to make "Jumpin' Jack Flash" his first-ever Stones cover tune.

"It came to me in a flash on the road," he explains, no pun intended. "I got so sick of people shouting out for bloody Rolling Stones songs, I thought sod them, I'll play one. We played it every night on that particular tour, just for a laugh." "Jumpin' Jack Flash" does top the list of his favorite Stones songs, which all predate his period with the band and include "Satisfaction" and "Street Fighting Man". But it's a particularly loaded choice for Taylor, who told me earlier tonight, "I don't think Mick has ever really forgiven me for leaving." For if ever there was a song intimately associated with Mick Jagger's stage persona, it's "Jumpin' Jack Flash."

To understand Taylor's decision to leave the Stones and his struggle to regain his own power, we have to backtrack to beginnings.

Taylor had just left John Mayall's Bluesbreakers after a four-year stint, and was intending to form his own R&B band—"Something elemental and earthy about blues and R&B reached a very deep part of my soul," he says—when he got a call from Mick Jagger. Brian Jones was being eased out of the Stones, and the segue to Taylor was so natural he simply walked into the studio where the band was finishing up *Let It Bleed*, recorded "Live With Me" and overdubbed "Honky Tonk Women", and that was that.

"They hadn't played live in three or four years, and Hyde Park was incredibly nerve-racking for everybody. But I felt totally comfortable once I got onstage and didn't spend too much time brooding about Brian Jones, because it was a really new period for the Rolling Stones. I think that's when they found their voice as a great live rock 'n' rock band. Keith and I had a very unconscious, instinctive relationship; we didn't work anything out, even in the studio, and onstage we really inspired each other. In fact, the whole band was inspired. That side of things was great."

Taylor would like to have toured more extensively, and was frustrated by management disputes that precluded the release of an official live album during those years. But what really began to wear on him was the "dual personality" of the band. "On the one hand, they were just this bunch of English guys who loved rhythm and blues. On the other hand, they were also famous pop stars, who were incredibly spoiled by their own success at that time, and who were surrounded by so many dubious hangers-on and users. I hated that. And I never ever felt that being a member of the Rolling Stones was the pinnacle of my musical career."

During 1974, amidst the parallel split-ups of Mick and Bianca, Keith and Anita Pallenberg and his own first marriage, Taylor decided he'd had enough. "The spark had gone out of the group, there were lots of drug problems and nobody seemed to be having fun anymore. I felt the Rolling Stones were becoming a caricature of themselves, that *Goat's Head Soup* was parodies of rock 'n' roll instead of real rock 'n' roll, and that they were losing something very elemental and real. I felt that very strongly, and it turned me off. I was the one that left, but I can assure you I was not the only one who said openly we'd better quit. And in fact, things did fall apart for quite a while."

While the Stones floundered collectively, Taylor got lost in his own swamp. "I was very clear about why I was leaving, but I wasn't clear about what I was going to do next. And it wasn't until after I left, and had to deal with things as an individual, that I realized how much being with the Rolling Stones had affected me. When you're part of something like that, everything's taken care of: You don't have to go to the bank, you don't have to do anything. I had to learn to grow up all over again and pay my dues."

The next decade twisted and turned inside a no-exit labyrinth. A potential supergroup pairing with Jack Bruce misfired, a 1979 solo album went nowhere and a 1983 tour with Bob Dylan, which segued into several album tracks, was but a flicker of light in the darkness. "I learned a lot from Bob Dylan, because he's unpredictable; the looser things are, the more he likes it. But I was still a sideman standing in the background shadows." In 1984, shortly after his father died, Taylor bottomed out for two blurred years.

"I was just sitting around wasting time, taking drugs. Which I've got nothing against, morally. But there's a difference between taking drugs to get high and taking drugs to blot everything out. I finally said enough is enough: I want to carry on." When Taylor moved to New York to get a band together and start playing club dates, a parade of people advised him to get a front man. Instead, he reached inside himself for his own voice, for the call-and-response of the singer and his guitar is one of the heartbeats of the blues tradition. "I was self-conscious about singing at first, but now I enjoy it. It's made my guitar playing more real. The blues comes naturally to me now: It's part of my experience, part of who I am. I'm basically a blues guitar player who improvises. Always have been, always will be."

I don't have to take Taylor's word for this. I can hear it onstage with the ad hoc musicians who may well coalesce into the band he's been seeking: Jon Paris, a blistering Johnny Winter vet, trades rhythm and lead like Taylor once did with Keith Richards; keyboardist Teo Leyasmeyer plays sly New Orleans-style riffs that make Taylor smile; and two young Brooklynites—Chulo Gatewood on bass and Damon "Delicious" DuWhite on drums—provide a rhythm section that swings. I can also sense Taylor's commitment to being a pass-it-on torchbearer in the wisdom he received from legendary bluesman Albert King. "He said, " I got no time for cats who think they know everything. I'll still be learning how to play the guitar when I die." And I've seen him sit at the feet of contemporary Texas blues maestro John Campbell, soak in the phrasing of his National Steel slide, and incorporate nuances into his own playing. Taylor has a humility in the face of the force of the blues that reminds me of what he said about Jimi Hendrix: "I think he knew he was blessed, and when you know that, you don't take too much credit for yourself."

Taylor still has to contend with industry types who want to exploit the old glory days, but he's gradually making his peace with his own history. Keith Richards played on one of his recent demos, and asked Taylor to take a turn on his solo album *Talk Is Cheap*. "You Don't Move Me" was Richards direct address to Mick Jagger, and I think the Taylor cut he used—which harks back to their mutual roots and features Chuck Berry keyboardist Johnny Johnson—was a subtle message that validates Taylor's belief that "Keith understands why I left": "I Could Have Stood You Up (But I Didn't)."

I must ask him, of course, the bottom-line question. If a genie came along and said poof! You're on the *Steel Wheels* tour; would he abandon the path he's chosen?

Taylor doesn't hesitate: "Absolutely not. I've had lots of success and money, and I don't think it really makes you happy if you're not fulfilled as a human being. I like what I'm doing, I feel it's going somewhere, and even if I were offered millions of dollars, I wouldn't trade places."

## Delta Blues

### *James "Son" Thomas; Roosevelt "Booby" Barnes; Jessie Mae Hemphill; Eugene Powell; Atla Simmons; Rev. Leon Pinson; Lonnie Pitchford*

**_Spin_, June 1990**

DELTA BLUES DIDN'T DIE when Howlin' Wolf, Muddy Waters, John Lee Hooker and BB King headed north for Chicago. The music wrenched from the cotton field oppression of the past remains a vital voice in the black community: it wails above the whir of crickets at backwoods picnics, penetrates the haze of hot summer nights on creaky front porches and stomps hard luck into good times on the dance floors of rowdy juke joints. Every blues song tells a different story, and the lives of Delta musicians give us glimpses into the culture that gave birth to rock'n'roll.

James "Son" Thomas plays bottleneck that slides back to boyhood Saturday nights half a century ago, when Elmore James let him sit in with his $8.50 Gene Autrey guitar, but his rhythmic phrasing is far older; it speaks from the graves of long-buried slaves.

"You don't just tum into a skull all at once," observes Thomas, whose fingers are as finely-tuned to the native hill clay he sculpts into hollow-eyed skulls as they are to his steel-stringed guitar. "You lies in the ground a good while before you get to be that skull." So it is with his blues, which strips the Delta tradition down to its essential roots. "It's the old-time way of playin' the music," he says on his front porch in Leland, where a clay-sculpted lady resides in a baby blue coffin. "And if you be out on these farms, you already have the blues."

After long years of sharecropping, Thomas, sixty-three, only began recording twenty years ago; now he's as close to being a star as a Mississippi-based artist can be. Accompanied by Swiss harmonica player Walter Liniger, with whom he shares an uncanny musical affinity, he regularly tours the US and European festival circuit.

But back in Leland, Thomas's life goes on pretty much the way it always has. The roof still leaks and the refrigerator's bare in the small wood house he shares with his son Pat, a part-time grave digger. He's still paying off hospital bills from a gunshot wound back in '81, when his old lady shot him with a .22, and he recently had to raise bail for a son gone bad on crack.

"I owe so much, there's no way for me to pay it all off," he says. "One of these days, I'm gonna get lucky and do some of the things I wanna do, before I get too old. You know, we all goin' to the same place, and that's down in the clay."

"Mama ain't happy with me, 'cause my soul can't be saved with me movin' around singing the blues," says Jessie May Hemphill, a descendent of four generations of musicians going back to the percussive rhythms of fife-and-dmm. "But she's proud I'm takin' care of myself. Ain't nobody got no say-so over me."

On stages throughout the US and Europe, the 'Delta Queen' flashes sequins and rhinestones, driving her foot-powered tambourine with a gold high heel. Tonight she's holding court outside her Como castle, a dilapidated trailer with no running water, where overdue utility bills are stashed in a bedside Bible near her sawed-off shotgun and an unkempt menagerie of poodles yammer to be fed. "Train's comin: look out y'all," she calls to neighbors lured by the hypnotic drone of her electric Gibson, as she launches into "Train Train." "Gonna run right through you!"

Jessie Mae picked up guitar watching her mother, Virgie Lee, play spirituals, but laid it aside until years later, after she'd lost five babies and buried her mama. "I started playin' the blues because my heart was broken and I was tired of all those guys who be lyin' to me. My songs come just like somebody was writin' 'em on the wall, and I got a whole lot of power that I ain't even used yet."

Sunday evenings, several country miles outside Greenville, Mississippi, the raucous echoes of a blues band lead to a juke joint called the Tin House. Smoke rises from the barbecue grill out back, where a crap game's cookin' along with the chicken and ribs. But the real action's inside. Roosevelt "Booby" Barnes and the Playboys rattle your bones with raw electric blues. Attacking his guitar with gold-ringed fingers and what's left of his teeth, Barnes roughens up the edges of Chicago-style tiffs with Delta grit, and works the crowd like a tent-show preacher.

Barnes first got into the blues when he picked up a harmonica at the feet of Sonny Boy Williamson, but there are other past lives he wouldn't care to relive; he was forced to leave the state in '68 when he hooked up with the white ex-wife of a local cop, and he battles the alcohol demons that make men show fangs. Today, sober in his sharp-pressed double -breasted suit, he runs the Playboy club, the hottest dive on Greenville's notorious Nelson St. strip, and scrapes by on weekdays with pick-up games of pool and the catch-of-the-day he sells from a cooler.

"I never had the breaks I should have," says Barnes, "but the blues is comin' on back, and it makes me feel good when the younger ones is comin' on playin'. The blues comes from a lonely feelin' when your heart been broken or anything kind of discourages you. And then you play the blues and be happy."

Eugene Powell grew up in Lombardi where he had a close-up view of Parchment prison life. "They'd make the prisoners tow those big logs, and if one stop and fall, the log would fall over and kill him." As a small boy, he entertained the prison bossmen's kids with his Sears & Roebuck guitar. "They'd watch us like we'd be on TV," and his fingers flew so fast that white townsfolk often perched him on boxes to play blues over the telephone lines to Memphis and St Louis.

Though glaucoma has veiled his eyes and a tumor has nearly crippled one arm, Powell still receives blues pilgrims on his front porch, where his guitar invokes the gracefully intricate pickin' of his 1930s recordings as "Sonny Boy Nelson." "'Things is more easier than they used to be," he says of today's Mississippi. "But old colored people like me, we're used to bein' in fear, and that's still with me. I know my place."

Napoleon Strickland, a cherubic man in his mid-'60s, is the Pan of Mississippi. The haunting notes of his fife, a hollow of sugarcane hand-punctured with holes, call the backcountry ritual of a 'picnic' into life, and seduce dancers in a circle of hypnotic rhythms that reach back to Africa.

Fife-and-drum music may have been cross-pollinated by the military bands of the Civil War; Jessie Mae Hemphill, who's played drums with Strickland since childhood, believes "the soldiers got it from the Indians, who beat them war pieces on the tom-toms. But now you can't get nobody to play the fifes, and if somebody don't start playin' 'em it's gonna die."

Strickland shares a small shack with his mother, Dora, who gleefully rolls her belly to prove she's every bit the dancer she was in her prime. "People be dancin' down at those picnics, Lord!" recalls Jessie. "Dust would get all over 'em, but they still be dancin'."

"The blues never get old, because blues is a feelin'," says Atla Simmons, who at seventy-two still has that feelin'. She punctuates an a cappella rendition of her signature song, "Rubber-Hipped Mama," with armchair gyrations and sassy smiles, evoking the sawdust stages she once shared with Bessie Smith on the 1930s carnival and tent show circuit.

After a long stretch up north, where she toured with Champion Jack Dupree, Simmons returned to Mississippi because "I got tired of the rat race." She now pens poetry and exercises her still powerful vocal cords at both blues and gospel gigs. "One is servin' the Lord and the other is entertainment. I read in the Bible that when Christ went to weddings, they'd sing and dance—and I'm sure they weren't singing gospel songs!"

"I ain't a real reverend, I'm a minister of music. And I don't play no blues." Though his strong bass line testifies to the Delta's blues and gospel crossbreeding, the Rev. Leon Pinson's repertoire is "sacred music": old time spirituals like "Amazing Grace" and church-printed "ballads" from the 1930s. His "talking guitar," which often plays in unison with his vocals, inspires congregations to "shout and get happy, according to how the spirit strikes them."

Legally blind since infancy, Pinson, seventy, relies on friends to drive him to supper at his sister Irma's for the best fried chicken in the county, and to church-house and festival gigs. At home, he keeps busy recording tapes for special requests. "Two white folk asked me once, how come your music feels different than the blues? I said it's supposed to make you feel different—if you listen to the words and what the Good Lord says."

"Young black guys aren't into the blues so heavy. They don't understand they're listening to their own culture, their own heritage." Lonnie Pitchford, thirty-four, one of the few blues artists to play in the style of the near-mythic Robert Johnson, reaches even further back in time with the diddly bow. In his hummingbird hands, this simple one-stringed instrument, whose earliest incarnation was a vertical string nailed to a porch pole, has a resonant complexity of rhythm and tone.

"All my life is blues," says Pitchford, who was initiated into Robert Johnson's unique chord tunings by one of his last remaining heirs, Robert Jr. Lockwood. "I'd like to be able to make a living making music and not punch any time clocks." A construction worker who's continually on guard against accidents that might damage his hands, Pitchford believes he'll have to leave Mississippi to realize his dream. But wherever he goes, he'll take the Delta with him.

"We need to teach black kids more about the blues, so they can find out what it's all about. Rap's cool, but it's a passing thing. The blues is here to stay. And today's problems is enough blues for anyone."

## Son Thomas Makes a Ladyhead

*Oxford American*, July 2014

LATE SEPTEMBER, 1989: THE Zion Tabernacle Church in Leland, Mississippi, sits directly across from James "Son" Thomas's house, so that Hutson Street cuts a literal swath between God and the Devil, that old Southern dichotomy. Gospel belongs to God and the blues is the Devil's business, and here the blues takes the form of Son Thomas, whose spare bottleneck slide strips the tradition down to its roots. Son's blues run deep into the Delta soil, wrenched from the cotton-field oppression of a past that still hangs heavy over the present. Just last week—while blues fans were gathering in Greenville for the annual Delta Blues Festival—Ole Miss frat boys dumped naked pledges on the historically black Rust College campus as part of an Ole Miss hazing prank. The pledges were painted with racial epithets.

The neighborhood kids on Hutson Street are a little spooked by the baby blue coffin on Son's porch, and the life-sized clay lady who resides inside. Dressed in go-to-meetin' finery—a hot pink dress and orange plastic beads—she has sculpted hands folded across her belly, the fingernails painted the same ruby red as her lips.

Son's been sculpting figures and heads and skulls from clay gathered in the nearby hills for just about as long as he's been playing the blues, which is to say: all his life. (His first guitar was a Gene Autry, ordered from Sears Roebuck.) He's particularly fond of skulls embedded with human teeth, like the one that gave his Grandpa the heebie-jeebies when he showed the old man his artwork a half-century ago. Son sells his pieces as fast as he can make them, and he's got a backlog of orders that will help him pay off his debts. Hospital bills have been piling up since his old lady, now his ex, surprised him with a .22 rifle almost a decade ago. (She shot him in the stomach.) He needs bail money for the son, gone bad on crack, who's waiting on a trial date over in Greenville. A retread to replace the tire gouged by broken glass on his way home from the Delta Blues Festival. The $125.00 rent he pays on the railroad flat with a leaky roof he shares with his other son Pat, who's hard of hearing and picks up whatever shifts he can as a gravedigger at the local cemetery.

Son had intended to spend the last couple of days working clay into life, but that was before his dog, Snow, a white German shepherd he got in a package deal with a used amp for $100.00, took a nip out of his three-year-old nephew. The kid's going to be okay, but Son had to lay down $70.00 in the ER because his niece with the Medicaid card was nowhere to be found. Son's afraid of what might happen if Snow's next victim isn't kinfolk but a neighborhood child. "He's a good dog, but you can't trust the breed."

I'm here to buy a sculpture, a transaction we discussed last week when I came to the house to interview Son for a story on the Delta blues. He waves me up to the porch with a languid lift of an arm bas-reliefed with veins from the long years of sharecropping. "I didn't think you was comin' back," he says. Son was skeptical that I'd return to complete the deal, though I'd sealed the promise with a hug when I left the other day. ("This is the first time I've ever been hugged by a white woman," he'd told me, accepting the embrace somewhat warily. "Except for Nancy Reagan. But she only put her arm around me, so it wasn't a real hug.") There's a photo of Son and Nancy hanging on the wall, taken when his sculptures traveled to Washington, D.C. for a national folk-art show. Nancy is beaming her photo-op Samaritan smile, but Son looks rather grim. The shot was taken seven weeks after he took the bullet in his belly, and he was still drinking and having periodic seizures, one of which resulted in third-degree burns on his right hand when he collapsed on an electric heater.

Son is wary of outsiders. Too many white folks have paraded past him, taking his music and his image and his stories and giving nothing in return. But he seems pleased to find my word is good, and he accepts my takeout chicken dinner from Lili Robinson's Soulfood Cafe, handing it to Pat to "put it up" for later. Then he smiles, the light returning to eyes as deep-set as the hollows of his clay skulls. "I do believe I feel like workin' now," he says. "Gonna make me a ladyhead."

While Pat softens up a batch of the hard hill clay in a washtub, stirring it with his gravedigger's shovel—"it don't hold much water so it dries fast"—Son tells me he rarely allows people to watch him work. "Too damn distractin'." I promise to stay quiet. He nods. "You learn more by keepin' quiet."

Son slips a piece of cardboard under a raw lump of coarse mottled clay, then molds it into an oblong shape about the size of a five-pound loaf of bread. Later, he'll paint the clay a color closer to his own skin tone, but right now it's yellow-beige, like the skin of a jaundiced white man. A backless chair serves as his work surface, with a tray underneath that holds a clutter of wire, marbles, clippers, and beads. The first tool he reaches for is an empty whiskey pint bottle. He uses this to make the initial cuts that determine the shape of the skull, the shape that "just comes out of the clay."

With four practiced whacks of the bottle, he carves out the base. Then, with a series of gentle taps, he refines the chin line and neck and makes a rough outline of the nose. "This looks easy but it ain't," Son says. It takes years to get it right, to exert just the right amount of pressure without cracking the clay. He works quickly with no wasted motion, smoothing the surface with long, tapered fingers fine-tuned to the hidden bone structure of clay. Using his thumbs, he makes two deep hollows for the eyes, pausing to regard his handiwork. A frown flickers across his face. Then he rises and crosses to another corner of the porch. Rummaging through a box, he plucks out two marbles: "They just feel right."

Son presses the marbles into the clay sockets, two startled-looking cat's eyes. "I'm workin' slow today," he notes. "What takes time is when you have to keep gettin' up and down to find things you need." As if on cue, Pat appears with a cardboard box containing two dozen wigs: afros, wavy and straight styles in a palette of browns and blacks, none of them blonde except for a snarled wiglet.

But Son's not ready for those yet. As I watch him work, the ladyhead begins to come to life, transforming from what looks like an Etruscan relic into something softer, more sensual. Son dips his fingers into a plastic margarine tub of water and begins to mold the fine features—eyelids, a small, impertinent mouth—from the still-moist clay remaining on his palette. His movements are deft and delicate, almost feminine, in sharp contrast to his bluesman's hands. When Son plays steel string and slide, his fingers are emphatically masculine in their attack, forging rhythms that cut time with unexpected phrasing much older than the blues that pre-dates the twelve-bar format. What bridges the two creative acts is the homing instinct of Son's fingers.

He reaches into the wig box. I expect him to try several styles on for size, but his hand goes immediately to a short, wavy head of hair. It works. The newly coifed ladyhead looks somewhat androgynous in her short-cropped waves, but the style makes a fine frame for her high, proud cheekbones. Son's own hair is a fine, grey-flecked stubble, and I ask him if he's ever tried on samples from his wig collection. "No," he says with a laugh, "but maybe I should."

## Raiders of the Lost Spark

*Willa Mae Buckner, Guitar Gabriel; Captain Luke*

***huH*, October 1995**

A FORMER BUS-DRIVING CONTORTIONIST WHO sleeps with a seventy-foot snake at seventy something? A resentful old hermit whose son wields a mean razor blade? North Carolina field recorder Tim Duffy has seen it all during his treasure-hunting quest to document an obscure, fleeting, and beautiful culture for his own *Music Maker* label. Cree McCree investigates the blues detective and the music he's revived from the dead.

She's raised eyebrows with sexy songs dripping with innuendo. She's raised temperatures with erotic-fantasy dances. And what she does in her own bedroom is definitely kinky. Madonna Ciccione, meet your great-grandmother, Willa Mae Buckner: the "Wild Enchantress" of the all-Black tent show circuit of the '30s and '40s, where her boogie-woogie blues were scandalously "blue" and she wrapped her bronze-painted body with undulating pythons—including seventy-foot Big Jim, who was still sharing her bed when Willa Mae turned seventy.

"I've enjoyed Madonna's efforts to get where she is today," says the sassy septuagenarian, who sings some of her old "dirty songs" on a new CD that documents *A Living Past*: acoustic blues recorded in the living rooms, kitchens and nursing homes of all-but-forgotten artists. "Madonna's story is different from mine," adds Buckner, whose resume includes stints as a carnival contortionist, session bass player, city bus driver in Winston-Salem, NC—and, most recently, Music Maker recording artist. "But we both stuck with it, you know."

So did Tim Duffy, a young white musician/folklorist turned amateur detective and field recorder. Now based in Winston-Salem, after stints in Africa and Appalachia, Duffy has spent the last few years in and around the Carolinas tracking down long-retired artists like Buckner and Captain Luke, who repertoire ranges from Kingfish stories and an onomatopoeic jaw harp to basso profundo vocals. Duffy uncovered one old-timer after another, each leading to the next in a chain reaction that eventually became the Music Maker Relief and Recording Foundation, which now funnels sales from CDs directly into the medical bills, roof repairs and living expenses of a dozen aging artists.

But it all began with Duffy's dogged pursuit of Guitar Gabriel, a legendary bluesman supposedly killed in a house fire years ago.

Determined to honor the deathbed request of his mentor James "Guitar Slim" Stevens, who instructed the young archivist to "find Guitar Gabriel," Duffy followed a convoluted trail to the rowdy "drink houses" concealed behind closed doors in the crack-infested projects of East Winston-Salem. Like the juke joints of the Mississippi Delta, where the liquor's cheap, the tales are tall and your luck can change as fast as a chord change in a twelve-bar, these nonstop house parties are the heart of a marginal community whose soundtrack remains the blues. Unlike the Delta's well-documented jukes, however, which have lately become a mecca for white blues buffs, the Carolina drink houses aren't in any guide books.

"I stumbled into this whole hidden culture," recalls Duffy, who got shot at by wary locals and hassled by equally wary cops. And when he finally flushed out a very-much-alive Guitar Gabriel, "it was a war." New recruit Captain Luke became Duffy's bodyguard during an all-out battle with Guitar Gabriel's family, who were dead set against any efforts to revitalize his career.

"No one in the projects wants to see anyone go up, because it breaks up the structure of the community," Duffy explains. "His son tried to kill me with a razor blade." Nor was he welcomed with open arms by Guitar Gabriel himself, who'd been holed up with his axe and a bottle since 1970, when his regional-hit single "Welfare Blues" netted him less than zero in a classic music-biz burn.

"Gabe was intentionally, and understandably, mistrustful of the whole world," he says of their initial meeting in 1991. "He had the most terrible case of the blues I've ever seen."

Guitar Gabriel spat it out in "Dr, Buzzard": "Whoa, I feel like a broke down engine, I swear done lost its driving wheel." But as Gabe later observed, "blues takes a lot of animosity out of your heart," and the best cure for the blues was The Blues.

"Once we started playing together, we began building a relationship that evolved into a marriage of sorts," relates Duffy, who'd bridged similar cultural gaps while making field recordings in Kenya. Thus, the sheepskin hat bequeathed to him by Kikuyu tribesmen ended up on the head of Guitar Gabriel, who wore it like a crown on the cover of his 1993 Duffy-produced CD, *Deep in the South*. And it never looked more regal than at Carnegie Hall, where he received a standing ovation after being named Living Blues Comeback Artist of 1994.

"Whenever you wear this hat, it gives you a feeling of what you are representing," explains Gabe, great-grandson of a slave, grandson of a sharecropper, and son of an itinerant blues man and "sideshow geek" called Razorblade (whose razor blade and glass-eating act Perry Farrell would have booked in a hot second for Lollapalooza.) "Anything you take on to do, got to have a basing to let people know what it is and what it stands for," adds the Philosopher King of the Blues, who built his foundation in the '40s touring with such now-legendary icons as Lightnin' Hopkins, Reverend Gary Davis and Muddy Waters, "You can drive a Cadillac, but if you don't got Cadillac on it, people still don't know what it is you're driving."

There's no mistaking the imprimatur of Music Maker co-founder Mark Levinson, however, whose Cello recording equipment is recognized worldwide as an audiophile's Ferrari. "What Tim's uncovered is a subculture thought to have disappeared: original acoustic blues artists who have only been recorded before with lo-fi equipment" says Levinson, who re-mastered Duffy's original recordings for the 1994 compilation *A Living Past* and sent him back into the field with a mobile Cello unit. And with the clock ticking on the available resource pool—Preston Fulp, pictured on *A Living Past*'s cover, died before its release—"it's our last chance to hear these artists," he adds. "High fidelity gives us the opportunity to hear what this music was, and is."

Remarkable though they are, the recent Sony re-releases of Robert Johnson are still sealed in a time capsule of tinny 1930s acoustics, which modern ears have come to associate with the "real" sound of the blues. Duffy continues to unearth other equally noteworthy artists dating back to the '30s and '40s, who come from traditions less well-documented than Johnson's Delta-to-Chicago line.

"In the Carolina Piedmont region, there's a real close thread between white hillbilly music and Black blues," notes Duffy, citing the classic conjunction of forces scholars have long credited with the birth of rock and roll. Thus Guitar Gabriel, whose blues are as deep as the Delta and as bawdy as a cathouse in heat (Jesse Helms would go ballistic over his XXX-rated "You Gotta Watch Yourself"), is equally conversant in the dueling banjos-style guitar picking perfected by Preston Fulp on the old tobacco warehouse circuit.

"The emotional impact of hearing these artists on high-fidelity is staggering," observes Levinson, who's not just tooting his own horn. When Gabe's sister Lucille Lindsay starts riffin' on the afterlife in "I'll Fly Around Heaven All Day," then spontaneously breaks into "Tryin' to Make 100" on the new compilation *Came So Far*, you're right there with her in her run-down nursing home, watching the Pearly Gates fly open through her old blind eyes while Gabe fingerpicks the lock off her door. When Captain Luke hisses and growls his "Dog and Cat Fight," the fur starts flying in his Carolina kitchen. And when Willa Mae lets you know in no uncertain terms that "I'm getting old, way up in years/but I can still climb a hill/without shifting my gears," on her slyly suggestive "Yo-Yo," her presence is as immediate as the living room piano Michael Parrish tuned just moments before.

"If you was outside and couldn't see it was a white boy playin' that boogie woogie piano, you'd think it was some of the famous ones," chuckles Willa Mae. "I'll tell you," adds Captain Luke, whose stunning reinvention of "Rainy Night in Georgia" is a highlight of *Came So Far*, "when I was just playin' the CD for my friends I made 'em all be quiet. I said, listen at that piano player when he comes in!"

Parrish, for his part, never dreamed he'd be backing contemporaries of Ma Rainey and Louis Jordan in the 1990s. "What's amazing is that this music is still around," he marvels. "And every one of these artists is such an individual personality. Willa Mae's an original feminist, Captain Luke's a great folk artist who also makes these beer can sculptures. And Guitar Gabriel? The guy's like a bottomless well of music and philosophy."

The master of "a rendition of life" he calls the "Toot Blues"—"because you're on the move"—Guitar Gabriel may have trouble walking these days, but he's still taking some musical leaps at seventy. In a move that may upset blues purists, the new *Guitar Gabriel Volume 1* ventures well beyond drink houses into his own private Birdland, an improvisational crossroads where the starkly pre-modern meets the startlingly postmodern and the Devil's "got his hair tied up in a ponytail to keep all the drunks confused."

And this is at it should be. The blues isn't a museum piece to be preserved in formaldehyde. It's an ongoing dialogue of dynamic tensions inside a tradition that loops back to Africa—and loops forward into everything from Sun-Ra's intergalactic explorations to PJ Harvey's inner space exorcisms.

"You don't find it in notes, it comes from the *heart*," says Guitar Gabriel in his oral liner notes that give *A Living Past* its name. "It's expressing about the things that you've been up against, what you have, what you didn't have. Your misfortunes and your good happenings." The $35,000.00 raised from CD sales to date by the Music Maker Foundation is definitely a "good happening"; Gabe and his fellow artists now have a little more than they otherwise would have had to live out their lives. But what we receive in return can't be quantified. As Guitar Gabriel puts it: "It gives you a living past and also a future coming in."

# The Genre-Busting Brilliance of Clarence "Gatemouth" Brown

***huH*, July 1996**

"Don't call me no blues player," warns Clarence "Gatemouth" Brown, spitting the words out like they were errant string beans that dared to cross his notoriously vegephobic palate. "I'm a *musician*. I'm growing and I always will grow."

Yeah, you right, as they say down in Louisiana, where Gate was born seventy-two years ago and currently moonlights as deputy sheriff for the town of Slidell during his rare respires from touring. (The badge on the Texas-sized belt buckle of the Texas-bred Brown is not merely honorary; he once stopped a drug-crazed mall marauder dead in his tracks by slamming the perp with his pickup truck and holding a pistol to his head.)

Gate may have launched his professional career in classic blues-showdown style the legendary night in '47 he commandeered T-Bone Walker's guitar for a spell-binding fifteen minutes at Houston's Bronze Peacock, earning $600.00 in tips from the crowd and the enduring enmity of Walker. But the blues was just the means to an end he's spent the past half-century expounding.

"Thank y'all for coming out to hear some planetary music," the wiry, cowboy-hatted Brown grins, introducing tonight's set to a packed house at New York's Tramps. Then he launches into an encyclopedic compendium of American musicology (jazz, country, bluegrass, Cajun, zydeco, folk, roots rock, R&B, and, oh yeah, the blues) universalized by the particulars of his singular style. And whether he's taking "The A-Train" to Abilene or daring "all you frustrated geniuses to snatch on this" with a hyperkinetic "Pressure Cooker," no laundry list can possibly encompass sleight-of-mind feats like referencing the classical roots of "Unchained Melody" while finger-picking his way to a slap-calypso finale on his violin.

"What's wrong with most musicians is they wind up playin' the same thing for years and years and years," observes Brown, puffing on his trademark pipe while pontificating from a supine position on his tour bus during pre-gig chill time. "T-Bone has a couple nice chords, but when the deal went down, he knew two songs: 'T-Bone Shuffle' and 'Stormy Monday,' After that, everything was the same. Me, everything I do is different. This last album's different from anything I ever did."

*Long Way Home*, his superlative new release, features a stellar guest line-up of Gatemouth disciples, including Eric Clapton, Ry Cooder, Leon Russell and Maria Muldaur. But the album clearly belongs to Brown, who exhibits his full range of capabilities—from introspective acoustic guitars studies like "Deep Deep Water" to a frenetic fiddle-and-mandolin fugue with Cooder on "Dockside Boogie"—while deftly using the stars as collaborators. With Gate on vocals and viola, Leon Russell's "Mean and Evil" becomes an improbably fell-good romp, as befits a guy who dismisses "them old hardcore blues guys" like the late Lightnin' Hopkins as "just too damn negative."

He even dips into the Dylan songbook with "Don't Think Twice," which he initially rejected until "I heard a version in my head of how I was gonna do it" and laid down some R&B harmonies with Maria Muldaur. "Long Way Home" becomes a subtle, sepia-toned acoustic duo with Eric Clapton, whose rockin' "Blues Power" (written with Russell) opens the album with Brown on vocals and Clapton on lead guitar and is the only track that doesn't quite meet Brown's exacting standards. "You should have heard my solo before he was on it," jibes Brown, who toured all over Britain with Clapton and played his entire two-week stint at London's Albert Hall. "Whew, it was smokin' honey, and I'm not lyin'!"

Honey, I'm sure you ain't. Clapton's a young whipper snapper compared to Brown, who attributes his prodigy—he played the guitar at five, the fiddle at ten and first debuted on stage as a drummer—to his father, a local string band musician. "That's who I got my gift from," he reflects. "Got nothin' to do with God. I don't believe in all this religious stuff." As a blues apostate, he bows his knee to no one, including the iconic Delta hellhound Robert Johnson. "Robert Johnson?! I don't even listen to that shit man," he laughs. "Don't like that backwoods blues."

Nor does his cotton to urban blues clones playing Muddy Waters and Chuck Berry. "Them people are easy to play," he scoffs. "And when too many people play like one individual, God almighty, it becomes like garbage. I'm not worried about them copying me because they can't do it." And don't even get him started on the alleged musical mecca of New Orleans. "I won't play New Orleans music," declares Brown, his legendary album with Professor Longhair notwithstanding. "And I don't go to no Mardi Gras. It's all Dixieland, street bands, and a lot of clownin'. It's embarrassin'."

Gate's aversion to crowd-pleasing ploys dates back to a memorable night in Detroit, where as a youthful guitar stud, he started "doin' them stupid little tricky things" to impress Duke Ellington. "When I got through, Duke say, 'boy, I'm gonna tell you somethin,'" he recalls. "You got the makin's of being one of the finest guitar players in the world, but you don't have to play the fool just stand up and play that instrument."

He also took Count Basie's crash-course in dynamics. "There's four stages to music: loud, mid-range, soft—and off. "And he heeded Louis Jourdan's all-in-the-groove advice: "You can get out of the pocket but be sure you know how to get back into it." But the "final word" from his short list of mentors is what defines his career: "Find your own way to play, that way it be you playin' instead of someone else."

That Gatemouth Brown has no imitators among his legion of admirers is ultimately a tribute to his own Zen-like approach to music. "I don't make no plans, I grab 'em as they comes," he notes. "One should dwell in the present." Thus, he doesn't miss a beat when asked a really stupid question: if forced to choose, which one of your many instruments would you take to a desert island?

"The one I feel like takin' at that precise moment," he retorts, breaking into uproarious laughter. That's why I'm gonna be here longer than the millennium, baby!"

## BB King: The King of the Blues on the State of the Blues

***Downtown Express*, February 1990**

BB King makes music that's meant to be shared, and brings the benevolent grace of laughter to his blues. Even offstage, under the harsh fluorescent glare of a spartan dressing room at New York's Beacon Theatre, he radiates a wash of sunlight that fills the room with warmth. It's nominally his break between two sold-out February shows—a mere pinpoint on a worldwide map of nearly three-hundred concert dates a year—but the once and future King of the blues is still on duty, recording a local radio spot. "I have to screw up just a little bit," he says, grinning, as he diverges from the script and begins to improvise a riff.

"Hi there, this is BB King, you know the guy who plays the guitar called Lucille? When I'm in Newark, or anywhere near Newark, I al-ways listen to WBGO." He pauses a beat, then adds: "Shut up, Lucille—they know!"

Indeed, we do. Long the world's most beloved blues ambassador, King and his electric lady Lucille just entered a whole new American ballpark; there's hardly a heartland home that wasn't touched by his recent MacDonald's commercial and Cosby Show guest spot. Though such mainstream forays raised a few eyebrows among academic blues purists, they're a natural extension of the missionary zeal King has brought to his music since he first began playing on his hometown streets of Indianola, Mississippi. Now he settles his formidable bulk in a chair, adjusts the jaunty twist of a plaid scarf over the bold red stripe of his sweatshirt, and addresses the current state of the blues.

"I have to disagree a little bit when you say 'revival,'" says King, sixty-five, his eyes sparkling with youth. "Blues has never been as popular as it is today, so it can't be a resurgence. Most of the people who's doin it now, like Robert Cray and Stevie Ray Vaughn and Jeff Healy and so many others, are new kids on the block, new blood, and I'm so glad we got 'em. I been tryin' forty years to get blues to become part of the mainstream of music, and that's starting to happen. I think it's fantastic."

As King recalls, it was back in the early '60s—just before the Brits brought the blues back home to the States and made it listener-friendly for white folks' ears—that the form felt its biggest pinch. "The clubs we used to play didn't want to bring blues in no more. Even in Memphis, where I was livin' then, we couldn't walk down Beale St. and hear the blues like we used to. Anyplace in the world you went if you said blues, they said, oh, Chicago. Well, I wanted all places to be Chicago—from Jackson, Mississippi to Moscow, Soviet Union. I could see it was needed."

When we discuss the Mississippi Delta, where King returns annually to his roots, he reconsiders the word 'revival.' "I kind of disagreed with you before, but now I think you're right, because there is a kind of resurgence down there. Blues music had its origin there, and it wasn't there for a long time, and now it's brought people together.

When I go to the park right off BB King Road, all kinds of kids, black and white, come up around me as if they know me, and I'm the guy who's gonna tell them a good story. That makes me very happy and proud."

King also gives his blessing to black urban youth's infatuation with rap. "I think as long as it's positive, and not too many four-letter words, rap music is great. We all need something we can feel that this is what I'd like to pattern my life after."

It's time for King to suit up for the stage, and when I thank him for his time, he responds with characteristic graciousness: "I should be thanking you, because you're helping us to make this work."

Then I slip into my seat in the darkened theatre, and rediscover, as always, that the thrill remains in 'The Thrill Is Gone.' Despite his grueling schedule of one-night stands, King's show is as fresh as it was when I first saw him open for the Rolling Stones two decades ago: the marvelous mime of his gestures, the honey-rich texture of his voice, and, most of all, those effortlessly elegant guitar solos in his bittersweet dialogues with Lucille.

"Blues music is a tonic that's good for whatever ails you," King has often said. Now, once again, I drink in the tonic of his traditional ovation ritual, when the audience streams up the center aisle. Flanked by two double-breasted deacons, BB King, minister of the music, dispenses pins and guitar picks like communion wafers to our outstretched hands, with a smile as wide as the heavens.

# John Lee Hooker: The King of the Boogie

***PleaseKillMe*, April 2020**

*Born in the Mississippi Delta, the son of a sharecropping pastor, John Lee Hooker absorbed the blues of that region before heading north and picking up an electric guitar. That was a seminal moment in music history, as his driving rhythmic style earned him the nickname "King of the Boogie" and influenced generations of rock guitarists. Cree McCree chronicles a memorable encounter she had in 1989 with John Lee Hooker for PKM.*

"I don't play a lot of fancy guitar," John Lee Hooker once said. "The kind of guitar I want to play is mean, mean, mean licks."

It doesn't get much meaner than the stripped-down, hypnotic stomps that defined Hooker's several-decade career, which cast a long and mighty shadow over the crossroads where blues and rock collide.

Born the son of a sharecropping pastor in the Mississippi Delta, Hooker ran away at age fourteen to the north Mississippi hills, where he learned that region's distinctive drone guitar style from his stepfather, Will Moore. Then he headed north and went electric when he hit Detroit. One of his earliest recordings, "Boogie Chillen" (1948) was a million-selling jukebox hit out of the gate, earning him the mantle of King of the Boogie and setting his course for decades to come.

The number of rock & rollers influenced by the one-and-only "Boom Boom" man along with way is legion, from the Rolling Stones to Eric Clapton to Bonnie Raitt, with whom he recorded the Grammy-awarding duo "In the Mood" on his best-selling album *The Healer* (1989). The Rock and Roll Hall of Famer also earned a Lifetime Achievement Grammy, among many other major awards, and continued to mesmerize audiences until just a week before he passed at age eighty-three in 2001.

Despite all his well-deserved accolades, Hooker remained as down to earth as the rich Mississippi soil he was rooted in. "I don't feel like no legend," Hooker said in the 1989 interview that follows. "I'm just a human being. I drink with you, I dance with you, I go out with you, I party with you. I love people, I enjoy bein' with 'em. I'm human, just like you."

In the summer of 1989, the blues was in the midst of one of its periodic revivals among young, mostly white music fans. The first wave coincided with the folk revival of the 1950s, when earnest, scholarly fans sat in reverential silence while giants like Texas bluesman Lightnin' Hopkins set his acoustic guitar ablaze with propulsive riffs born in raucous backwoods juke joints where the drinking gets harder and the dancing gets dirtier as the night goes on.

The second wave was more like a tsunami: the British Invasion of the 1960s, spearheaded by blues-drunk rockers like the Rolling Stones, who got the music's down-and-dirtiness from the get-go. That's when the blues first hit this then-small-town Ohio girl in the heart and the groin, sparking a lifelong passion that eventually led me down the Mississippi to the fertile crescent of the Delta and North Mississippi Hill Country blues.

The third-wave blues revival was in full swing in '89, when I had my brief but memorable encounter with the great King of the Boogie, John Lee Hooker. Hotshot blues guitarist Robert Cray was making waves, proving rap wasn't the only platform for young black artists, while elder statesman BB King was in heavy rotation in McDonald's TV spots. And at age seventy-two, Hooker himself was a hot commodity: he was about to release *The Healer*, which snagged a Grammy for "I'm in the Mood"; had just sung the title role on Pete Townshend's rock opera album, *The Iron Man*; and was on deck to help the Stones cap their wildly successful Steel Wheels tour with a monumental performance of his own "Boogie Chillen."

The buzz about the blues was so big, in fact, that I had managed to pitch—successfully, I thought—an article called "Mainstreaming the Blues" to *Us Weekly*. Which isn't as implausible as it sounds. Back in the '80s, *US* had not yet devolved into the dishy celeb tabloid it is today and was still giving *People* a run for its money as a snotty kid sister that had its finger on the pop culture pulse.

Armed with press credentials (I thought), I took the train from New York to Philadelphia for the Second Annual River Blues Festival at Penn's Landing in late July, where Hooker was slated to perform and topped my list of interview "gets" for the *US* story. For a few weeks that summer, I'd been dating the River Blues Festival's promoter, New Orleans Jazz Fest honcho Quint Davis, who I met at Crossroads on Houston Street, where Texas bluesman John Campbell was tearing the roof off the joint. So, I clearly had an inside track for backstage access. Or so I thought.

Boy, was I wrong! Long sad story short: Quint distanced himself from me in Philly. When I walked up the backstage stairs to greet him in the red suede boots he bought me, Quint told security to block me. It went from bad to worse when, far from facilitating my press access, he essentially closed the door.

But the intrepid reporter in me was determined to get my coveted interview with Hooker, especially after I watched his blistering set. The King of the Boogie slithered through Big Joe Williams' "King Snake Crawling," hit hard with his own badass "Boom Boom," evoked "Stormy Monday" with razor sharp guitar licks, among many highlights, and closed with (what else?) "Boogie Chillen," his signature boogie-till-you-drop stomp. Yowser! And, somehow, I managed to pull it off.

During a series of frantic phone calls on Sunday morning, made on the hotel's pay phone in this pre-cellphone era, I managed to track down my *US* editor—at home—and put her on the line with Hooker's manager, who was a real pit bull of a guard dog. While my editor couldn't confirm that my "Mainstreaming the Blues" piece was definitely a go (and they ended up killing it), she did confirm that I was a writer for the magazine, which gave me enough legitimacy to get me in the door. I was granted a brief half-hour with Hooker, whose bags were already packed for a trip to the airport.

Sharply dressed and already sporting his trademark fedora, Hooker greeted me warmly and invited me to sit on the bed across from the one he was seated on, looking every inch the gentleman, he always was, no matter the circumstance or time of day. What follows is a lightly edited transcript of a lively conversation he seemed to enjoy as much as I did. In fact, I know he did, because less than a month later, when I saw him blow out the candles on his birthday cake in a New York club, his face lit up with recognition and he gave me a big old hug when I told him that it was my birthday, too.

All these years later, I'm thankful to The Healer for helping me bind the wounds of one of the worst weekends of my life with his music, his laughter and his words.

**PKM:** I've been down to Mississippi lately, because I'm doing a story on Delta blues. What is it about the Mississippi Delta that's made it such a fertile crescent for the blues?

**John Lee Hooker**: Well, practically all the blues singers you know of come from Mississippi at a really early, young age. They was just born with it. It wasn't hard times, it wasn't depressed. Mississippi just drew a lot of talent. Out of every state, Alabama, Georgia, any of 'em, Mississippi's got the most blues singers.

**PKM:** Why do you think that is?

**John Lee Hooker:** I don't know. It wasn't that they grew up and got the blues from hard times. I was born with it; I was born with the talent. I was ten-years-old, singin in the church, spirituals, and my father was a minister. I come from a good background. And I left when I was fourteen. A lotta other young people who was good singers and drifted up here, they all come from Mississippi.

**PKM:** What made you leave Mississippi?

**John Lee Hooker:** Well, cause I never would have been a star stayin in Mississippi, cause there wasn't nothin there. My mom and dad had a big farm, he was a sharecropper, horses, cows, mules, donkeys, you name it, he had it. Plenty of food, we never had a hard time for food and stuff like that. But I knowed it wasn't the place for me if I wanted to become famous. I had very, very little smarts up here [points to head], but I knew I couldn't do it there! And so I said the heck with school and everythin, and I ran away when I was fourteen. I was stayin with my stepfather, cause he didn't mind guitar playin in his house. He was a musician, and a guitar player, his name was Will Moore. And I left my real dad.

**PKM:** What did your real dad think of the blues?

**John Lee Hooker:** You mean when he was livin?

**PKM:** Yeah.

**John Lee Hooker:** Well, he was glad that I finally reached my peak and got so famous. He accepted it then. But, you know, they call it the devil's music…

**PKM:** Yeah, what so you think about that? There's some traditional players down in Mississippi who say you either play the blues or you do gospel. You gotta make a choice.

**John Lee Hooker:** Well, you don't have to make a choice, but that's just how it is down there. I don't know whether it's still like that, things have changed so much. The South has completely turned around; it's kind of like here now. Back when I was a kid comin up, they was completely separated from each other. So, I don't know what they think about that now. I think they still think it's the devil's music. Some of 'em think that way up here, they call it devil music.

**PKM:** What do you think it is?

**John Lee Hooker:** It's not devil music. It's music that's good for the soul, that's good for the people, it makes people happy all over the world. Just like spirituals. Matter of fact, it's more stronger than spirituals to people. More people into what I'm doin than is into church songs. And in the church, they just can't make a living singin in the church. [Blues] makes you a good livin, makes you more money, makes you more friends, makes you more popular. I don't see anything wrong with it, but still, some of 'em call it devil music.

I don't think there's nothin wrong with it. I know I do love it; I love making people happy, I enjoy people, I love people, and I go out of my way to meet my fans. I love 'em. A lot of stars run and hide when they get through with entertaining, they run in their dressing rooms and hide from the public. Sometimes I have to, because they try to rip your clothes off and sometimes you got to get away, but when people just stand still out there, I'm willin to just talk to them.

**PKM:** So you love your audiences?

**John Lee Hooker:** Oh I love 'em, I love people, I enjoy being with 'em. When I'm home, I go to small bars, people think I wouldn't go in, they surprised to see me in there. But I'm human, just like you.

**PKM:** You've been a legend for so long. What's it feel like being a legend? Do you think of yourself as a legend?

**John Lee Hooker:** No, I think of myself as being just like you, just like a normal human being. I don't feel like no legend. Sometimes I say to myself, what is a legend? I'm just a human being, I'm just like you, I drink with you, I dance with you, I go out with you, I party with you. I ain't never heard I'm a legend until maybe a few years back!

**PKM:** You know, Moses Rascoe told me the funniest thing. He's seventy-two, the same age as you, born the same year, but he doesn't keep up with the current scene that much. And when he heard he was on the bill with John Lee Hooker, he said, "you must mean John Lee Hooker, Jr. You mean that old man's still alive?" I said, "Moses, he's the same age you are!"

**John Lee Hooker**: I ain't that old. You know, I put my age up when I went in the army. I wasn't born in 1917, I was born in 1920, really. I put my age up to get in the army.

**PKM:** Oh really? I didn't know that.

**John Lee Hooker:** Yeah, and they kicked me out of the army.

**PKM**: Why'd they kick you out?

**John Lee Hooker**: Because I lied to get into the army. Because at that time, the army was a thing to get a lot of girls. In an army suit, you could go out and get 'em. And when they found out—it took them two months, maybe three—and I was so good playin the guitar, they all liked me. And when they found out my identity wasn't true, they let me went, but everybody loved me. That sergeant or whatever, captain, he kind of hated to see me go but he said I had sworn to tell the truth. He said, you could go to jail for this, but everybody loves you so much we're just gonna discharge you. But I still have that brand [the age]. I didn't change it myself, it still says 1917.

**PKM**: Why not? It's a good year, 1917.

**John Lee Hooker:** It's a good year and everybody knows me by that. Now I enjoy sayin that I'm that old, cause I know I don't feel like that.

**PKM:** I know, I see you onstage and it's amazing. When you stood up yesterday, it was like you were 15. I don't know where you pull that out, man. But you sure do!

**John Lee Hooker:** I just got a lotta energy, a lotta energy.

**PKM**: You sure do! Well, what do you think about the whole current revival of the blues? It seems like we're in the midst of a new revival.

**John Lee Hooker:** Well, it's gettin bigger and it's gonna get bigger. People are learnin what the true identity of the blues means, and what the true identity of what the real music is. True identity is there's definitely other stuff come from it they call rock n roll and pop and rap—it all come from that. Forty years ago, you ain't never heard of rock n roll. Wasn't such a thing as rock 'n' roll. Just called the boogie. Which I created and called the boogie. Used to be the boogie woogie, but I called it the boogie. And everybody jumped on the band wagon. It was a neat name. And I'm a very intelligent writer. I can write songs just like [snaps fingers]

**PKM:** Where does that come from?

**John Lee Hooker:** Heart and soul. Just heart and soul. If you look at me, you think this guy don't know nothin. But I can look right through a person and tell what they're thinkin. I can tell if it's a kind-hearted person. I never got much schoolin cause I didn't care. But I'm fine, I'm blessed, and I love people. That's what keeps me goin, I think.

**PKM:** Do you think with Robert Cray being out there, one of the younger people, and BB King's doing McDonald's commercials…

**John Lee Hooker:** Ridiculous! I don't like to see him doing McDonald's. Old BB! It's nice, though it's nice. I love him! I'm sure he don't eat 'em! I love him though.

**PKM:** You made a comment one time that you thought one reason young black people for a long time were not really getting into the blues is that they didn't want to be reminded that that music came out of a past they would rather forget. Do you think that's changing?

**John Lee Hooker:** Well, I don't know whether I really said that, but I might have said that.

**PKM:** I read that as a quote in an article, but that doesn't mean you said it.

**John Lee Hooker:** Well, somebody could have quoted me wrong. Young people love the blues, a lot of 'em love it, but not as many of 'em. But I think they're learnin, I think they're gonna finally come around to it, the true things. Some of 'em do like the dance music, and stuff like that. And then there's a lot of white kids don't be into the blues either, there's more of them than black.

**PKM:** A lot of white rock and rollers have said how much you've given them, over and over you've been cited. What do you think you got from some of these white rockers? Did you get anything back?

**John Lee Hooker:** Yeah, I got more well known, more money, 'cause they did my thing and I got paid.

**PKM:** I also wanted to ask you just quickly about the project you just finished, *The Iron Man*. That's a kid's story, right? And you sing and play a part in it?

**John Lee Hooker:** Just sing. I sing on some of the lyrics.

**PKM:** Was that fun for you to do?

**John Lee Hooker:** Oh yeah.

**PKM:** You did this with [Peter] Townshend, right? And Clapton?

**John Lee Hooker:** Just Townshend.

**PKM**: And is there a message in that story?

**John Lee Hooker:** No, just somethin that was out of my line of work. But it was fun.

*[crosstalk about having to leave for airport]*

**John Lee Hooker:** Once I get goin, I'm hard to stop.

**PKM:** One last quick question. You sing a lot about women, what have you learned about women in your life?

**John Lee Hooker:** What else you gonna sing about? I'm not gonna sing about men, cause I'm not gay. I love women. Every man sings about women, every song you hear got a woman's name in it—rock, ballads, spirituals, any music got something about a woman. There's somethin about a woman—and a woman sings about a man. So it's just that simple. I can't sing, ooh, I love this man!

## Obituary: Chris Whitley (1960–2005)

*OffBeat*, January 2006

Chris Whitley always played as if his life depended on it. Sometimes, as in his 2004 manifesto *War Crime Blues*, the emotion was so raw you could practically taste the blood on the strings of his National steel guitar. Other times it was more of a throbbing ache, as in this year's *Soft Dangerous Shores*, his last dispatch as an expat in Dresden, Germany. He came home to die in Houston, Texas, where he was born in 1960, and passed on November 20th, of lung cancer.

The news of his death came hard on the heels of Katrina and out of left field, like She did. The intensity of the last few weeks as he lay dying, smack in the middle of the Houston diaspora of New Orleans evacuees, was straight out of a Chris Whitley song. A menacing "City of Women" where "everywhere I go is wet and red." A city of "Soft Dangerous Shores," where "no one lives to tell of paradigm shifts you know so well." A city not unlike New Orleans, where Whitley recorded his classic 1991 Columbia debut *Living with the Law* in Daniel Lanois' fabled Kingsway studio. Malcolm Burns produced both his first and his final album, which bookend a career that was born on the streets of New York, honed in juke joints and Euro dance clubs, and produced a wildly eclectic, emotionally consistent body of work that was sometimes uncannily oracular. He always told the truth.

When I watched him coming up in New York on the cusp of the '90s, he was a driven, driving, incredibly sexy guitar slinger and the only serious rival to John Campbell, who was making a heavenly noise with his National steel around the same time. (There were even a couple to-die-for double bills). What set Whitley apart were his songs. The sepia-toned portraits on *Living with the Law*, which cast him as a Sam Shepard antihero, had the harsh, bright beauty of "Big Sky Country" with just enough Big Easy ooze to make a lot of smart chicks want to "Kick the Stones" out of his bed. Then he disappeared for four years. He came back with a bang on *Din of Ecstasy* (Sony, 1995), turning the volume up to eleven with screaming existentialist blues that anticipate 9/11. Later, in a fine series of albums for *Messenger Records*, he followed his muse wherever she led him, from his father's Vermont barn, where he recorded *Dirt Floor* in a single day, to the *Hotel Vast Horizon* of his adopted home of Dresden, where dreadful memories of the Allied firebombing linger to this day. "No one was spared and nothing was learned," he sings on "Fireroad," a cautionary tale for post-Katrina New Orleans. But it doesn't have to be that way. Faced with "the news how the world gave way tonight," he sets a "Medicine Wheel" spinning and tells us to "sustain your heart and protect your light." Fortunately, we have Whitley's music to help us do that. He, and it, will be mightily missed.

# Memphissippi Sounds: Blues at a 21st Century Crossroads

*DownBeat*, February 2022

THE DEBUT RELEASE BY Cameron Kimbrough and Damion "Yella P" Pearson, *Memphissippi Sounds* (Little Village), establishes the singular duo's distinctive genre: Kimbrough's hill country drone meets Pearson's Beale Street blues in songs infused with R&B and spiced with the poetry of straight-out-of-Memphis rap. Opener "Who's Gonna Ride," launched with harp-driven blues you might have heard forty years ago at the legendary juke joint run by Cameron's granddaddy Junior Kimbrough, speeds straight to 2021 with an invocation of "I can't breathe" that practically spits out the clincher: "Get cha foot off my neck, boy."

Though they speak truth to power, Kimbrough and Pearson also write plenty of songs about every bluesman's favorite subject: women. "After you get through getting your neck stepped on, you need a little love," says Kimbrough, who was raised in rural Potts Camp, Tennessee, with a population of about five-hundred, but now lives in Memphis. Case in point: "You Got The Juice," a boudoir call-and-response on which both singers whisper sweet little somethings into your ear buds. Yowser! Kimbrough and Pearson sat down for a conversation via Zoom last October, when they talked about everything from their own "driving while Black" encounters to their remarkable bond as collaborators.

This interview has been edited for length and clarity:

***DownBeat***: Memphissippi Sounds wouldn't exist if you hadn't met onstage on Beale Street one magical summer night in 2017. How did you both end up in the club that night?

**Damion Pearson:** Another hill country player hired both of us to play a pickup gig. I was called to play harmonica and Cam was on the [drum] set.

**Cameron Kimbrough:** I had never even heard Damion's music. He was onstage when I walked in, checking the levels.

***DownBeat***: Checking the levels—a professional!

**Kimbrough:** Yeah! And I made up my mind, that night, we gotta do some jamming together.

*DownBeat*: Both of you are singers and multi-instrumentalists. But you're also incredible songwriting partners. Did you start collaborating right away?

**Pearson:** Yes. Because musically, it just flowed. The second time we played together, Cam called me out of the blue for a two-hour show, and we didn't have any songs. So, we were just throwin' it down on stage, but there was a vibe from the very beginning.

**Kimbrough:** Yeah, there was. Backstage, after the show, when the guys asked what our names were, I said, "I don't know. This is just the second time I've met this guy!"

*DownBeat*: "Who's Gonna Ride" sets the tone for the album and brings it into the present. How did that come about?

**Pearson:** The lyrics I wrote in the midst of the pandemic, where I was just thinking about some of my experiences with the police. I've had several! One of the first was when they changed a law and said three or more people gathered together can be considered a gang. And I have four brothers, so just walking home, we're a gang. And the police would stop us. Ask us what we were doing. You learn very early on that anything can happen, bad things go down with the police, and seeing what happened to George Floyd really touched me. The whole world was marching for George Floyd, and I wondered what the impact would be if the same thing happened to me. "Who's gonna ride with me?" was a personal question. Like, dang, what if something like that happened to me?

*DownBeat*: Have you also had encounters with cops, Cameron?

**Kimbrough:** I've had several. But I don't even want to get into talking about what should have been really innocent encounters.

*DownBeat*: Yeah, driving while Black. Did you both work together on the music for "Who's Gonna Ride"?

**Pearson:** Yeah, we do on every song. It's like we're talking to each other.

**Kimbrough:** It's a conversation.

**Pearson:** Playing with Cam, I stripped down, and I've been learning so much. Cam kind of showed me a different sound. Deeper and more bluesy.

***DownBeat*:** Yeah, that hypnotic hill country drone digs deep. You recorded this at the famous Sun Studios, right?

**Pearson:** Yeah, it's pretty surreal. So is how well it's been received, because a lot of what's on the album just came off the back porch. And when we got in the studio there just happened to be microphones there.

***DownBeat*:** And now your back-porch conversation is going out to the world. What do you hope to achieve?

**Kimbrough:** I want the world to be inspired and the youth to be inspired by what we're doing, and make us a household name.

***DownBeat*:** Worthy goals, all. And the Yella P Manifesto Damion wrote for the album will help you reach them. Can you send that out to DownBeat's readers, Damion?

**Pearson:** *Memphissippi Sounds*: A voice for the blues people, the sons of sharecroppers. A voice for the marginalized. An escape from the mainstream. A swim in muddy waters. A testimony to time, grit and grime. A healing sound. A mantra. A shot in the dark. A real awakening. A sign of the times.

# The Many Lives of Little Freddie King, New Orleans Blues Royalty

*DownBeat*, January 2023

The elder statesmen of New Orleans blues—Little Freddie King and Guitar "Lightnin" Lee—are both octogenarians. But King has seniority and bragging rights over friendly rival guitarist Lee, a native New Orleanian who just turned eighty.

"We're not grown until we get eighty," King explained at his home in the New Orleans' Musicians Village shortly after he mesmerized the overflow crowd celebrating his eighty-second birthday at BJs, his longtime 9th Ward headquarters. "So, thank God I made eighty-two."

Little Freddie King is also the undisputed monarch of New Orleans blues whose down-home, gut-bucket style emerged from the fertile crescent of the Mississippi River. Born Fread E. Martin in Bo Diddley's hometown of McComb, he crafted his first guitar from a cigar box tossed out by two "big shots" in a Cadillac while he was walking home from a seven-mile trek to the nearest store. The guitar was a project born out of necessity—after his guitar-picking father gave him a whipping and revoked his picking privileges for breaking the old man's strings.

"I just play what come to me from my heart," King said about a sound that evolved over decades of hard living and hard drinking. (He got sober forty-eight years ago.) "And it come out clear, there's no false sound to it. I've been dead so many times, it's crazy."

Again and again, King snatched life from the jaws of death, surviving a bloody litany of shootings, stabbings, electrocutions, near-fatal accidents and killer hurricanes, all while gigging almost constantly and recording a prodigious catalog of work that dates back to 1971, a year after he started his fifty-year run at the New Orleans Jazz & Heritage Festival.

*Blues Medicine* serves as King's latest release on Made Wright Records, a label he jointly owns with his drummer/manager, Wacko Wade. Back in 1993, Wade abandoned his career as an R&B drummer to play with King. In 2021, King was also enshrined on 180-gram vinyl by Newvelle Records, shortly before the prestigious jazz label recorded Jon Batiste, who King calls "that Black kid from Kenner."

Sporting a red vest, vintage tie and trademark flat-brimmed straw hat, the ever-dapper bluesman welcomes friends to a home bursting with memorabilia, outrageous stage wear and a world-class guitar collection that includes a custom Dr. Bones model. Back in the kitchen, the one-time TV repairman and auto mechanic tinkers with his Flying V guitar, the sole survivor of his Hurricane Katrina-destroyed home. Even after such tragedy, King spins fantastic tales about his long, almost-mythic life.

**Let's go back to the very beginning, when those big shots threw away that cigar box.**

When I spotted that box in the ditch, I said, that's just what I need to make my own guitar. So, I bring it home and cut holes in it with bottle glass, pulled pickets off the fence for my neck and made little tuner keys out of hickory. Then the horse started swishing horse flies off his tail, and when I hear that sound I said, wow, maybe I make strings out of them hairs. So, I pulled some out, put 'em on and tightened 'em up. And when I plucked it, it made a sound! But those hairs are delicate, so I kept going back for more until I pulled a great big bald spot in the horse's tail. And I said, "Uh-oh, now I'm gonna get another beating. But when my daddy got home, he got so high on that corn liquor that he didn't pay no attention. He just run out like Gene Autry, jumped up on the horse and went down through the woods. So, I missed that whooping.

**They say a cat has nine lives, and you may have already outlived nine.**

Yes, Lord, I'm telling you. One time, I went to the hospital with a hemorrhage, but the doctors couldn't stop the bleeding. So, I prayed, "Lord, please spell my life a little longer." The next morning, when the vampires come, that's what I call the nurses, I said I ain't got no blood. The good Lord stopped me from bleeding. And they brought about thirty or forty doctors and nurses to see me because they couldn't believe it.

**You keep amazing people, like that time you nearly electrocuted yourself.**

I was high, and I had to tune this man's TV and forgot it was plugged in. So, when I grabbed it, boom! This big, blue-and-purple ball of fire popped outta my mouth. Then my heart started beating fast and funny. So, I called the cab and went over to Charity Hospital and the doctor said, "What's your problem?" I said, "I just got hit by five-hundred volts." And he said, "You didn't get hit by no five-hundred volts, because you would be dead." I said, "Well I ain't dead." Then I passed out and fainted.

**That's pretty scary. What was your scariest close call?**

My bicycle accident [in 2017]. I had to play at [the nightclub] DBA that night, so I goes down early to get my cigarettes, going as fast as I can go. When I got halfway there, I didn't see this lumber piled on top of a garbage can, and all that wood hit me and bust me up inside. I was in the middle of the street so I said, "Jesus, please help me." And wasn't five minutes before a white dude come by in a Cadillac and said, "Mister, you hurt? Want me to call the paramedic?" I said, "No, just pull me out the street, so another car don't come by and finish me off." Another guy helped me get up, and I got a piece of the same lumber that nearly killed me and made a crutch out of it. Then I called Wacko [Wade], and he took me to the emergency room. They wanted to operate but I didn't want to stay, so he took me home, and I laid on the couch for three days squeezing this little rubber ball to get my fingers back. I had to. We were going to play a New Year's Eve show at this jazz festival in [Orvieto] Italy. I played wearing a neck brace, and I couldn't bend my fingers right. But I just pushed through and faked it. Sounded good! We played the whole week at a cafe that packed 'em in three-hundred people a night.

**I love the title of the new album, Blues Medicine, because all music, and the blues in particular, really does have the power to heal.**

That's the inside we put in. It's better than the doctor's prescription, a dose of medicine that will make you well. All the songs [on the album] are brand new, except for two. "Dust On The Bible" was originally done by Hank Williams, and "Caress Me Baby," that's a Jimmy Reed song. But they should be considered new because of the way I play them.

**They've been Freddie-fied. There's no mistaking a Little Freddie King.**

The gutbucket, see, is really tribulation from stress and hard times. You don't have nowhere to stay. You got to lay out there and sleep with your head on a hollow log. Get up the next morning for breakfast you gotta drink muddy water. So that's gutbucket blues, all that heart and soul.

**You've spread that heart and soul all over the world. Got a personal highlight?**

Bourbon Street in Sao Paolo [Brazil]. It's a real high-end club with ladies in long dresses and high heels that also has this free block party for the people of Sao Paulo. We play on a small stage by the club, but they put up big-screen TV sets so the party stretches for blocks. That's a good one, mmm-hmm. Eighty-thousand people.

# II.

## Soul Sisters: Marianne Faithfull, Janis Joplin and Other Uppity Women Who Shook Things Up

### *Introduction: Sisterhood Is Powerful*

Sisterhood is powerful: I feel a deep personal bond with many of the women I've been fortunate enough to write about.

It was, of course, the white and black magic of their music that sparked our initial connection and lit the flame deep inside me that continues to burn. But the wisdom I gleaned from our encounters also continues to guide me. Whether we cemented our bond over the course of many years or one intense conversational communion—conducted with her banshee spirit in the case of Janis Joplin—they all taught me something important.

Three-and-a-half-years sober when we first met, Marianne Faithfull was taking her first baby steps back into the public spotlight after a two-year hiatus following her storied 1987 *Strange Weather* comeback shows at New York's Bottom Line, where I was among the lucky few who witnessed her rebirth. She was still in the process of mastering the art of receiving, a tough one for me as well, when Marianne gifted me this insight at the end of our epic 1989 interview: "Being able to receive has always been hard for me, because it's a far humbler position to be receiving than to be giving. It's very important to master that."

Yes, Marianne, it is hard. It was only after cancer put me on the ropes last year that I started to fully understand this.

Years after I stabbed the heavens with a power drill while dancing to her version of "Working Class Hero" on *Broken English* (1979), Marianne continues to be a deeply personal role model for me. Her will to survive and create art in the face of death, not just once but repeatedly, has challenged me to receive whatever the universe gives me, and accept the healing bounty of love we've both been given.

In 2019, when I flashed back to our original 1989 conversation for the PleaseKillMe.com story that opens this section, Marianne had just released Negative *Capability*, her 21st studio album. Arguably her strongest since *Broken English*, she revisits "As Tears Go By" from a septuagenarian's "evening of the day" perspective and, as always, is acutely attuned to the moment. "They Who Come at Night" rages at the random terror that haunts modern life and hit the Bataclan in Paris just blocks from what was then her home. Drawing on the Keatsian power of "negative capability," which enables great artists to stay true to their vision amid chaos and confusion, she poses on the album's cover proudly with the cane she was using to battle arthritis.

When the pandemic hit, Marianne began battling more than just arthritis. In 2020, she had to be hospitalized following a serious infection with Covid-19 that nearly killed her and still makes it hard for her to breathe and sing. But she soldiered on to fulfill a lifelong dream of reading Keats, Byron, Shelley and other favorite romantic poets on *She Walks In Beauty* (2021), accompanied by the Bad Seeds sonic architect Warren Ellis—who like Nick Cave, remains a frequent collaborator. Marianne makes a cameo appearance reading a poem in *This Much I Know To Be True*, the 2022 documentary that explores Cave's creative relationship with Ellis. A trouper to the end, Marianne slipped this mortal coil in early 2025, surrounded by her family and loving friends.

It's Marianne's power to receive their gifts of love that gave her the strength to endure, just as I've been empowered to survive cancer through my own artistic community. So once again, "Marianne Faithfull saved my ass," as I wrote in *PleaseKillMe*. "It wasn't the first time. And it probably won't be the last."

At the opposite end of the survivor spectrum (though both fell under the spell of "Sister Morphine") is Janis Joplin, equally influential on the woman I became. The Goddess Immediata's multiphonic cries of rage become rapture, pain become prayer, set loose my spirit dancers, and split my hot boogie queen persona wide open when she crashed the boy's club of live-free-die-young rock stars who ruled the world in the late '60s. Though I never saw Janis live, she was in heavy rotation on my hi-fi, and I spent several months chasing her ghost for a deeply reported *High Times* cover story in 1993. One day she even spoke to me:

*Talk about the Kozmic Blues, man. It's like a joke in itself, I mean it'd have to be, wouldn't it? To get shot down when YOU'RE ALREADY FUCKIN' DEAD!?!? That's supposed to be your ticket to ride, man, that's the Great*

*American Way: This is my body, take, eat! This is my blood, take, drink! Take another little piece of my heart! Sure, it kills you but, hey, you get to live forever. That's supposed to be the tradeoff. Everybody knows that.*

Yeah, Janis, you're right. In 1993, when I wrote that story, Janis really was in danger of slipping into oblivion. She didn't join fellow dead rock stars Jimi Hendrix and Jim Morrison in the Rock and Roll Hall of Fame until 1995, and while both of them remained in heavy rotation and became requisite rocker fashion statements, you rarely heard Janis on the radio or spotted a Joplin t-shirt. Morrison was even enshrined in Oliver Stone's 1991 movie *The Doors*, which I bet really stuck in Janis's craw—and for good reason. Like I told her banshee spirit during our *High Times* seance: "It's legend that you bashed Morrison over the head with a whiskey bottle, but it wasn't until I got an eyewitness account from your old Texas pal and Big Brother manager, Chet Helms, that I knew exactly WHY: 'He unzipped his pants and put his penis in her face, and she hauled off and whacked him good.' Right on, sister!"

An uppity woman if ever there was one, Janis showed me "a woman can be tough," like she sings in "Piece of my Heart," just like Marianne Faithfull did a decade later when she broke free from her lovechild past and came out swinging on "Broken English." Janis taught me you don't have to be a great beauty like Marianne to become beautiful. Even a pudgy ugly duckling, like we both were as adolescents, can transform into a swan if she switches her inner spotlight on when she steps onstage (or in my case, the dance floor, where Janis always encouraged fans to join her).

Both Marianne and Janis made my list of the '10 Best Albums Recorded By Women' when rock eminencia Ann Powers put out a call for submissions in 2018, as did many of the other women in the pieces that follow. And while I never had the opportunity to interview the great Patti Smith or even see *Live Through This* survivor Courtney Love live, PJ Harvey worked her mojo on me during a scorched earth performance in New York. And years after she cast her spell on me with *Illuminations*, Buffy St. Marie knocked me dead in full warrior mode when she rocked the New Orleans Jazz Festival. Jazz Fest was also where I saw my longtime hero, Lucinda Williams, for the first time with my true-blue soul sister Pamela Des Barres—who made my '10 Best Albums' list for *Permanent Damage*, her classic girl-talk album with The GTOs—one of the greatest pieces of dada performance art ever committed to vinyl.

Pamela and I first bonded when I was asked to profile her for *Us Weekly's* Seven Deadly Sins issue when *I'm With The Band: Confessions of a Groupie* was burning up the bestseller lists. She was predictably typecast as Lust, complete with a sleazy, very un-Pamela backseat slut photograph we both detested. But that 1988 story documents the beginning of a lifelong sisterhood, during which she encouraged me to "let it bleed" on the page, hooked me up with some key writing outlets and sent healing chants my way to help me confront cancer. There's also no question that Miss Pamela shook things up when she burst onto the scene.

So did Divine, who while not born a woman, created the most outrageously flamboyant female impersonator ever to blaze across the screen with her partner-in-crime John Waters. At the beginning of my journalistic career in Santa Fe, NM, I spent a couple weeks watching a heavily corseted Divine enthrall goggle-eyed cowboys as a bawdy saloon singer in Paul Bartel's "Lust in the Dust," a once-in-a-lifetime experience I resurrected for a 2021 *PleaseKillMe* story. I also got up close and personal in a long interview with her offscreen progenitor Glenn Milstead, during which we exchanged growing-up-as-a-fat-kid stories and I revealed I'd also worn glasses and braces. "Oh Jesus," a horrified Glenn responded. "You're lucky you're still around."

And I'm *still* here today, thanks in part to all of my Soul Sisters, the most recent of whom I bonded with in New Orleans.

I took a couple deep dives with my now-fellow New Orleanian Rickie Lee Jones. We initially met when she bought one of my star Cree-ations—a three-babydoll bustier, complete with babydoll pussy—a few Mardi Gras seasons ago. The first was a pandemic-era cover story for *OffBeat*, pegged to what would have been live performances at French Quarter Fest and Jazz Fest.

A year later, we spent a lively afternoon discussing Rickie Lee's compulsively readable memoir *Last Chance Texaco: Chronicles of an American Troubadour* for a *PleaseKillMe* story, when she opened our conversation by asking me what I liked about her book: "You get so deeply inside me that I feel like I *am* you," "Oh excellent," she responded before she reached over to swat a mosquito off my head. Our conversation explored the funhouse mirror of a life only Rickie Lee could have created and hit on key episodes both public (being half of the ultimate hipster cool couple with Tom Waits) and private (hiding in a cupboard as a child after a horse kicked her in the head). It was also a mother lode of hard-earned wisdom: "Life is fucking hard. But we all keep going on. And we're talking to each other in the invisible world. And we keep going."

That afternoon, Rickie Lee encouraged me to write my own memoir, which this book turned out to be, and she checked in with me frequently after I was hit with cancer. So did Tiana Hux Dews, whose creative career I've been tracking for years. Most recently, as the leader of her mighty band Malevitus, she calls down our collective demons and confronts the world's impending apocalypse by urging us to "Celebrate While We Incinerate."

But the deepest Soul Sister of them all was Jessie Mae Hemphill, who became my giggle-under-the-bedcovers girlfriend during a years-long connection that ranged from New York City to the hill country of Mississippi, and crossed many cultural and color boundaries. One of eight foundational blues artists I profiled for a 1990 *Spin* magazine spread pegged to the late '80s blues revival, Jessie Mae Hemphill first appears in the Deep Blues section of this book. But the scant three-hundred words I was allotted in *Spin* barely scratched the surface of her story and our experiences together.

Thirty years later in 2020, I finally had an opportunity to revisit "Hangin' With the She-Wolf of Como" for an in-depth spread in PleaseKillMe.com, which traced the arc of our relationship.

We first bonded like a couple of schoolgirls on the dance floor at a blues festival in New York. Then Jessie invited me to visit her in the crossroads town of Como, Mississippi, where we raised eyebrows traipsing through the aisles of the Bag 'n' Save in matching Crown Royal caps and shared a bed in her dilapidated trailer with a menagerie of poodles. Not long afterward, she returned to New York City for another festival and stayed in my fourth-floor walkup on Sullivan St., which failed to pass muster. ("Lordy, girl! You tryin' to kill me? I thought all the buildings in New York City had elevators!") But we had a blast hanging out and hitting the town together, both of us dressed to the nines.

After a stroke forced her to hang up her guitar in 1993, we kept in touch periodically, and I wore the necklace Jessie gave me in Como when I got married in 1995. Years later, in 2004, shortly after she recorded her swansong double CD, *Dare You to Do It Again*, I drove up from New Orleans to visit her in Senatobia, Mississippi, where we had the last of several lengthy interviews before her death in 2006.

The story of our relationship, drawn partly from contemporary journal entries, ends with an oral history of Jessie Mae Hemphill, told in her own words. Here's one quick preview from my 1989 journal: "Jessie has sworn off men for the moment, and sleeps with a loaded shotgun to fend off potential intruders. But her spirit rises far above circumstance: in her music; in the vibrant luminescence of her watercolors of guardian angels; and in the backwoods magic that whips up a fife-and-drum picnic that feeds an entire neighborhood of children, young blades and do-ragged grandmas on a rack of barbequed ribs intended for two."

My journey with Jessie Mae Hemphill bears witness to what I said at the beginning of the intro for this section: Sisterhood is powerful. I am blessed to have communed with Marianne Faithfull, Janis Joplin and all the other uppity women who shook things up, and am proud to introduce them to you in the stories that follow.

In 2018, Ann Powers put out a call for readers to name the ten best albums ever recorded by women. Here's the annotated list I submitted then, in no particular order, which I might update at some point. (The Ryan Adams reference clearly has not aged well, though I let it stand as a matter of historical record). Diverse it's definitely not. Nor is it au courant; these albums are all pretty old, like me. But it is heartfelt and true (at least to me):

***Broken English* by Marianne Faithfull**

Blasted it nonstop when it first came out, and created a killer interpretive dance careening around with a power drill to her raw, visceral version of "Working Class Hero." Years later, my live-in lover dropped to his knees and proposed to me while we were blasting the title track in our apartment. I said yes.

***Horses* by Patti Smith**

One for the ages, for "Birdland" alone. "I am a helium raven and this movie is mine." Yes, Patti, it most certainly is.

***Strange Weather* by Marianne Faithfull**

Sadder and a thousand times wiser, Marianne Faithfull moved me as deeply with her definitive post-career hiatus comeback album, forged in the 9th circle of hell, as she did with "Broken English." Her bone-dead-weary "Boulevard of Broken Dreams" cuts to the quick with shards of a shattered funhouse mirror, and her "As Tears Go By" flashback strips her early hit down to the marrow. Not a single track is wasted on this oft-overlooked masterpiece.

***To Bring You My Love* by PJ Harvey**

Has there ever been an invocation of erotic obsession as vividly visceral as Harvey's slow-blues crawl through hell in the title track? Or a lament as deeply sorrowful as the cries and whispers of the young mother who drowns her own daughter "Down by the River"? Harvey's "Dry" may have made the NPR best-of list, but I like my Polly Jean bloodier and wetter.

***Essence* by Lucinda Williams**

Everyone cites "Car Wheels on a Gravel Road," which is a fine debut album. But it didn't dig as deep, or reach me "where the spirit meets the bone" (to cite a later Lucinda lyric) the way "Essence" did. The title track, which doubles down on erotic obsession with its waiting-room stations of the cross—"I am waiting in my car/I am waiting at this bar"—inspired one of my down and dirtiest dance performances ever. The fact that it's rumored she wrote it for Ryan Adams, who she supposedly had a fling with (and on whom I had a crazy-bad crush on myself at the time), adds an extra frisson of danger to an already dangerous song.

***World Without Tears* by Lucinda Williams**

When this album first came out, Peter Blackstock of *No Depression* magazine had the unmitigated gall to take Lucinda to task for her "Righteously" lyrics, which he deemed unseemly for a fifty-something woman: "When you run your hand/All up and run it back down my leg/Get excited and bite my neck/Get me all worked up like that." Fuck you, Peter! Sexiness is ageless, and Lucinda is still one of the sexiest singers alive. And "Real Live Bleeding Fingers and Broken Guitar Strings," her tribute to the great Paul Westerberg, captures the wild, untamable spirit of real, raw rock 'n' roll.

***Live Through This* by Hole**

Courtney Love's fierce, ferocious "fuck you" to the world after Kurt Cobain shot himself and left her to pick up the pieces while a surreal circus of media vultures picked them both apart not only cemented her place as an artist in her own right. It also revealed the excruciating vulnerability of the little girl inside, the "Doll Parts" girl with the bad skin who "wants to be the girl with the most cake." I'm particularly fond of "Olympia," one of the more ostensibly unassuming tracks on the album, which speaks for anyone who ever escaped a town and a high school where "everyone's the same."

***Illuminations* by Buffy St. Marie**

"God Is Alive, Magic Is Afoot." Spooky and otherworldly yet rooted deeply in the soil, these mystic revelations from a First Nations warrior priestess reached me deep in my soul and tore back multiple veils of illusion. Years later, Buffy knocked me dead in full warrior mode when she rocked the New Orleans Jazz Fest with hard-driving "Medicine Songs" full of rage against injustice and laced with intimations of hope. She's only just begun, but I first pledged my allegiance to Buffy with "Illuminations," which shine just as brilliantly today.

***Pearl* by Janis Joplin**

I worshiped Janis out of the gate when she first careened onto the stage and let that magnificent voice loose with Big Brother and the Holding Company. But when Janis stepped out unvarnished for "Pearl," she dug deeper into her own soul than she'd ever dug before, and revealed a whole other woman behind her brassy, hard-drinkin' persona. Has there ever been a prayer as crazily plaintive as "Mercedes Benz"? And while many artists have put their own stamp on "Me and Bobbie McGee," including the man who wrote it, Janis' scrappy take on her own rough-hewn life remains the definitive version.

***Permanent Damage*** **by The GTOS**

Frank Zappa may have been the wizard behind the curtain. But it's the Girls Together Outrageously who turn what could have been just a bunch of out-of-tune chicks whooping it up at a pajama party into one of the greatest pieces of dada performance art ever committed to vinyl. Who wouldn't want to eavesdrop as "Miss Pamela and Miss Sparky discuss stuffed bras and some of their early gym class experiences"? Or ponder the significance of Captain Beefheart's "Fat Theresa Shoes"? And while many have mourned the premature loss of the Rolling Stones' Brian Jones, only the GTOs would ground their obsession with a prepubescent lookalike who inspires "Love on an Eleven-Year-Old Level."

# Blazing Away with Marianne Faithfull

**_PleaseKillMe_, August 2019**

AFTER A HARROWING DECADE *of personal and medical travails, Marianne Faithfull staged a remarkable musical comeback with the 1979 release of Broken English. Still battling her demons, Faithfull got fully sober in the mid-1980s and staged a grand personal comeback with a concert at St. Ann's church in Brooklyn (later released as the live album Blazing Away). Cree McCree met, and talked at length, with Faithfull around this time. McCree recently revisited the recordings of those conversations, presented here in their entirety for the first time.*

Marianne Faithfull saved my ass. It wasn't the first time, and probably won't be the last.

During a recent hurricane scare in New Orleans, where TS Barry was threatening to strike with the Mississippi River at historic highs, I was cocooned in a 1989 time capsule with Marianne, transcribing an interview I did for *Details* right after her glorious comeback performance at St. Ann's church in Brooklyn, released in 1990 as the live Island album and concert film *Blazing Away.*

So, while the rest of the town was angsting out with Katrina PTSD jitters, I had Marianne's smoky voice and easy laughter in my ears. It flashed me right back to Noho Star in New York City, where we chatted over two Caesar salads and numerous cigarettes before heading to the SoHo boutique Morgane Le Fay to find "something rather elegant" for her encore St. Ann's performance in *Seven Deadly Sins.*

Three-and-a-half-years sober when we met, Marianne was taking her first baby steps back into the public spotlight after a two-year hiatus in Ireland following her storied 1987 *Strange Weather* comeback shows at New York's Bottom Line. She'd only just started doing press, and since this was her first major interview, I was a little trepidatious. But she put me at ease immediately with her radiant warmth, animating her words with expansive gestures and an almost childlike exuberance. And when I finally dared to broach the subject, she didn't shy away from addressing the elephants in the room: Mick Jagger, Keith Richards and the despoiled innocence of the Stones years.

At that point in time, she was adamant about cutting off all ties:

"I've been quite ruthless in putting a great deal of distance between myself and the Rolling Stones. I don't dream about them. I don't think about them. I don't want to have anything to do with them again. In this life and in all others."

She also allowed, almost in passing, that "that might change with time." And so it has.

In 2004, Keith Richards co-produced "Ghost Dance," with Charlie Watts and Ronnie Woods backing her up, for *A Collection of Her Best Recordings*, released to coincide with *Faithfull*, the autobiography she told me in '89 that she would never write.

Richards later dueted with her on the Merle Haggard classic "Sing Me Back Home" on *Easy Come Easy Go* (2008) and remains a close friend. And while she and Mick haven't collaborated since they co-wrote *Sister Morphine*, "I'm very fond of Mick," she told *Interview* writer Evelyn McDonnell in 2009. "I really am. And he taught me so much. It was Mick who first played me 'Ooh Baby Baby.'"

Still, the Stones really *are* ancient history for Faithfull. Since her 1979 breakthrough album *Broken English*, which spit in the face of her lovechild past with the punk-rock rage of a street-junkie survivor, she's forged a formidable career.

After a few hit-or-miss albums and rehab stints, a newly-sober Faithfull re-emerged in 1987 as the ravaged chanteuse wandering "The Boulevard of Broken Dreams" on *Strange Weather,* creating the world-weary stage persona she fully concedes is an act. ("And it's a good one.") Long a nuanced interpreter of Kurt Weill and Bertolt Brecht, she later turned her live cabaret show "An Evening in the Weimar Republic" into *20th Century Blues* (1997), another landmark album of signature covers that channels "this dreary twentieth century din" on the Faithfull-penned title track.

Unlike most '60s relics cranking out hits on the nostalgia-tour circuit, Faithfull continues to reinvent herself and seeks out collaborators, many of them younger. *Kissin' Time* (2002) found her "Sliding Through Life On Charm" with Beck, Blur, Billy Corgan and Jarvis Cocker, while *Before the Poison* (2005) cemented her longstanding relationship with kindred spirits Nick Cave and PJ Harvey. And *Easy Come Easy Go* (2008) capped a years-long partnership with producer Hal Wilner that dates back to *Strange Weather.*

*Negative Capability*, her 21st studio album—and arguably her strongest release since *Broken English*—was recorded at La Frette studio in Paris, where she now lives. Produced by Rob Ellis and the Bad Seeds' Warren Ellis, it includes "The Gypsy Faerie Queen," a haunting duet co-written with Nick Cave, who captures the intimate spirit of their Paris sessions in this video interview.

Drawing on the Keatsian power of "negative capability," which enables great artists to stay true to their vision amid chaos and confusion, Faithfull poses proudly with the cane she uses to battle arthritis on the album's cover. And after decades of bushwacking her way through darkness into light, she's intimately acquainted with the key lesson of "No Moon In Paris":

*"Everything passes/Everything changes/There's no way to stay the same."*

Faithfull comes full circle on her latest album, revisiting "As Tears Go By" from a septuagenarian's perspective half a century after she first recorded it, and bringing a honeyed warmth to *Witches Song*, pitched an octave lower than on *Broken English*. She's also acutely attuned to the moment. "They Who Come at Night" rages at the random terror that haunts modern life and hit Bataclan in Paris just blocks from her home, while "In My Own Particular Way" is a paean to warts-and-all grownup love.

Forty years after I stabbed the heavens with a power drill while dancing to her version of "Working Class Hero" on *Broken English*, Marianne Faithfull continues to be a personal lodestar. And though I never got to take her lyric-writing class at the Jack Kerouac School of Disembodied Poetics at Naropa University, I've always considered her a teacher. At the end of our 1989 interview, she left me with this pearl of wisdom:

"Being able to receive has always been hard for me, because it's a far humbler position to be receiving than to be giving. It's very important to master that."

In that spirit, I give this moment in time we shared for you to receive, Marianne.

*The following interview, edited for clarity and length, was conducted in late 1989 for an article for Details magazine, which appeared in the March 1990 issue:*

***PKM*:** Was the St. Ann's show your first time performing in a church?

**Marianne Faithfull:** Yes. I was concerned from the beginning…I'm not actively religious, in the sense of being a practicing Catholic or anything like that. But I didn't want it to be sacrilegious, I wanted to do it with respect. So, I was astounded that some people were offended by the church. It was the last thing that I expected.

***PKM*:** That's really interesting, because the last performance I saw before your show was the Mississippi Delta Blues Project, which was also in a church. And some of the old blues guys were a little taken aback, because down South, a lot of people still believe that the blues is the devil's music. Booby Barnes was like, 'oh my god, am I going to get struck down by lightning?' But they all got into it, and people actually ended up dancing in the aisles.

**Marianne Faithfull:** That's exactly what a church is! What you're describing is exactly what worship should be: praise and celebration and communion with what people call God. Being human. And the Episcopalian priest [at St. Ann's] was delighted. He thought the show was wonderful. So, I was shocked that anyone would take offense, because I was really concerned that we did not abuse the privilege of working in a church. I did not want a big fuss to be made about "Why'd You Do It" in a church. I knew that "Sister Morphine" was a dream.

***PKM*:** It was. It sends chills up your spine when the scrim comes down, and that stained glass window becomes illuminated for "Sister Morphine."

**Marianne Faithfull:** "Sister Morphine" is probably the most transcendent song I do. In terms of facing my personal reality and going through it--not past it or over it, but just through it. "Sister Morphine" is always with me. But I'm not high. And that's a very powerful thing.

***PKM*:** I also feel, whether it's in a church or not--because I saw you at the Bottom Line a couple years ago, which was also extraordinary--that it's a real act of faith for you to perform in the first place.

**Marianne Faithfull:** It's a clear sign of my commitment to people. It's a thing I picked up from Allen [Ginsberg]. It's environmental generosity for me. I believe it is my form of service.

***PKM*:** There's also a literal unveiling that happens; you remove the gloves, and later the cloak. I feel like you need that, too, that peeling off of the layers, and that it's not just there for dramatic effect.

**Marianne Faithfull:** Absolutely. That's why that mantle is so ideal for me, because it gives me time and people will wait for the transformation to happen. It doesn't happen when I walk on. The first at least four songs might be technically proficient. But whatever it is that happens to me isn't there yet. And then at some point, I feel it too, it comes. And then something else happens. And God knows what it is.

***PKM*:** It's giving me chills just hearing you describe it.

**Marianne Faithfull:** I don't let myself worry about it or analyze it. The best thing I can do is not get in the way. Just step aside and let it do whatever it is. My job is to take care of myself: get enough sleep, and not smoke too much, and eat right. And when I do that, it happens. It's amazing how smooth it is.

***PKM*:** You're so animated in your gestures when you talk. And when you're on stage, you're so contained. One of the notes I wrote was "contained rage." Some of your songs have a lot of anger in them, and yet you're so cool about it, you let the musicians express of lot of that rage. It's a very powerful dynamic.

**Marianne Faithfull:** It's true. They all become one thing.

***PKM*:** Well, you have a really long-standing relationship with most of your musicians.

**Marianne Faithfull:** I do. And I always will. But I'm obviously interested and open to doing different things. You can never tie yourself down to one thing. That's always been my problem with popular taste in pop music or whatever you want to call it. They want you to find a formula and stick to it. And I'm not prepared to do that, ever. Not even now.

***PKM*:** How would you describe your formula if you were to stick to it?

**Marianne Faithfull:** Well, I'm not fixed! But I guess, oh very cool, wise, la de dah.

***PKM*:** And you don't want to be trapped by that? Having to smoke cigarettes for the next twenty-five years of your life?

**Marianne Faithfull:** No, no. What if I want to stop smoking? As you can see, when you talk to me, I'm not very world-weary at all. That's the thing. It's definitely an act. And it's a good one. I like it. There's a part of me that's extremely cynical and really does have that attitude.

***PKM*:** What would you like to do next as an artist?

**Marianne Faithfull:** I don't know. There are so many possibilities. All the people I work with, they all have different ideas. And at the moment, I'm sort of taking all these ideas and figuring out which I want to do.

***PKM*:** What about anything more theatrical? I know you were on the stage at one point.

**Marianne Faithfull:** I would like that very much. Because, in a way, being Marianne Faithfull is almost not enough. It doesn't use all my faculties, I know that. I'm still firing on four cylinders where I could be firing on eight, and I'm aware of that.

***PKM*:** Do you want to do more film work?

**Marianne Faithfull:** If I got something I really thought I could do, I think I might. But you must know well how exploited and awful the business is. Rock & roll is sleazy, but film is even worse.

***PKM*:** Really? I always thought rock & roll was the ultimate sleazy.

**Marianne Faithfull:** That's true. you're right. OK, rock & roll is the lowest level of human life there is. And then you have the fashion business. And then maybe film.

Sleaze is something you have to come to terms with. It's not that I can go around pointing at other people, saying you're sleazy and you're sleazy and you're sleazy but I'm not. If I work with sleaze and surround myself with sleaze, I am sleaze. And I have done that. But I really do try to put a distance between myself and the major sleaze.

***PKM*:** Do you think that's what you got caught up in the early days? I do want to ask you a little about the Stones, because I just saw their latest tour and they're very much on my mind. Did you see it?

**Marianne Faithfull:** No. The Stones, when I knew them anyway, were not sleaze. They may have become sleaze. I mean, there were elements of that. But they weren't really that sleazy. It's hard, because I've just seen that wonderful Michael Cooper book [of photos from the early '60s]. It wasn't really as beautiful as that, but he captured some wonderful moments, I remember them, and it's made me a little softer toward [that time].

But I really have been quite ruthless about putting a great deal of distance between myself and the Rolling Stones. And I know I'm right, for me.

***PKM*:** I wasn't sure if you even wanted to talk about it.

**Marianne Faithfull:** Well, I certainly wouldn't want to get into any kind of sliming.

***PKM*:** Oh no, that's not what I mean. I've sort of liked watching the evolution.

**Marianne Faithfull:** What did you think of the [Stones] show?

*PKM*: I thought it was incredible, it renewed my faith. I'd lost faith in Mick many years ago when he went off on that tangent. And there was Keith, stronger than ever, and goddammit they're still the greatest rock & roll band in the world.

**Marianne Faithfull:** I'm sure. And I'm sure they will always be.

*PKM*: And in a very different way, you renewed my faith in myself. Seeing your show was a very transcendent experience. Do you feel like things are coming a little closer again, and that you don't have to put so much distance?

**Marianne Faithfull:** The only area I've always felt really comfortable with the Stones is the Stones as artists. I really admire them as writers and I always have. That's the way I can handle it. I'm just still too diminished by it. And that's not the Stones' fault. That's my fault.

I was just furious with myself that I let it just get so important. My work is so important to me. And yet I continued to put it back and didn't really follow it through. I can't blame the Stones for that. But it makes me furious, and I feel like it was a very seductive detour in my life. That I frankly didn't need.

But at the same time, I obviously wanted it to happen.

*PKM*: I saw the Stones concert with a close girlfriend, and when those two honky-tonk women got blown up, who were so much larger than them, we saw it as a sort of homage to the goddess. It was like the old macho days had been transmuted into something much more powerful.

**Marianne Faithfull:** That's great! It's also *so* inaccurate to talk about "The Stones."

*PKM*: You're right. They're completely different entities. Do you feel a kind of kindred spirit thing with Keith?

**Marianne Faithfull:** I always have, yeah.

*PKM*: It always seemed strange to me that it was Mick that you ended up spending more time with.

**Marianne Faithfull:** No, I don't think so. I think it all happened as it was meant to happen, really. I think Keith is better as a friend anyway.

*PKM*: Are you still in touch?

**Marianne Faithfull:** I haven't spoken to him for a long time, about two or three years. Because I have consciously put a block on it. I don't want anything to do with him.

***PKM*:** Did you listen to Keith's new album [*Talk Is Cheap*]?

**Marianne Faithfull:** No.

***PKM*:** It's quite good.

**Marianne Faithfull:** I heard that. And I know one of the people who worked on it. I mean, I think I listened to it once but I really didn't let myself get involved. I have detached, quite consciously. I wish Keith really well and I know he's doing well, and that's lovely. But I don't feel connected. And I don't feel grateful either.

That may change with time. I realize that. I'm only three and a half years clean and I'm still having to confront these things. But I would not say my relationship with Mick Jagger was life-enhancing. I would also not say my relationship with Keith Richards was life-enhancing. And that's really got nothing to do with them.

What I do want to say is that I do not judge them. They're not in my present. They're in my past. And, of course, I do believe that we're all one. That's how I could detach. Because they're there in me anyway, I can sort of step back.

***PKM*:** And let it go for the rest of your life? You don't feel there ever has to be…

**Marianne Faithfull:** A moment of reconciliation? I used to think that. But I don't now. First of all, it's extremely unlikely. With Mick Jagger. With Keith Richards, if I saw him, I think it would be very positive. But why would I see him? What for?

***PKM*:** I could imagine you two writing something together.

**Marianne Faithfull:** I don't know. I'm very much not in touch with this. And I don't let myself get involved. People call me and try to tell me that this one said this and that one said that. And I don't give a flying fuck. So no, I am not open to that. And that's how I have to be for myself. The demeaning, the diminishing side of this, you wouldn't really understand it unless you'd been through it. I mean, every woman has had that experience, I'm sure.

***PKM*:** I've had parallel experiences, but they weren't on that grand public scale.

**Marianne Faithfull:** Actually, because of the grand public scale, that's why I have to be so ruthless about it. It's obviously how it was meant to be, I don't want to change a thing. It's all OK.

***PKM*:** Do you feel past life connections at all?

**Marianne Faithfull:** No, I really don't, actually. I have felt those things but I don't only not want to see those people in this life. I don't want to have anything to do with them again. In this life and in all others.

I'm naturally aware that we're all connected, we're all a part of each other. But I did not know, and I know now, that we do not have to actually physically have anything to do with each other. At all. That is the right of the individual to make that decision.

I don't dream about them. I don't think about them. I have to talk about them because it's part of my experience, people ask me. And every time I talk about it, it gets stronger. This is my will. I don't want to have anything to do with them and it's not because they're bad or evil. They're not. For me, it's just over.

***PKM*:** That's not the only thing that's over. I know you've been clean for the past three and a half years. Do you also not drink at all anymore?

**Marianne Faithfull:** No. Nothing. I can't. I was always sure there was a magical amount, and if I could get it right, not only would this extraordinary thing occur but I would feel good. That was my aim. And sometimes I got it right. Just the right amount of vodka, just the right amount of chicken salad sandwich. And then I couldn't really get it right and it got worse and worse and I was killing myself. And I knew that, for me, I would not be able to control it. And that the best thing I could do was to just stop. And that's what I did. And it all got a lot easier. I sometimes miss it, that sort of intoxication. The seductiveness of that. But it doesn't really measure up to just feeling sort of good most of the time.

***PKM*:** And you're certainly not going around spouting therapeutic platitudes.

**Marianne Faithfull:** I've worked hard not to do that. With the experience I've been through, I think it's only normal in the beginning to get sort of self-righteous and evangelical. And I did. I've come out it now, thank God. I believe that doing nothing else, except not using drugs and alcohol and doing what I do, is a powerful thing. And I don't have to say a thing. There's nothing to say.

*PKM*: What gave you the strength to quit? Is there a higher power? Is it inside you?

**Marianne Faithfull:** Well, it's something I don't really talk about or share. It's very private. My inner life is just that. Inner. Private. Completely mine. I don't share it with anyone. That's the one thing that is completely personal to me.

I do obviously exist within a community, and I am just one among many other human beings trying to live. How I do it, what I believe, what I think—and I do have an intense spiritual life and I always have had—and it's much more intense now, because I give it more time than I did. And I guess because it's important to me I don't want to talk about it. Because it's private.

*PKM*: You've also given yourself time to heal.

**Marianne Faithfull:** I've had two years, really, to be at peace. Some of the strength I have at the moment comes out of this time I've had in Ireland, where I live in the country. I have a lot of time to myself there, and I need that. I'm still healing. And I didn't like it at all. I wanted to be working.

I'm very conscious that every time I don't do a tour that's projected, people say that I'm still drinking. And I really want to shake that, very much. And it takes a long time.

I called up a top agent in America to talk about my projected tour in March. I'm going to see her on Thursday. And all she said—she knows me and she must know that apparently, I got clean—all she said on the phone was "are you well? are you well?" And I can't get offended. I just have to take it. And just say yes, I'm very well, I'm extremely well. I can't even say, well, I don't feel so great today.

*PKM*: You know, I think I might have a flu coming on [*laughs*]

**Marianne Faithfull:** No, I can't say anything like that [*laughs*]. The last thing I can say is a flu coming on. That's the classic sort of dope sick stance.

*PKM*: When you did those Bottom Line shows [in 1987], that was the first time you'd performed in public in a very long time, at least to my knowledge.

**Marianne Faithfull:** Oh no, it really *was* a long time. It was a sort of rebirth. And everybody regrets that they didn't film it. It would have been nice to have that show and this one. But what happened was that the Bottom Line almost became the shadow show. Because people kept saying, oh it's not like the Bottom Line. Of course, it's not like the Bottom Line! It's two years later, and a lot has happened, and it's not going to be the same.

*PKM*: But the St. Ann's show was so much more opened up. Not only because of the space but because of who you are now, two years later.

**Marianne Faithfull:** Sure. It's changed. And I like that! It gives me a lot of hope that two years from now it can just go on doing whatever it is. There's a lovely phrase in the tantra: self-existing energy. That just goes on working whether you know it or not, whether you want it or not, whether you accept it or not, there it is!

*PKM*: There's a line in that song you do on *Strange Weather*, "A Stranger On Earth": "The day's gonna come when I prove my worth." Did you feel like you were having to prove your worth for a while?

**Marianne Faithfull:** For years. All my life.

*PKM*: And do you feel you've gotten beyond that?

**Marianne Faithfull:** Well, on a good day. On a bad day, I don't feel any better. I feel just the same. It's very cyclical. It doesn't go in a straight line by any means. Every day and every way, I get better and better and better. I hope I'm not making it sound like that!

But I must say I do feel a lot more confident. Confidence in Spanish is *confianza,* which means "with faith." It's that simple. It doesn't mean I don't get deluded or get enmeshed in bullshit. Because I do. But I have hope. I think I have a lot of hope.

I'm also still learning. I'm still a little stuck in the human beings are all slimes bit. Because, although I try not to, I do feel like that a lot of the time. And that's not just men, that's men and women. Just people are basically awful.

But on the other hand, that's not really the truth. Because in my life I have a lot of people, and I meet a lot of people, who are not slime.

The point I've really got to, and I know this is a big breakthrough for me, is that I'm not going to judge people. I'm not going to idealize them and say they're wonderful. But I'm also not going to say these people are slime. Because I honestly don't know. I wouldn't be surprised if they *were* slime!

*PKM*: I think we all have our slime moments.

**Marianne Faithfull:** Yes. It's a moment-by-moment thing. All I can really do is examine the slime in myself. And not worry about other people.

*PKM*: Is there anything from your past, any trial by fire that had to happen? Anything positive that came out of it?

**Marianne Faithfull:** Well, yeah. A lot of things. "Sister Morphine" came out of my junkie phase. I couldn't have written that—I am that kind of person; I have to actually have the experience to be able to write about it. It has to be authentic. And it certainly was authentic! [*laughs*] I don't regret it, really. But enough already is what I think. I can't hurry that up. It just has to slowly get better.

*PKM*: First there's the private healing and then there's the public healing.

**Marianne Faithfull:** Yes. And that's what I'm doing now. I'm actively talking to people, and I'm keen on talking to the press, really. Because it helps my work. It helps my ability to get dates, to perform, it's all hooked into this. It's very important. Because the whole point of this is being able to get through these things. Not past them, not over them, but through them.

*PKM*: Do you think you'll ever write a book?

**Marianne Faithfull:** No, I don't. People are not really so interested me and my own life, and how I became the way I am. Which didn't happen in the '60s. [laughs] It happened in my childhood and all the rest of it. People are interested in what it was like to live with Mick Jagger. And I know that. But I don't need to write about it. Maybe I will write a book when I'm older.

*PKM*: Well, you are a writer.

**Marianne Faithfull:** It's quite likely that I might write a book. Certainly not an autobiography. I would like to do a book of essays.

*PKM*: What kind of essays would you write?

**Marianne Faithfull:** I really don't know. I did have a dream once, when I was very worried about my life at the moment. And in the dream, some people came with a book and it was my book. The book I was going to write. And they opened it for me and let me read it. And I did. It was actually songs, I think.

*PKM*: Do you think you've written some of those songs since you had that dream?

**Marianne Faithfull:** Yes, I do. And when I lose heart, and get depressed about it, I remember that dream. I know for a fact that I have many more things to write.

***PKM*:** I'm picturing something almost like an illuminated manuscript.

**Marianne Faithfull:** It was this huge book. I don't remember a thing in it. I woke up and I was just so pissed off that I couldn't remember. I don't know what it really meant. It might have even been my life. But it makes me feel safe because I know that there's more to do.

***PKM*:** So, you're ready to receive.

**Marianne Faithfull:** Yes. Being able to receive has always been hard for me, because it's a far humbler position to be receiving than to be giving. It's very important to master that.

## High Times Greats: Janis Joplin

***Fifty years after her death, we revere Janis Joplin as America's greatest female rocker ever, but still don't know what made her tick.***

***High Times* cover story, September 1993**

For the September, 1993 issue of High Times, Cree McCree provided an exhaustive profile of Janis Joplin, who died on October 4, 1970. She was the brashest of the brash, the life of San Francisco's flower-power party. To commemorate the half-century mark following her passing, we're republishing the story below, followed by a sidebar tribute featuring Debbie Harry, Exene Cervenka, Jennifer Barry, and Maria McKee.

Little Richard said you can hear the holy spirit in Janis Joplin's voice. She could (and did) sing clear as a bell, but it was the cracks in that bell—multiphonic cries that splintered a single note into a three-tone chord—that set loose the spirit dancers. Listening to her now—on a marathon "Ball and Chain" bootleg from late 1968—I hear an exquisite glossolalia of rage become rapture, of pain become prayer, her voice dipping and soaring like a host of fallen angels beating their wings in flight.

I never saw Janis live, but for the past few months I've been chasing her ghost. Perched atop my computer in an old Scavullo photograph, bedecked in beads and that gold crocheted vest she practically lived in on-stage, Janis grins at me, her eyes crinkled with glee in that mutable Play Do face. One day she even spoke to me:

Talk about the Kozmic Blues, man. It's like a joke on itself, I mean it'd have to be, wouldn't it? To get shot down when YOU'RE ALREADY FUCKIN' DEAD!?!? That's supposed to be your ticket to ride, man, that's the Great American Way: This is my body, take, eat! This is my blood, take, drink! Take another little piece of my heart! Sure, it kills you but, hey, you get to live forever. That's supposed to be the tradeoff. Everybody knows that.

Yeah, Janis, you're right. Death certainly didn't kill Jimi Hendrix, who's been more prolific posthumously than most living rock stars, and whose T-shirt-emblazoned face remains a requisite fashion statement for all aspiring guitar heroes. But that's cool, I know you're down with that; you bonded with Jimi bigtime, over Southern Comfort and your separate-but-equal missions to penetrate the very core of the blues.

I bet what really sticks in your craw is the canonization of that chauvinist pig Jim Morrison, who has never slipped out of heavy rotation. It's legend that you bashed Morrison over the head with a whiskey bottle, but it wasn't until I got an eyewitness account from your old Texas pal and Big Brother manager, Chet Helms, that I knew exactly WHY: "He unzipped his pants and put his penis in her face, and she hauled off and whacked him good." Right on, sister!

The Morrison-bashing incident is typical Janis, who also belted another oinker, Jerry Lee Lewis (true to form, the Killer hit back). An Uppity Woman if there ever was one, Janis Joplin pre-dated the feminist movement (she also pre-dated Roe v. Wade, flying to Mexico for a botched abortion while already a star). Considering how much Janis accomplished during her twenty-seven-year existence, it's no wonder she's pissed that her legacy seems to have been inherited by the wind. Think about it: When was the last time you saw anyone wearing a Janis Joplin T-shirt? Or heard her voice come over the radio?

Signs of Janis are everywhere, however. The simultaneous publication of three Joplin biographies last fall created a brief flurry of renewed interest, but neither Ellis Amburn's tabloid-trashy *Pearl*, Laura Joplin's sweet-sisterly *Love, Janis* or the reissue of Myra Friedman's still-definitive *Buried Alive* (a bestseller when it first came out in 1973) burned up the book charts. In 1991, Janis was in the news when the Joplin estate prevented a play based on the singer's life from continuing its Seattle run. Broadway producer Manny Fox (*Sophisticated Ladies*) currently owns the theatrical and film rights for future dramatic treatments of Janis Joplin's storied life. A play and movie are in the works.

But those efforts are still in limbo, as is Sony/Columbia Record's long-awaited Joplin box set, which has been mired in disputes between Sony and the Joplin estate for years. "We've been saying it's coming out soon for so long it's getting pretty old," admits Janis' brother, Michael, who along with Laura Joplin manages the estate. "Sony has one idea and we have another. It's been hard to come to terms."

Such complications have contributed mightily to the post-death demise of Janis Joplin, a vanishing act that borders on cultural crime. Shortly after her 1970 smack/booze overdose—a fate no less sordid than Hendrix's or Morrison's, but perceived as somehow more unseemly for a woman— the circumstances of Janis' death began to overshadow her life. Blame Bette Midler's grotesque portrayal of a vaguely Joplinesque singer distorted into an obsessive-neurotic in *The Rose* (she earned an Oscar nomination for the 1979 role). But what really did Janis in was the Reagan-era backlash against the fever-pitched excesses of the '60s. Having first deified her as the Goddess Immediata, cultural revisionists promptly circled her corpse like vultures, brandishing Janis as Everything That Went Wrong With Be Here Now-ism.

"It was Janis Joplin, in particular, who symbolized the tone and temper and mood of her time," Janis' former publicist/confidante Myra Freidman writes in the new introduction to *Buried Alive*. "She had espoused a philosophy of the immediate, a disdain for the future, an appetite for the instinctual. She voiced these beliefs repeatedly, and they were every bit as important as her fear—not really so distant from the wellspring of her credo either—that she was just 'an ugly chick from Port Arthur, Texas with not too much talent.'"

That this "ugly chick" forged a triumph out of that fear, transforming a raw natural gift into one of the most expressively nuanced instruments of any generation (and becoming a sex goddess in the process) is a remarkable achievement. Hopefully, Janis' probable, but by no means certain, induction into the Rock and Roll Hall of Fame in January will refocus attention on that achievement. Meanwhile, amidst the current '60s revival, whose bell-bottomed, lace-and-tatters gypsy chic Janis helped pioneer, there has never been a better time to reconsider Janis Joplin's brilliant art within the context of her brief but spectacular life.

## *The Texas Tornado*

WHETHER BY ACCIDENT OF birth or by cultural immigration, geography is often destiny. This was certainly true for Janis Joplin, who had two key coordinates on the geo-psychic map she trailblazed to stardom: her home state of Texas and her adopted home of San Francisco. "A mixture of Leadbelly, a steam engine, Calamity Lane, Bessie Smith, an oil derrick and rotgut bourbon funneled into the 20th century somewhere between El Paso and San Francisco" is how *Cashbox*, the music-industry trade publication, described Janis' nascent public persona in 1966.

Janis Lyn Joplin was born on January 19, 1943 in the then-booming refinery town of Port Arthur, with which she would have a lifelong, highly public feud. It was Texas (and neighboring Louisiana) that bequeathed Janis her deepest musical roots. It was also Texas that branded her a social outcast, ridiculing her as "pig," "whore" and pro-integration "n@gger-lover." "They laughed me out of the class, out of town and out of state," she told Dick Cavett in 1970.

What wasn't there to like about this bright, talented young woman from a good middle-class family? She dressed weird, for openers, in scandalously short skirts that did little to hide her pudgy figure. Her face was a teenager's nightmare, pitted with acne that would leave lifelong scars. She swore like a trooper and spoke up for civil rights in classrooms where integration was not yet open to debate. She scorned Top 40 radio and brazenly advertised her passion for black music and culture by crossing the color lines in local bars. She was the very antithesis of the nice suburban girl growing up in 1950s America.

Janis took refuge in painting, her violent slashes of vivid colors on canvas foreshadowing a voice still buried inside. She ran with an all-boy literati gang steeped in Leadbelly, Bessie Smith and Billie Holiday, Burroughs, Kerouac and the Beats. Tary Owens, one of the gang members, recalls across-the-river escapades into Louisiana honky tonks and blues bars that often culminated in barroom brawls with the bartender firing shots into the ceiling. Janis more than held her own in this hard-drinking posse, and booze became—and would remain—a constant companion.

But, more importantly, such forays were Janis' introduction to live music. "The thing about being from Texas," says Owens, "is musicians have always played everything. The same band plays blues, soul music, R&B, country, straight rock 'n' roll, and usually two or three guys can play jazz. So, it was natural for Janis to embrace all of that."

Janis graduated from high school on the cusp of a new decade in 1960. She boomeranged between attempts at "normalcy" (attending Lamar State College of Technology in nearby Beaumont and Port Arthur College) and stabs at Bohemia (an extended stay in Venice, California) before finally merging the two lifestyles in Austin as a student at the University of Texas in 1962. One night Janis stunned her new friends in UT's hip enclave called "The Ghetto" with a tape she'd just made.

"It was a Bessie Smith song. We went insane when we heard it, absolutely bonkers," recounts Clementine Hall, a close friend and founding member of the 13th Floor Elevators. "Her voice was magnificent, rich and clear, with a deep burr in it. We didn't even know she could sing!"

The discovery that Janis could for-real sing, not just in the church choir or in classically oriented family musicales, was a profound revelation. Ever so humbly, she ventured into Austin's flourishing folk music scene, playing autoharp in solo gigs and singing with the Waller Creek Boys bluegrass band. "Janis had to be literally dragged onstage the first few times she sang in public—threatened and told, 'You can do it, you can do it, you can't run away,'" says Hall. "She wore all black from head to foot and tried to disappear as much as possible."

Janis' hypersensitivity about her singing ability—which she never really outgrew—co-existed inside a powerful persona. "We listened to her like an oracle," Hall recalls. "I know it sounds absurd for a 19-year-old girl to have that kind of influence, but honest to God, she spoke with absolute authority on every subject—and we listened." The only woman on campus who didn't wear a bra, and one of the few to make the Dean's List of designated "troublemakers," Janis was UT's one-woman liberation army.

However, all was not well on campus. In a cruel déjà vu of her high-school humiliations, the frat houses nominated Janis as the "Ugliest Man on Campus." She tried to laugh it off, but the reopened wound festered beneath her bravado, and hastened her next move—to San Francisco, in the company of fellow Texan and fledgling San Francisco entrepreneur Chet Helms.

### *The Post-Beatnik Years*

THE VERY FIRST NIGHT they arrived in San Francisco, still road-weary from the long hitchhike from Texas, Janis launched a beer-and-change career on the coffeehouse circuit. Word spread fast that this new chick from Texas could really wail. Her performances from this era—a few of which were released on the posthumous *Janis* in 1975—are stunning, some as stark as the Texas flatlands, others almost uncanny invocations of Bessie Smith's smoky jazz-club blues.

Never much of a pothead, Janis preferred the hyperactive rush of speed, the drug of choice for San Francisco's fading beatnik community. "People like their blues singers miserable," Janis later said, and at this point she seemed hellbent on proving it. Despite interest from record labels, Janis managed to sabotage most of the opportunities. "Whenever she'd be on the verge of moving up to the next plateau, some disaster would happen," says Helms, her manager at the time. Deals regularly dissolved in the wake of speed-and-booze-steeped accidents and brawls.

Things went from bad to worse when Janis first escaped to, then from, New York, where she continued shooting speed in the summer of 1964. Back in San Francisco and hooked on methedrine, Janis weighed just eighty-eight pounds. In the spring of 1965, friends pooled their cash and sent her packing on a Greyhound home to Port Arthur.

Kicking her habit and re-enrolling at Lamar State in a valiant attempt to "go straight," Janis tried to compromise that year, says Laura Joplin, "but the one thing that felt honest and right for her was music." It wasn't long before she was drawn back to Austin, where the 13th Floor Elevators were rapidly transforming the folk scene with the same psychedelic rock that was about to explode in San Francisco. Janis was particularly taken with lead singer Roky Erickson, who would stretch his voice way past the usual limits for a white vocalist. "She was always a belter, but never a screamer," says Helms. "That aspect of her [the screaming vocals] was pretty directly derived from Roky." Adds the Elevators' Clementine Hall, "Roky showed her how to scream in a way that you didn't injure your vocal cords." It was excellent training for a woman whose cords were about to get the workout of a lifetime.

## *The High Priestess of Hippiedom*

Janis loved to say she was "fucked into joining Big Brother." Chet Helms had called in June of 1966, summoning her back to San Francisco to join Big Brother and the Holding Company, the hottest attraction at Helms' Avalon Ballroom. The "fucked into" talk made great copy, but it was hardly the whole story. As longtime roomie and style guru Linda Gravenites observes, "Janis wanted to succeed in capital letters, on her own terms. To be famous and show everybody."

And show 'em she did. The mix of Janis' bare-your-soul vocals and Big Brother's garage-band psychedelia was an instant ticket to ride on the kaleidoscopic rollercoaster of the Brave New World whose epicenter was San Francisco's Haight-Ashbury. With the "Summer of Love" a year away, the burgeoning hippie scene was still untainted by gawking tourists and *Time* magazine reporters. Life was an open door of endless possibilities, and the music never stopped. The Grateful Dead, Jefferson Airplane, Quicksilver Messenger Service and Santana all melded together with Big Brother in communal celebrations where free outdoor concerts were the rule and a couple of bucks bought entree into night spots like the Avalon and Bill Graham's Fillmore Theatre.

Everyone loved Janis and Janis loved everyone. Her lovers at the time included Country Joe MacDonald (of Country Joe & the Fish); Peggy Caserta, the beautiful junkie who later cashed in on their liaison with the book *Going Down with Janis*; and Big Brother guitarist James Curley, whose wife Nancy remained a close friend. It was, after all, the "whatever" era, and arguably the happiest period in Janis' life, when she could be a star without being a Star.

Janis' overnight emergence as the Haight's High Priestess of Hippiedom was an ironic twist for someone who rejected LSD, the hot drug of the moment, in favor of dope. "We considered ourselves beatniks," reports Pat "Sunshine" Nichols, Janis' roommate, confidante and long-since-recovered fellow junkie. "We were literate, we read Huxley and Kerouac and Rimbaud way before the Haight happened. Our set was elitist, we considered ourselves the most creative people, and we used [heroin] to enhance our creativity. The only thing [the hippie scene] gave Janis was the opportunity to do her own thing."

Just a year after returning to San Francisco, Janis baptized thousands of born-again pagans at the legendary Monterey Pop Festival in 1967 with her electroshock treatment of Ma Rainey's classic blues, "Ball and Chain" (Jimi Hendrix, who torched his guitar, also emerged as a cultural shaman). Monterey had a dramatic effect on Big Brother: shortly thereafter, Bob Dylan's kingmaker Albert Grossman took over management and Columbia Records signed the band to a contract (a previous deal with Chicago-based Mainstream Records had resulted in the group's low-budget debut). Big Brother's New York showcase in early 1968 incited what would now be called a media feeding frenzy. But they could care less about Big Brother. What they wanted was Janis.

"As soon as we started to achieve some success, the media jumped on us," recalls Big Brother drummer Dave Getz. "They picked Janis as the star and the band as kind of dragging her down. There's some truth to that. Janis was like a rocket. She became an incredible singer very fast."

Big Brother's Columbia debut, *Cheap Thrills*—featuring R. Crumb's cover illustration—laid down a body of work synonymous with Joplin: the gut-wrenching wails of "Piece of My Heart," Big Brother's steamy reinvention of "Summertime" and, of course, the show-stopping "Ball and Chain." Despite mixed reviews ("it's a real disappointment," *Rolling Stone* pouted), *Cheap Thrills* went gold just three days after its July 1968 release.

Janis was on her own trajectory now. In September, she told the band she was planning to form a new group as a solo artist. Big Brother's last show with Janis Joplin, on December 1st, appropriately took place in San Francisco. Twenty years later, the breakup remains a sore point for guitarist Peter Albin. "I still haven't forgiven her for the way she handled it," he says. "She made the decision and that was it." Albin also hasn't forgiven the people he believes pressured Janis into the break-up: management and the media-mongers.

"Big Brother was an incredible band," explains Tary Owens, Janis' Texas pal, "but they couldn't play a shuffle. They never had that backbeat rhythm Janis loved." Guitarist Sam Andrews, the sole Big Brother member to segue into Janis' Kozmic Blues Band, offers this perspective: "She wanted more of a soul and R&B sound, and also the power to control her own thing. People were shocked seeing a woman take that much power all of a sudden. She loved us and was good to us, but she was management and we were labor. That was a definite change."

As Kozmic Blues Band leader Snooky Flowers puts it, "Janis wanted to be as powerful as we were. And she was."

## *The Full-Tilt Boogie*

WHAT BEGAN AS A hippie home movie had accelerated with the jump-cut speed of an MTV video. The mainstream media, desperate to translate the chaos of the '60s into captions, found Janis so totally NOW, so soundbite-able. "Man," she told the *New York Times* in a magazine profile, "I'd rather have ten years of superhype-most than live to be seventy sitting in a goddamn chair watching TV. Right now, is where you are, how can you wait?"

Almost overnight, the Ugly Chick from Texas was making trend-setting fashion statements in *Glamour* and *Vogue*. A peacock's worth of feathers and an arsenal of bracelets and beads topped Linda Gravenites' "pirate-chick" combos of hip-hugging bell-bottoms, recycled lace and sumptuous velvets and silks. Draped over her shoulders was the foxy lynx coat Janis "extorted" from the makers of Southern Comfort, the sweet whiskey that became her trademark drink. But neither the ascendence of Janis' floozy alter ego, "Pearl," nor the continual lure of the needle, clipped the wings of a glorious voice that knew no bounds.

Though her seismic performances throughout 1969 incited fans to frenzy, Janis' new band—a horn-driven team of seasoned session pros assembled by Nick Gravenites (Linda's husband) and guitarist and fellow user Mike Bloomfield—was cold-cocked by the same rock pundits who urged her to ditch Big Brother. Again, *Rolling Stone* led the charge, first challenging the band's R&B authenticity, then attacking Janis in a particularly mean-spirited cover story that dubbed her "The Judy Garland of Rock and Roll." Released in November to lukewarm reviews, *I Got Dem Ol' Kozmic Blues Again Mama!* deserved better. A baptism-by-fire into the soul of R&B, these sessions produced some of Janis' best work, including "Try," "Maybe" and her born-again gospelizing on "Work Me, Lord."

Speeding towards a new decade in her psychedelic Porsche, Janis ran afoul of the law in Tampa, Florida, where she told the pigs to fuck-off when they tried to dampen a dancing-in-the-aisles crowd (Janis also inspired the FBI to monitor her self-proclaimed mission to "get them standing up when they should be sitting down"). Unhappy with the band's revolving-door personnel changes, she played her last gig with Kozmic Blues in December. By the following April, Janis regrouped with the Full Tilt Boogie Band.

On the road all summer—highlighted by a multi-orgasmic train tour across Canada of rock 'n' roll royalty including the Grateful Dead—Janis was raring to record again. The *Pearl* sessions in September found Janis expanding the dimensions of her kozmic blues and rediscovering her country roots, especially on the acapella "Mercedes Benz" and her still definitive take of Kris Kristofferson's "Me & Bobby McGee," with its gradual acceleration from down-home twang into, well, full tilt boogie.

The new band satisfied both Janis' own artistic vision and her ever-vigilant critics. Unfortunately, her collision course with alcohol and heroin was about to take its toll. Janis already survived an overdose once in 1969, the year heroin exploded on the Haight-Ashbury scene. Her off-again, on-again habit was bound to catch up with her. And doctors, alarmed at the swelling of her liver, pleaded with Janis to stop drinking (one binge with Kris Kristofferson, known as "The Great Tequila Boogie," lasted three weeks).

Alone in her room in Los Angeles' Landmark Hotel on October 4, 1970, Janis shot up a too-pure batch of heroin that fatally intersected with her booze-bloated veins. Just three weeks earlier, Jimi Hendrix was found dead in London. Now Janis was gone too.

Unlike the lingering mystery that still surrounds Jimi's death, Janis' death was incontestably accidental, and can only be construed as suicide on a symbolic level. "In a sense," says Linda Gravenites, "she lucked out. She had a successful, though too short, life and she went right out on the top. That was her choice."

"What most people forget about Janis is that she had a real good time," Sam Andrew observes. Most of Janis' intimates agree. As evidence, Linda Gravenites cites her old friend's beyond-the-grave blessing. While leafing through a photo-essay tribute to her own contributions to hippie-chic style, Linda suddenly heard Janis' voice. "She said, 'See, it's fun, isn't it honey!' And I had to admit to her, 'Yes, it was fun.'

## *The Cosmic Voodoo Child*

For the forthcoming Janis film project, Michael Joplin, an accomplished glass artist, was asked to create a visual collage in homage to his sister. The image he chose looks uncannily like a voudoun altar. Votive candles burn amidst velvet, feathers and lace strewn with Joplin icons: a bottle of Southern Comfort, a pack of smokes, a well-worn copy of *Cheap Thrills*, faded photos and magic mojos from deep blues country. And this is as it should be.

I believe Janis was a mambo, a voudoun priestess—and not only in the general sense of rock 'n' roll possession so compellingly traced to its roots in Michael Ventura's revelatory essay "Voodoo and the Origins of Rock and Roll" (*Whole Earth Quarterly*, Spring, 1987). She was ridden by and, as a mambo, conducted her audience to be ridden by, "divine horsemen": ancestral archetypal forces that the Haitians call "loa." Particularly, she was the serviteur of Ghede, the most paradoxically complex of the loa: Lord of Death, Lord of Eroticism, trickster/clown, taboo-breaker, insatiable glutton, teacher and healer. The parallels between the highly codified behavior that inevitably signals possession by Ghede—and Janis' summoning of and eventual submersion in *Pearl*—are startling.

The "pinched, W.C. Fields-type voice" Janis used when inhabiting *Pearl* is clearly evident in documentary footage of her Port Arthur high school reunion trip in 1970. "*Faaaantaaastic*," she responds to a "how-ya-doin'?" query from a local reporter as she sweeps into town in floppy black hat, purple feathers and amber-tinted shades.

"Indeed," writes Maya Deren in her definitive study of Haitian voudoun, *Divine Horsemen*, "wherever and whenever men assemble, Ghede may choose to appear among them with his nasal voice, his black or purple colors, his smoked glasses and his perpetual hunger…Ghede speaks in a nasal voice because a perfectly buried corpse would sound that way, and because, incidentally, it projects perfectly his cynicism." The "perfectly buried corpse" is an eerie reminder that "Buried Alive in the Blues" was the song Janis was set to record the day after she died.

Like Ghede, Pearl was a devotee of strong drink and good cigars (she even appeared in a TV cigar spot). She would sometimes arrive, as Deren says of Ghede, "unbidden, at a ceremony for another loa, to 'spoil it.'" One such incident occurred at a Grateful Dead concert just months before her death, as Chet Helms reports. "Janis was onstage, very drunk, kind of trying to upstage Jerry Garcia, goosing him onstage, very sexually provocative." Indeed, sexual provocation is a primary function of Ghede, who Deren describes as "both tattered and beautiful. He confounds sex with sex, dressing men as women and women as men." Just like Pearl, he's a terrible tattle-tale—" he will tell all the juiciest morsels in public to the amusement and embarrassment of everyone"—but he's also "generous with his wisdom," as Janis' friends and family confirm.

Most tellingly of all, perhaps, Ghede connotes "the anxiety, fear and ultimate withdrawal which he senses in all men, and which all his clowning and all their laughter can never quite obscure. Indeed, this ruler of men is, of all loa, probably the most lonely." The correlations between Ghede and Janis' Pearl—and there are more, many more—are so overwhelming they're impossible to dismiss.

Whether or not Janis actually studied the rituals and history of voudoun is irrelevant (though it's worth noting that Janis went to Rio for Carnival, when Ghede's counterparts among Brazil's "Santeria" rule the streets). The forces she invoked and grappled with both onstage and off are inherent in the music that found her as much as she found it. Beneath its ostensible subject matter of hard luck, hard lovin' and hard livin', the blues encodes the language of shamans and shapeshifters, the mojo hands and juju sticks that loop back to West Africa via the West Indies and, of course, New Orleans. An ultrasensitive like Janis, bred on the Texas/ Louisiana cusp of the Caribbean Gulf and steeped in country blues, could hardly escape those forces. How such forces interacted with American pop culture, with the omnivorous (and very Ghedeian) Zeitgeist of the '60s—and, most profoundly, with Janis herself—is an essential part of her story that has never been directly addressed and which bears further study.

Like any great artist, Janis transcended her time and place. That she was also quintessentially of her time and place makes the magical subtext of her story all the more compelling, for the loa continually replenish the ancestral gene pool by serving the living in present time. As Michael Ventura writes, "Spirit always adheres to forms. That is why forms survive. Because even when specifics are forgotten, a form can retain the aura of what originated it and so pass on not the doctrine but the sense of life."

Long live Janis Joplin.

### *Sister Stories*

Debbie Harry, former lead singer of Blondie: "Janis has endured, because people do her when they don't even know they're doing her. You know what's funny? A lot of these guys in metal bands and hard-rock blues bands all sound like Janis. The guys have got her down."

Exene Cervenka, former lead singer of X, now a solo artist: "Janis was very brave, even though she had to drink and get fucked up to do what she did. It's easy for Madonna to be brave—she's got a great self-image, she's pretty, she's healthy, she's got a trainer and so on. For Janis Joplin to step in front of a camera took a lot. The fact that everybody embraced her is really pretty amazing."

Jennifer Barry, lead singer of Halfway Home: "I came across a copy of *I Got Dem Ol' Kozmic Blues Again Mama* in a bargain bin and that song 'Maybe' just totally tore me up. She's so soulful, so raw, so real. I was totally an outcast, a complete loser too. Janis kicked the door right open for people like me."

Maria McKee, lead singer of Lone Justice: "*Janis Joplin's Greatest Hits* changed my life. It made me realize that you could be a woman and open your mouth and let something like that come out."

## Jessie Mae Hemphill: Hangin' with "The She-Wolf of Como"

**_PleaseKillMe_, August 2020**

*A five-time W. C. Handy award-winner and the fourth generation of a venerable musical family, Jessie Mae Hemphill (1923–2006), from the North Mississippi Hill Country, sang songs wrenched from her own life experience, celebrating the transformative power of the blues for audiences throughout the U.S. and Europe. Cree McCree met Jessie at the Mississippi Delta Blues Festival in Brooklyn, N.Y., in 1989 and stayed close to her over the remaining years of her life. Cree recounts some personal encounters for PKM.*

Jessie Mae Hemphill was at the peak of her career as one of the few female country blues artists to emerge since Memphis Minnie when I first saw her perform in 1989. Flashing sequins and rhinestones, her high heel driving a foot-powered tambourine while her voice soared above the hypnotic drone of her electric Gibson guitar, the She-Wolf of Como, a.k.a. the Delta Queen, was the North Mississippi Hill Country's high priestess of hard times. A five-time W. C. Handy award-winner and the fourth generation of a venerable musical family, Jessie sang songs wrenched from her own life experience, celebrating the transformative power of the blues for audiences throughout the U.S. and Europe.

She was also just a hoot to hang with. Though I was in my early forties, and Jessie was a decade older, we hit it off like a couple of schoolgirls when we met in May 1989 at the Mississippi Delta Blues Festival at St. Ann's Church in Brooklyn, New York. After her own mesmerizing set, we forged an instant bond when we teamed up for some impromptu boogie during Big Jack Johnson's "Catfish Blues" that set the whole crowd to dancing.

Before she left New York, Jessie invited me to visit her in the crossroads town of Como, Mississippi. I took her up on that offer that September, when we enjoyed raising eyebrows traipsing through the aisles of the local Bag 'n' Save in matching Crown Royal caps. I'd been sent to Mississippi by *Spin* magazine to do a big spread on Delta Blues pegged to the late '80s blues revival, and Jessie was one of eight artists I profiled in that piece. But the scant three-hundred words I was allotted for the Delta Queen barely scratched the surface of her story and our experiences together.

In November 1989, when Jessie returned to New York for the Benson & Hedges Blues Festival, she stayed in my Sullivan Street apartment and we hit the town together. After a stroke forced her to hang up her guitar in 1993, we kept in touch periodically, and I wore the necklace Jessie gave me in Como when I got married in 1995. Years later, in 2004, shortly after she recorded her swansong double CD, *Dare You to Do It Again*, I drove up from my current home in New Orleans to visit her in Senatobia, Mississippi, where we had the last of several lengthy interviews before her death in 2006.

The story of our relationship, drawn partly from contemporary journal entries, montages those interviews with my memories and ends with an oral history of Jessie Mae Hemphill, told in her own words.

### *Hangin' with the She-Wolf in Como (September 1989)*

There's no running water in the Delta Queen's castle, a dilapidated trailer lit by the static of an old TV, where overdue utility bills are stashed in a bedside Bible and an unkempt menagerie of poodles yammers to be fed. After one too many heartbreaks, Jessie has sworn off men for the moment, and sleeps with a loaded shotgun to fend off potential intruders. But her spirit rises far above circumstance: in her music; in the vibrant luminescence of her watercolors of guardian angels; and in the backwoods magic that whips up a fife-and-drum picnic that feeds an entire neighborhood of children, young blades and do-ragged grandmas on a rack of barbequed ribs intended for two.

### *Jessie Mae Hemphill Throws a Picnic (Journal Entry, 9/27/89)*

DORA STRICKLAND SITS FRAMED by the open door of a small wooden shack tucked behind one of those tidy brick bungalows in Como, Mississippi, that Jessie Mae Hemphill is determined to buy someday. She's a big-boned woman, and a handsome one, though she's long since parted company with her teeth and the toes of her tennis shoes have been cut open to allow her bunioned feet to breathe. She's also crazier than a loon, Jessie tells me.

Though her son, Napoleon, is a full-grown man of sixty-odd years, Dora keeps a tight rein on the legendary fife player. She managed to hold sway over two wives and now rules singlehandedly over Napoleon's comings and goings—no small task, since the Pan of Mississippi is in constant demand at fife & drum picnics in the surrounding hill country. Dora's iron will may explain Napoleon's boylike demeanor; he's roly-poly round with a cue-ball head, apple cheeks, and an open-faced smile that seems perpetually delighted at the ways of the world.

Dora likes to hold center stage and was quite the dancer in her day, Jessie tells me. As if to prove this point, Dora shuffles to the front porch and begins to roll her belly in a sinuous motion under the faded print of her house dress, grinning at the audience of neighborhood girls who've gathered to egg her on. She's a sight to behold, this 80-year-old woman with a do-rag tied round her balding head, heaving that belly for all it's worth, as sensuous and snake-like as any veiled belly dancer charming the men in Istanbul.

"I don't know how Dora does that," says Jessie. "My belly goes out but it don't go in! Can you do it?" Turns out I can (though not with Dora's practiced grace); long-ago belly dancing lessons stand me in good stead. As I roll my stomach for the onlookers, Dora claps her approval, and I am transformed from a curiosity—Jessie's white-girl trophy—into instant acceptance as a participant in the culture.

Once the ice has been broken, Jessie invites Napoleon and Dora over for barbecue. Dora's not about to budge, but we cajole her into letting Napoleon on the loose, on one condition: he catches a ride with a neighbor later on. "That's Dora," whispers Jessie. "She don't want him ridin' in a car with two women, no way."

Back at her trailer, after we've stopped to pick up beer and a pint of vodka ("Napoleon loves his 'wodka'"), Jessie asks the young boy who's been mowing her lawn to haul out the barbecue: a sturdy unit of hand-wrought iron set in a car-wheel base. We're still not sure if it will be much of a gathering; will Napoleon even show? Then Jessie's neighbor Patty Ann pulls up, jumps into action with the charcoal briquettes, and it's clear we have a picnic in the making. Once Dora makes good on her promise to dispatch Napoleon to Jessie's, it's time for the party to begin.

The Mississippi moon, three days past the fullness of its prime, is still puffed up with pleasure. Napoleon plays a siren call of notes on his fife—as true and clear as a piccolo, though it's only a hollow of cane. Soon the drums join in, Jessie beating out the earth tones on her big bass drum, Rabbit the rapid-fire staccato on the snare.

Though the only bonfire is the smoldering grill, and we're surrounded not by the leafy camouflage of the woods but by the open expanse of the trailer court that serves as Jessie's front yard, our informal barbecue morphs into a full-fledged hill country picnic when the fife and drum music kicks in. Copped from the white man's military corps, and steeped in the rhythmic thrum of indigenous tribal drums, the hypnotic repetitions evoke not the battlefields of war but an ecstatic celebration of the senses, a dance older than the hills dipping down to the Delta. The fife seduces, insinuating itself into the body as the bright major key segues into minor, and the drums roll like waves onto shores delineated by the fife.

Now the neighbors come, drawn from their surrounding homes by the mesmerizing call of the music. And they come not to complain about the noise but to participate in the magic. Even Jessie's nemesis, the dog-killing driver she suspects of running over her favorite poodle, is drawn to the outer ring of concentric circles converging on the lawn. Though she doesn't dare cross Jessie's property line, her sons are bolder, moving to the ring of cars and lounging tentatively on an old Caddy. One is brazen enough to ask for a beer when he learns that the beer isn't for sale, as per local custom, but has been provided gratis by Jessie's guest as her ticket of admission to this ad hoc musicale.

Close to the drums, in the inner circle, sits Miss Dee, an ancient Black woman with a ramrod spine and immense dignity. Jessie wraps one of her furs around Miss Dee's frail shoulders; it's late September and the first snap of fall is crisping the air. Miss Dee never moves from her spot, but keeps her cane in constant motion, beating out a cross-rhythm with the drums. She was one of the great dancers of her granddaddy's day, Jessie tells me, and Miss Dee's eyes are alight with the flickering forms of a past now recaptured in the old, familiar cadences.

Also close in are the little girls, who begin to move, shyly at first and then with increased abandon, giving themselves up with laughter. Jessie's worked up a sweat on the bass drum, her hair is flying and the straps slip off her shoulders, the warm brown curves of her back glistening under the moon while her gold teeth flash in the light from the trailer's single bulb. And she's just warming up for the main act.

"Hey y'all," Jessie announces, after she unstraps the drum and tunes up her Gibson guitar. "This is Jessie Mae Hemphill speaking, so listen up. Everybody out there wanting to catch up, catch up now. Cause there's a big train comin' and it don't carry no hypocrites."

A few trademark cackles later, Jessie launches into the chugging rhythms of "Train, Train," and the music gets downer and deeper as the She-Wolf carries us down the tracks and segues into the slow burn of "Used to Be."

Then it's Napoleon's turn to switch gears, take a swig of vodka, grab his guitar, and start begging "Baby Please Don't Go." The one-two punch of "I Feel It" and "Sure Don't Worry Me" inspires one of the Caddy-leaning guys to shout "I'm gonna grab me a fox!" as the party starts getting rowdier, spurring Jessie to take back the ad hoc stage with "Shame on You."

Patty Ann's keeping time with her feet while she stands guard over the slabs of ribs charring to perfection on the grill, the pungent smell of smoke whipping clouds around the dancers. Her twelve-year-old boy is rubber-hipping a kind of backwoods breakdance, while I get down with Clemmonce.

He's a virile six-footer with a crystal and gold chain looped around the grey-flecked hairs of his chest, his movements loose and lanky as a teenager. Clemmonce purrs an ongoing seducer's plea in my ear, detailing potential delights, and is unphased by my refusal to succumb to his ploys.

Always I walk a fine line here, as the living emblem of Black men's fantasies about northern white girls. Everyone makes their bid, even elder statesman Son Thomas, and with time I learn to deflect these offers gracefully, citing my role as a working journalist. The men seem to accept this, and tonight I am bolstered by an unspoken pact with Jessie. This is our night, a night for girl talk and giggling under the covers in her trailer after the ribs have been eaten, the beer has been drunk, and the drums have been put away. And the men understand that Jessie speaks for me as well, when she clears her yard at the end of the evening by announcing, in no uncertain terms:

"Ain't no legs going up in the air tonight!"

### *Hangin' with the She-Wolf on Sullivan Street (November 1989)*

"Lordy, girl! You tryin to kill me? I thought all the buildings in New York City had elevators!"

Jessie Mae Hemphill has finally reached the top landing of my fourth-floor walkup on Sullivan St., bitching and moaning all the way, while my pal Linda Kelly and I play sherpa toting the bulky suitcase, makeup case and wig box that hold all her glitzy stage gear. John Allison, son of blues and jazz piano great Mose Allison and my tour guide into the blues, is carrying Jessie's Gibson, and he's not just along for the ride. As the founder of The Mississippi Blues Project, John organized the St. Ann's concert where Jessie and I met to shoot footage for a documentary film. This weekend, as part of the nine-day Benson & Hedges Blues Festival, where Jessie will be performing, he's screening the trailer for *It Hurts Me Too* and hosting an evening with R.L. Burnside, another great North Mississippi artist.

But all that's still on the horizon. Tonight, after she freshens up and settles into my bedroom (I'm couching it for the weekend), Jessie treats us to a private living room concert while my cassette tape is rolling.

"That was Muddy Waters," she says after putting her own spin on "Baby Please Don't Go." "And this is Howlin' Wolf, Jessie Mae style," she adds, launching into "Baby, Where'd You Stay Last Night." "I don't play like anyone but myself."

You sure don't, Jessie. I uncork another bottle of bubbly when Jessie announces "I need more champagne!" Then she's off and running with "Used to Be," prompting Linda to shout "Woot! That was nice!"

"I put some new stuff in there," Jessie notes with a sly grin. *I play all six of them strings, when I'm playin like that. And every one of them be havin chillun. I be feelin good!"

The good times keep on rolling when we walk down West Houston to Brothers BBQ, where Mark Grandfield's blowing harp with his blues band Mystic Chain. Jessie and Linda and I get down on the packed dance floor, where the crowd makes way for the Delta Queen when Mark calls her up to the bandstand. When she busts out "Jessie's Boogie," everyone goes ballistic, transforming Brothers into a smokin hot backwoods juke joint.

Tomorrow night, Jessie will play a fine solo concert at Harlem's Schomburg Center while the audience sits respectfully listening (except for me, of course, who finds a spot in the back to dance.) But tonight's the real deal, and almost as rowdy as the Como picnic, complete with grilled ribs and plenty of beer to wash 'em down. By the time we drag our danced-out asses back up those four flights of stairs, it's nearly 3 a.m. Jessie lights one last Virginia Slim before hitting the hay, and leaves me with a final pearl of wisdom:

"You gotta slow down, girl," she says, as much to herself as to me.

Jessie gave the same advice to Linda that weekend, when we were all running on empty amped by blues, booze and adrenaline. "And she was right," says Linda, who still recalls Jessie vividly more than thirty years later:

"Jessie Mae Hemphill made me feel safe. She was grounded, and she gave me a green card to let my spirit ride: It's OK to be strong and female. You never have to apologize, you just ride. And never hold back. I had just moved to New York City, and Jessie gave me courage. She made me feel so comfortable and loved."

### *Hangin with She-Wolf in Senatobia (July 2004)*

Jessie Mae Hemphill don't sing the blues no more. (Or so she claims). Just spiritual songs like she learned at her mama's knee. And since a stroke left her partially paralyzed a decade ago, she can no longer play her propulsive open-tuned guitar. But when the spirit moves her, she can still "Boogie All Night Long," like she sang on her first record, She-Wolf. Jessie jammed till 5 a.m. making *Dare You to Do It Again*, a two-CD benefit album of spirituals recorded live with a cast of dozens at Sherman Cooper's farm in Como, MS. And right now in her trailer in nearby Senatobia, she starts to boogie in her wheelchair listening to "Porch Logic Remix," the album's last track.

"I kinda like this," she says, warming up to DJ Logic's deep house spin on the clamorous fife & drum and droning guitars of the Mississippi session, remixed in a New York studio. Then her own voice loops into the mix—complete with samples of her pealing cackle, which ricochet off the walls as the drums dive deeper. "Oh lord, we're gettin down now!" she hoots, lifting her lapdog Pookie on her hind legs to shake a tailfeather. "That be good for dancin, chile!"

Recorded well into the session when spirits were starting to fly, Jessie also cuts loose with "Treat Me Right," a twenty-four-minute-deep drone epic that could almost be an outtake from the Velvet Undergound's infamous Austin sessions. About ten minutes into her stream of consciousness vocalizing, which makes no mention of the Lord and sounds suspiciously like the blues, she brings in the tambourine, driving the band to dig deeper.

"That wasn't no blues," retorts Jessie, scratching Pookie behind the ears while flashing me a gold-toothed grin. "That was just somethin I was doin. Whatever jumped outta my mouth that's what I done. That's the way I do all of them. When somethin come up, I just let it roll out."

## *Jessie Mae Hemphill In Her Own Words On Her Musical Heritage*

All my daddy's brothers and sisters, and mama's, way on back to the first generation was musicians. I'm the fourth generation. Granddaddy never did go in the fields. He raised his girls playin music. They'd go with him, help him make the money. One be playin guitar, one banjo, one floor bass. So, he had his own daughter band. When I came along, I got up there.

I was playin drum when I was nine. The big drum, too—always be some man to hold the big drum up for me and I would stand up on the Coca Cola box. I made more money than my granddaddy did. They just gave me money, money, money. I was so little and could beat that drum and wouldn't miss no time and people just be hollerin.

I done learned myself guitar. My mama played too, I learned by lookin at her, I had music in my head all the time. When I was nine, ten years old I hear something on the record player and come home and play it. I could play anything.

Fife and drum come from Indian peoples and all my daddy's people are Indian peoples. And all my mama's folk, too, back to the fifth generation. Indians used to beat on them drums, on the tom toms. Rum tum tum, rum tum tum. I was dancin with the big drums at the World's Fair in Nashville when Reagan came to that, and I dedicated an Indian war song to Reagan. But he don't help the poor people none. He help the poor get poorer and the rich get richer.

### *On Her Songwriting Process*

I GET THE WORDS FIRST. And when they come, I go get the guitar so that the title'll come to me. And as soon as I sing that first verse, another one be there just like somebody be writin it on the wall for me. I don't know what I'm gonna say, but it be there for me to sing. I keep on singin and pickin, and the tune of the song be right there too. The tune be right there already when the tune come to me, the tune is already in the song.

"Shotgun" and "Standing in the Doorway Cryin," those come when my heart was broken, I said I'm gonna make me a record and get on away from him. And I went to town and bought me a mic and and amp. I already had my guitar. And I went back home, and when I got "Standing in the Doorway Cryin" goin, I played it all night. Till the sun rose, girl, I picked it all night. Drinkin coffee all night and played it all night. And I said I know this gonna be a record.

"My Daddy Blues" and "Train Train" come to me fast. And "I Feel It," that's my theme song, come to me fast. On stage, I just line 'em up in my mind when I get up there. I can go from one to the other and just keep on doin that all the way through. And not play the same one twice, less someone ask me to.

Religious songs come to me just like the blues. I was out there workin in the yard, nobody home but me and my granddaddy, and I went to hummin and hummin and I went to singin "gonna be a fire you can't put out." Don't nobody sing it like me, you hear it in churches everywhere now, but nobody had the verses I had. And when I quit, Granddaddy said, woman—he called me woman—where'd you get that song? I said, I don't know, Grandpa, it just come to me a while ago. He said sing it again, and let's play it on the fiddle and guitar.

### *On Being a Black Musician and the Legacy of Alan Lomax*

I'LL TELL YA ONE thing. My granddaddy and mama and them all made records and never got any money for 'em, never did get to make no movies, nothin. At the time, they didn't want no Blacks to make no kind of records and things, they didn't let 'em. All the ones making records when granddaddy and them was playing was white hillbillies and country music. And they wouldn't allow a Black to make nothin like that.

Then Alan Lomax came down and recorded my granddaddy in Sledge, Mississippi, when they was playin for a picnic. And he made a record, that was in 1960 somethin and now things done change a little better for Blacks to make a record. And that's why Alan say he came down, cause they wasn't given the Blacks a chance to make records and be on the radio.

When Alan was doin granddaddy's record I was livin in Memphis. And Alan wrote to me, he was gonna come down. But he had a flat that night and didn't have no spare so he couldn't get over. Or I would have made one with Alan too.

### *On the Life of a Touring Female Musician*

WELL, IT'S HARDER ON her travelin than it is for a man. Because she's got to be kind of scared all the time that somebody gonna hurt her or somethin. I don't be scared, but I kinda watch out for myself. When people call me on the telephone I say look, I'm comin by myself but y'all gotta take care of me. You have somebody to stay with me and take me to my motel. Get me to my room cause I ain't comin back out! So they always have somebody to take care of me and I don't be scared. I'm not gonna be searchin around here tryin to get a cab for myself, not me.

The way I gets my jobs is, I give people my telephone number and they calls me, like they used to call David [Evans, her former white touring partner and manager]. And I set my own job up, I say this is my price, and I get my money now. Before, they would set price of a thousand dollars maybe, and he'd tell me the folks was just gonna pay me $300.00 or something. The rest of the $1,000.00 David would get. But I'm gonna make all my money from now on.

The first concert I played that I made my first thousand dollars in was New York. New York's been good to me, and I love it too. When I get [to a venue] they all be so nice to me. They so crazy about me cause I be so friendly with them. They say Jessie, you don't act like them other movie star women that acts like they has rocks in their jaw, don't wanna say nothing to their fans. They crazy—that's where their money comes from. When you be friendly with your fans then the man enjoys payin you for playin. I love my audience, I talk to them and tell them I love 'em. I say, don't count me as no big shot, you just count me as regular old Jessie. Just myself, that's all I want to be.

I always think I can do anything I wanna do and I tries it. You never know what you can do until you tried it, and you got to wanna do it to try it. And when you try it, boy, boy, boy—if it don't work out one way, it'll work out another. Right?

### *On Fending Off Bullies & Lecherous Guys*

I NEVER LET MY STEPDADDY do nothin to me. And when my stepdaddy try to do somethin to my mama, I get the shotgun. And if mama hadn't went to cryin, I'd a blowed his brains out.

The boys like the girls that go into the bushes with them, the back seat riders. But when I was goin to school, I was the one they liked. They be tryin to get at me all the time. I scratch 'em in the face, they was scared of me. I said I'm doin like a cemetery: I'm just takin in, I ain't puttin out nothin.

I told all these girls who were goin to school and got pregnant, I said you all is crazy cause you all gonna carry these babies home to your mama. I ain't carryin no baby home to my mama. I said, I'm gonna knock these boys down, give em bleedin noses, boy. Those boys scared to come up to me! I hit them guys in the nose! [laughs] I'm a mean little sucker. I scratch their eyes out. I glad I did it. I didn't never get pregnant. Those other girls, after those boys get them pregnant, they was gone.

### *On Helping Old People, and the Wisdom of Age*

I MET AN OLD MAN one time, when I was livin in Memphis. I used to help old people cross the street and things. One day, I met an old man when I was goin downtown. I was sharp as a tack and this was a real old man. And the sun was shining pretty, you know. And I said hi, we have a pretty day today, don't we? He said yeah, and I stopped and talked to him. I hadn't decided to play no blues then. He said, you know, you're the only young person that ever stopped and said somethin to me. These young people don't have time to talk to old people. I said yes, but I do, cause someday I'm gonna be an old lady too. I might get treated bad, but I might get treated good by somebody.

I love old people cause I can learn more from old peoples than I can from young peoples. And he said you's a beautiful girl, that smile you got is so beautiful. He said I wanna tell you this and then I let you go. Keep smilin he said, that smile you got will take you all over the world. And it has! I didn't even believe it was comin true! I got a whole lotta power I ain't even used yet.

## Seven Deadly Sins: Lust—Pamela Des Barres

*Us Weekly*, July 1988

Back in the lusty Sixties, the big F-word was free love. Charged by rock & roll, a generation's libido was liberated. Rock gods ruled, and their consorts were groupie goddesses. Among the most celebrated of these young Aphrodite's was a woman called Miss Pamela, a member of Frank Zappa's all-girl band, the GTO's (which stood for Girls Together Outrageously). In July 1968—when she'd already been swept up by Jimi Hendrix's bass player but was yet to have Jimmy Page and Mick Jagger vying for her affections—Miss P described herself thusly: "Pamela Ann Miller, nineteen and three-quarters, blond hair, blue eyes, one-hundred-and-sixteen pounds, ready, willing and able to LIVE LIFE TO THE FULLEST! TAKE ME, I'M YOURS!!!"

Pamela Des Barres, nee Miller, thirty-nine and three-quarters, has red hair now. The other vital statistics remain the same. She still lives her life in capital letters and triple exclamation points, and she's on a roll. Her book, *I'm with the Band*, hits the paperback racks later this summer (Berkley)—about the same time she'll be lustily displayed in a *Playboy* spread—and Ally Sheedy just nabbed the film rights in order to portray Miss P on screen.

Des Barres says she wakes up every morning and goes "YAY!" She warmed up for this interview at the Atlantic Records fortieth birthday bash, which reunited her Led Zeppelin pals Robert Plant and Page.

During the interview itself, she sprawled across a comfy double bed in the guest room of friend Melanie Griffith's New York apartment.

**How would you define lust?**

First of all, I don't consider it a sin. It's just passion! You can have lust for inanimate objects, like a painting you want really badly. But I usually associate it with human beings and I think it's one of the great things in life to feel lust for somebody. Sometimes I can see lust on someone, or feel it on myself, like a film over your body that's kind of shimmery, stick, slurpy—and ooze. I feel sorry for people who don't experience it very often.

**Do you think everyone is capable of experiencing lust? I remember Jimmy Carter, in that famous *Playboy* interview, talked about lusting "in his heart."**

God bless him. I admired him so much after that. Because we all lust. I do think some people turn inward, all those celibates and Zen masters. So maybe you can transcend lust. But I'm really happy I haven't transcended it yet. It was a life force of its own, lust, it grabs at your insides without warning and it's such a thrill.

**There's a great line in your book: "Something came over me in the presence of rock idols, something vile and despicable, something wondrous and holy." Isn't that dichotomy part of what lust is all about?**

It's true, it really is a cross between pornography and heaven. You're in touch with your body and soul at the same time. That's why I never saw lust as being a sin.

**And rock evokes both the pornographic and the holy?**

Yes, yes, yes! They're up there flaunting their stuff at you, and the power of the music mingles with the passion and creates lust. I wanted to be with the source of the music, the source of inciting that desire in me.

**So did hundreds of thousands of other women. What was there about you that attracted these rock gods?**

I don't know. Passion, maybe, the passion scent, the pheromones—that stuff that comes out of your skin. When you have a whole lot of feelings oozing out of your pores, they sense it. It pours out into a puddle around you.

**But you also seemed to have this almost breathless innocence about you. It wasn't a complete flaunt.**

No, you're right. It was innocent oozing, because I was real sweet. Maybe it was a combination of wanton passion mixed with that baby fat!

**You were elusive, too. The first time Jimmy Page sent for you, you didn't go.**

But that wasn't calculated. Jimmy scared me to death, his reputation preceded him mightily. I figured if he was sincere, he'd try again—which he did.

**You also turned down Jagger—not just once but several times.**

Well, I was in love with Jimmy Page, and at that point in my life I was looking really hard for love. There's a huge difference between lust and love—the lust wanes and the love stays—and I was a cross between sex-crazed and love-crazed. I was still lusty after Mick, and when he gave me those hickeys all over my thighs...

**And you left?**

Yeah, but eventually had some wonderful times with Mick. All the leading up to it was kind of nice. Mick came on the scene when the baby-boom girls were on the edge of almost being allowed to fulfill our fantasies. Whereas the Fifties girls could only wish about Elvis. I would listen to Mick sing "I'm a King Bee, baby...let me come inside" and absolutely get off. When I finally made it with Mick, I kept thinking about "King Bee," it was such a part of my life.

**Did it live up to your expectations?**

Sure, it did, it always did. I never had a complaint about any of the celebrities I found myself with.

**Of course, Don Johnson wasn't a celebrity when you two fell madly in love.**

He had an incredible sense of who he was, and when you meet someone who has a passion for themselves, you took to it. Oh, God, the first time I laid eyes on Donnie those pheromones came spurting out. I still have a great passion for Donnie, and that's part of our friendship. When I sent Donnie his chapter—it's called "I Met Him on a Monday and My Heart Stood Still"—he sent me a dozen red roses with a little card that said, "Da Doo Ron Ron Ron, Da Doo Ron Ron."

**How did you view yourself as a woman through all this?**

I considered myself very much a feminist because I went after what I wanted. It took a lot of rebellion to get me out of Reseda, California, and into the Hyatt House with Jimmy Page.

**Do you think the Sixties were the golden age of lust?**

As far as now is concerned, yes. But, please, it's been going on forever and ever.

**Early on, weren't you split between religion and lust? When you were at a revival meeting in Kentucky with your relatives, you wrote: "Thunder crashed in my head and I shivered all over knowing I was all tangled up in the age-old pressure of living inside the flesh."**

Yeah, it was a bad battle I was having between what I perceived to be my soul, and my body. I've united the two now. I'm totally unguilt-ridden about sex. The televangelist scandals pissed me off, because they were doing one thing and saying another, but I certainly never blamed Jessica Hahn. I met her when we were doing our *Playboy* layouts, and God, she's a lusty broad.

**Can the concept of sin make lust more exciting?**

It adds a little titillation, sure. It's like entering the danger zone. But the only thing that really makes lust a sin is if you want something you can't—or shouldn't—have, at the expense of someone else. There's no such thing as casual lust, it can take over your life for a while. *Fatal Attraction* is real-life stuff. I'm sure some people ruin their entire lives over lust.

**How do you deal with lust in the age of AIDS?**

Well, I'm happy I got to go through the sixties, I'll tell you that. Rock stars are throwing rubbers out into the audience now, and that's great, but I don't think it's the answer to anything. AIDS is here, and we gotta be real responsible about it, and I'm real tired of the litany of it, but it's the truth. So people are squelching their lust and that's got to be unhealthy. It's depressing.

**That's reality. But dreaming is still safe, and even married men are fair game for that. Let's talk about your fantasy wish list. Who would you pick?**

Prince. Terrence Trent D'Arby. Robert Plant, even though I've known him twenty years—he's such a big, blond hunk of majestic royalty. Richard Gere—he's been a fantasy of mine for a long time. Bruce Springsteen is hot; besides the fact he's got an amazing rear end and gorgeous arms, he's just so inspiring. And Marlon Brando, he'll never be over-the-hill.

**Have you met Prince?**

I met him briefly at Helena's [restaurant] one night, and I lost all cool with the man. Usually, I have some semblance of cool, otherwise it doesn't work. But I went right up to Prince, I danced in front of him to his own record, "Kiss," and went over to his table and said, "I love you, I love you." Can you believe it? I was thirty-eight years old!

**What about Terance Trent D'Arby?**

I saw him for the first time in concert the other night, and I hadn't been struck like that by a new act since Prince. I thought, God, if I were just ten years younger, I'd find a way backstage. And I would have found a way. It's the idea of making your mind up to do something.

**What would you do, once you got back there?**

It's so hard to say. I never had a one-through-ten way to meet somebody. You know what it was? If I could just get into the room, I was okay. I think if you're in the room, and put out the vibe, your chances are good. It's getting into that room that's the hard part. When I first met my husband, Michael [musician-actor Michael Des Barres], I was inflamed with lust. We had a very passionate relationship. And nothing could have kept me out of those rooms in the sixties.

And today?

Well, I'm just recently separated, so I don't think I'm putting out the vibe. At least not yet. But I was so inspired by Terence Trent D'Arby that while he was onstage I was writing stuff for my new book, *Blush.* I'm going to create a character around him. It's a very sexy novel, and I've never written sex scenes before, except my own sex scenes from my past. I get all excited writing them. I get full of lust. And desire.

## Malevitus Celebrates While We Incinerate

**_OffBeat_, February 2020**

Tiana Hux is a force of nature, a long-stemmed rose studded with thorns that draw blood. A gifted performance artist, she frequently sheds skins and has appeared in many different guises, in both her home state of Texas and her spiritual home of New Orleans, where she released her first record, *Story*, just before Katrina, and put down permanent roots in 2016.

As a properly starchy Mary Poppins, Hux delights kids at birthday parties. As the booty-shaking MC Sweet Tea, she leads her Tastee Hotz dancers in feminist rabble-rousers like "Why Don't Saint Sensations Get Paid?" In "A Day Late and a Dollar Shot," an immersive Hux production staged at the New Quorum in 2019, she was a bourbon-swilling Storyville denizen who knows how to play all the angles. And when she steps up to the mic with Malevitus, she's a high priestess of rock and roll who calls down our collective demons in an ecstatic exorcism.

"Read my lips: 'Apocalypse.'"

Hux cuts right to the chase on "Golden Toy Soldiers," the opening track on *Malevitus*, the band's stunning debut CD, which foreshadows all the landmines ahead: climate change, societal breakdown, families torn apart by war, death and incarceration. It also throws down the musical gauntlet: hard-driving rock laced with rap, psychedelia and snotty punk 'tude, that crackles with enough kinetic energy to make us dance through the apocalypse on our own graves.

Malevitus may pivot on Hux's searing narratives, but it's her crack team of musicians that spurs us to celebrate while we incinerate as the world goes up in flames.

Rob Cambre's guitar annotates the "clicks in the Big Machine" of "Toy Soldiers," and the dead-of-the-night shivers in "Night of the Dog," while his trademark supernatural solos have never sounded weirder or more beautiful. Longtime Hux collaborator Marcus Bronson provides ample ballast with both his bass and vocals, propelled by the fire-stoked engine of drummer Mike Andrepont, who gives *Malevitus* its heartbeat.

This tight-knit unit really hit its stride in the studio, where the group co-created the album, first at Studio in the Country and later at Embassy Studio. But Malevitus didn't coalesce overnight, and the origin story dates back to Hux's pre-Katrina New Orleans days.

"I'd had a big success here with my burlesque rapping act, and a lot of people took *Story* with them when they evacuated for Katrina," recalls Hux, who formed the Headbands in Austin but yearned to return to New Orleans, where Bronson and Cambre were among her closest friends. She first came back in 2010 to work on new material with Bronson, which premiered as Animal Ball, a performance piece with dancers, at that year's Voodoo Fest. Several years later, Cambre helped lure her back for good.

"I'd always been dying to work with Rob," says Hux. They sealed the deal on the banks of the Bayou St. John, where Cambre christened the band at Greek Fest.

"Tiana mentioned her early ancestors were Greek, and the family name they came over with was Malevitus," recalls Cambre. "And I'm like, that's the band name! Malevitus!"

The name translates roughly as "bad life," as befits a band that looks through a glass darkly. (It also bequeathed them an old Malevitus family photo for the album cover.) But the fledgling group still lacked a drummer, and didn't need to look far. Cambre was already playing in Rough 7 with Mike Andrepont, also of the Morning 40s and Happy Talk Band, who jumped right in.

Three years later, Andrepont jumped out to move to New York, on the cusp of finishing the record. But they completed the final track ("Light Years"), which Andrepont nailed in one take, and found a new terrific drummer: Jeff Massey, who also replaced Andrepont in Happy Talk.

"Not only did Jeff come to a lot of gigs, he was playing close attention to what was happening musically," says Cambre. "And we didn't have to talk him into it. It was almost like the call he was waiting to get."

"We loved Mike and hated to see him go," adds Hux. "But this project is definitely moving forward and we've fully embraced Jeff as our drummer, not just a fill-in guy. The d.b.a. gig was a real breakthrough. I was like wow! You had all this in reserve!"

The whole band killed at its d.b.a. debut in early December, where the group hit with all sirens wailing on "Fire Department," and amped it up with "Rapscallion," when Hux stripped down to a black fringed mini-dress and fish-nets and let loose on her tambourine. And the dance floor filled up, like it always does, for "Sugar & Salt," one of the best songs ever written about addiction.

As good as the album is, for the full Malevitus experience you need to see them live. In these days of escalating madness, purging the insanity on the dance floor is the only sane thing to do. At least you'll get the last laugh.

## Divine: Laughter and Lust in the Dust

**_PleaseKillMe_, December 2021**

*In 1984, Cree McCree sat down with Divine during the filming of the Lust in the Dust, directed by Paul Bartel and co-starring Tab Hunter. For this campy Western, Divine was "Rosie," an exotic cantina dancer. At the time, Divine, who grew up with John Waters in Baltimore, had just risen to national attention as the drag queen star in Waters' films Pink Flamingos, Female Trouble and Polyester. He/she had also embarked on a disco singing career and was in fine fettle. Cree recently discovered the unpublished interview in her files and shares it here, a holiday gift to PKM readers.*

Temperatures are rising in a rowdy saloon, where a seedy crew of goggle-eyed cowpokes are drooling over Rosie. She's one big red-hot mama. Heavily corseted in yards and yards of antique lace, she's belting it out for all she's worth: "These lips (boom boom) were made for selectin', these hips (boom boom) were made for connectin'," she sings, brazenly raising her skirts to reveal a voluminous pair of bloomers.

Welcome to *Lust in the Dust*, the campiest Western to ever blaze across the screen. Played by the inimitable Divine, Rosie became the cover-girl star of *Pasatiempo*, the Santa Fe New Mexican's weekly entertainment supplement, which gave me a plum assignment in 1984: tracking the *Lust* production from the soundstage cantina to the fictional town of Chili Verde at the J.W. Eaves Ranch, site of many Western shoots.

Directed by Paul Bartel, whose cult classic *Eating Raoul* was playing at a local theater during the shoot, *Lust in the Dust* lifted its title from the industry name for *Duel in the Sun* and co-starred Tab Hunter, Divine's leading man in *Polyester*, as a "Clint Cooper" mash-up named Abel. Lainie Kazan played the voluptuous Margarita, Rosie's rival for Abel's affection; Cesar Romero was a sanctimonious, greedy priest; and Henry Silva—with whom I had a hot one-night stand—played a comically inept villain. But Divine, as always, was the main attraction.

Thirty-seven years after I got up close and personal with Divine during a poolside interview at the Santa Fe Hilton, I revisited the transcript of our conversation, which plumbed his long and storied history with director and fellow Baltimorean John Waters. Then I streamed *Lust* on Tubi and teleported back to Chili Verde, via Divine's juicy commentary on many of the scenes, including Rosie's bawdy musical number.

"I think we should have dancing cactuses in it, and make it surrealistic," Divine enthused about plans to turn "These Lips Were Made For Kissing" into an MTV video. Though that video never materialized, and *Lust* didn't set any box office records, Divine's dream of going mainstream was fulfilled just four years later, in 1988, when *Hairspray* catapulted both Divine and Waters out of the underground into the multiplex. Unfortunately, the outrageous female impersonator, who first achieved cult superstardom as the dog-shit-eating "filthiest person alive" in *Pink Flamingos*, wasn't around long enough to enjoy the growing fame that cemented Waters' legacy in the years ahead. Divine, nee Glenn Milstead, died of a heart attack not long after *Hairspray* was released.

But he was very much alive during our 1984 conversation, when he vividly recalled rolling around in the titular dust during a catfight with Lainie Kazan—"I told her 'watch it, honey. Under this dress is a throbbing steel rod of passion!'"—and bemoaned his frustration with a skittish mule he was never able to ride. And Divine shines brighter than ever today in a host of fan sites and the work of countless imitators.

He is also enshrined in my tribute to "The Divine John Waters," a miniature float I pulled through the streets of New Orleans during Mardi Gras season as part of my microkrewe's 'tit Rex parade of shoebox floats. Though Waters didn't see the float in person, he told friends who sent him photos that he loved it. And why wouldn't he? Center-pieced by a John Waters votive candle, it's festooned with glittery piles of dogshit—a much-coveted throw that year—and features cardboard cutouts of Waters shooting Divine back in the Baltimore days with Edie the Egg Lady looming above them.

Though my *Pasatiempo* story had a few *Lust*-specific quotes in a special box devoted to Divine—"'Lust' star ecstatic about appearing in his/her first big budget film"—the lion's share of our long and lively conversation has never been published anywhere. At the time, I had high hopes of placing the entire Q&A in a national publication. But I was a little ahead of the curve, and it sat in the back of my file cabinet for nearly four decades. To put the interview in context of the time it was conducted, I included my 1984 introduction. Enjoy!

Conversation with Divine, Santa Fe, NM 1984.

Flamboyantly outrageous on stage and screen, where he's played everything from the world's greatest stripper to the unchallenged queen of suburban bad taste, the private Divine is genuinely unassuming. A big, balding man with gentle eyes and a laugh that comes from deep within, Divine wore his civvies to our poolside brunch interview at the Santa Fe

Hilton. And he takes his career as seriously as the smoked salmon, sausage and eggs he inhaled without missing a beat.

While covering the shooting of Paul Bartel's *Lust in the Dust*, I was continually impressed by Divine's good-natured professionalism. For long, grueling hours under a relentless New Mexico sun, his girth heavily corseted for the role of Rosie, Divine managed to turn the slightest gesture—a lift of the eyebrow, a pout of the lips—into moments of high hilarity on the screen in the dailies. As Bartel puts it, "Divine is worth his weight in comic gold."

Divine is betting on *Lust*, which also stars Tab Hunter, Lainie Kazan and Cesar Romero, to launch him beyond the notoriety he achieved in such John Waters' cult classics as *Pink Flamingos* and *Polyester*, and he's aiming straight for the heart of Middle America. With a budding singing career here and abroad, and a climate of growing tolerance evidenced by the success of such films as *Victor/Victoria* and *La Cage aux Foiles*, he seems likely to make it. Even his parents talk to him now.

[*The following conversation was edited for length and clarity.*]

***PKM:*** I'd like to go back to Baltimore, if Baltimore was indeed where it all began. Born in Baltimore?

**Divine:** Born and raised in the suburbs of Baltimore. And actually, I spent a very happy childhood, swimming with John Waters, who was a neighbor, and eventually we started making movies together.

***PKM:*** Before we jump to John Waters, do you mind my asking the name on your birth certificate? Unless—were you christened Divine?

**Divine:** No, Baby Divine, no. I was born Glenn [Milstead]. And I guess I was your American spoiled brat. An only child, I never wanted for anything. I had too much of everything.

*PKM*: When you were growing up, were you a big child?

**Divine:** Was I what?

*PKM*: Were you a chunky child?

**Divine:** You mean fat? Yes, uh-huh.

*PKM*: Okay, let's not mince words. So that wasn't something that came later.

**Divine:** No, I was always overweight. And then when I was about sixteen, I got tired of it because kids can be very cruel.

*PKM*: Sure, I was a fat kid too.

**Divine:** I always felt sorry for people who were fat and wore glasses, because they got it from every direction.

*PKM*: I wore glasses and braces.

**Divine:** Oh, Jesus. You're lucky you're still around. But anyway, at sixteen, I thought 'I'm going to go on a diet'. And I did, and it was quite difficult, but I lost one-hundred pounds and got down to one-hundred-and-forty.

*PKM*: Did you stay at that for a while?

**Divine:** About a year. But I realized at the same time, which was a very rude awakening, that it wasn't necessarily me they liked, it was the way I looked. So, I said 'well, I'm still the same person I was when I was fat'. And eventually my weight got back to normal. Took a few years, but it all came back.

Now people accept me this way, so I don't fight it anymore. I still cut down sometimes because I'd hate to get so big I couldn't fit through the door. [laughs] And I keep aware of my blood pressure, because when I work, I'm active and the last thing I need is a stroke. But I just had a physical before I came here, and I was in perfect health, which always seems to surprise the doctors more than me. They're dying to find something wrong with me, you know.

*PKM*: Were you already performing when you were in high school?

**Divine:** Well, I was in the glee club, because I loved to sing, but never in a theater group. I did some in elementary school, though.

*PKM*: What did you play in elementary school?

**Divine:** In one, I was a beaver. I'll never forget, because some kids backstage ripped my tail off right before the show.

*PKM*: Oh dear, that must have been traumatic.

**Divine:** I had to flip it, you know, the way a beaver flips. I got it sewn back on just before I went on, thank God. I was a wreck! Imagine—being a beaver and you lose your tail before your big chance. And in another play in sixth grade, I played Nero.

*PKM*: That's a pretty sophisticated theme for sixth grade. Nero fiddling while Rome burns.

**Divine:** I picked it. He was one of my favorites, Nero. I loved all those *Quo Vadis*-type movies. If you ever get the chance, you must see *Quo Vadis.*

*PKM*: Oh, I have. Peter Ustinov played Nero in that. Who were some of your other childhood heroes or heroines?

**Divine:** I always loved Elizabeth Taylor. She was my favorite movie star. And at that time movie stars weren't like real people, they were somewhere between gods and humans. And Elizabeth Taylor, my god, she was a queen. She still is.

*PKM*: Have you ever met her?

**Divine:** Oh, yes. I'd been invited to a party for her daughter, but I wasn't going to go because I thought she wasn't going to be there and what do I care about seeing her daughter? So, I went to bed to read and watch TV, and the phone rang. It was this friend of mine, and she said 'I'm at the party, where are you?' I said 'I'm in bed.' She said 'well, then, you are an asshole because she is here and you can't believe what she looks like. If you don't hurry up, you're gonna miss her.'

I didn't bathe or anything. I jumped right into my clothes and got in a cab and halfway downtown I thought, 'I'm making a mistake. She probably weighs five-hundred pounds and she's not going to have a stitch of makeup on and I'm gonna run out of there screaming.'

But finally, I walked into the room, and it was like everything went into slow motion. A friend of mine had done her makeup that day for a magazine cover and he was standing between us. He moved aside and said 'there's someone I'd like you to meet'. She was sitting there all in orange, with this huge diamond on, and looked like she'd just walked off the screen. It was perfect. She smiled and batted those eyes and I couldn't believe what they looked like. I was completely starstruck and dumbstruck. Elizabeth Taylor was my biggest childhood fantasy, and she was no disappointment at all.

*PKM*: Lucky you! So when was Divine born as a recognizable entity?

**Divine:** About sixteen years after Glenn. Divine was a name given to me by John Waters. The summer before my senior year, we became very, very friendly. John said he felt I was Divine, so that's what people should call me.

*PKM*: I imagine you and Waters weren't your typical American high school students, going to the prom and making out in the back seat.

**Divine:** Oh, we did all that. Went to the prom, went to the ring dance, went on dates.

*PKM*: You had double dates with John Waters?!

**Divine:** No, no, I was on my own. I had a wonderful girlfriend. Her name was Diane Evans. I wonder what happened to her? I also dated a girl named Stella. I liked her a lot and I wanted to marry her. But she was older than I was, and my mother and father didn't want to hear about it.

*PKM*: What else were you and Waters doing? Were you wild and crazy?

**Divine:** Not really. I mean, we liked our share of beer, but we didn't rob anybody or break into stores. We weren't really juvenile delinquents. Although our parents thought we were. We were like all kids. You go through a period when you talk back and think you know it all and I went through that. But I think everybody does.

*PKM*: So was John already playing around with movies?

**Divine:** Yeah, he loved cameras, he loved the whole idea of movie making. And he did it all on his own. I admired him. I still admire him, because a lot of people can do a movie for forty million dollars, but there aren't that many who can make a full-length color feature for $12,000.00. That's what *Pink Flamingos* cost. It looks like it, too. But he did do it and he's done it more than once. We never took any of this seriously, you understand. It was just fun and games. And whoever thought anything would happen?

*PKM*: Were you surprised at the success of *Pink Flamingos*?

**Divine:** Very surprised. I think we all were.

*PKM*: What did your parents think of *Pink Flamingos*?

**Divine:** They didn't care for it. They didn't care for anything in it. We didn't speak for about nine years.

*PKM*: It's not exactly the kind of film you write home to mom about.

**Divine:** But it's the kind of film that mother finds out about because it was so popular.

*PKM*: Yeah, and it got a lot of press. So what did it take to make a reunion happen after nine years?

**Divine:** Well, the Christmas before last, I decided to give them a call because my father has multiple sclerosis and I was very afraid he would die and I wouldn't have been able to live with that. Because he's always been very good to me and never did anything to me except disapprove of what I was doing. And that's also his right. Whether I listen to him or not, he's certainly entitled to his thoughts on the matter, so I called them up and we had a lovely conversation, and I started to write to them, and invited them down to the house in Key West—they live in Fort Lauderdale now—and everything was fine. And my father's health has gotten a lot better in the warm weather.

*PKM*: Are they excited about *Lust in the Dust?*

**Divine:** Oh, very excited. When I first got to New Mexico, I called them, and my mother said 'hi, hi, hi, how's Cesar Romero?' I said I'm fine and she said 'yeah, yeah, yeah but what about Cesar Romero?' I said 'well, he's not here yet'. She said 'oh, I gotta go. Will you call me when he gets there?' She said 'if you don't send me a picture of him, just don't leave New Mexico.'

Then my father said, 'are there any gals in the movie?' I said, 'besides me, there's Lainie Kazan'. He said, 'oh yeah, she's sexy. Big tits.' And he was quite thrilled. So I think for the first time, out of all the things I've done, they are just in ecstasy. I'm glad they're happy.

*PKM*: What's shooting *Lust* been like for you?

**Divine:** Well, the whole thing's been unbelievable. I mean, first they told me Paul Bartel was directing and that Cesar Romero and Henry Silva were going to be in the film. And I thought 'sure, sure'. Because in this business you hear about things so often that fall through and don't happen. Then they said 'George Masters is doing your makeup', and I said 'mm hmmm, yeah, yeah, yeah'. I used to read about him in the movie magazines, doing makeup for Marilyn Monroe and all these other big stars. And there he is, right on the set! Not to sound corny or anything, but it's been one thrill after another.

This is the most Hollywood-type film I've made, so it's all a brand-new experience for me. We have sets built with walls you can move to change the camera angle. When I worked with John Waters, if we filmed in a house, we filmed in a house. If you wanted to move a wall, well tough luck because you couldn't. And when we came out to the ranch, and I saw my name on the trailer, I almost cried.

At first, I was so nervous I couldn't enjoy it. I felt like an amateur with all these pros, I felt like Little Lotta stuck in the middle of a real Hollywood movie. But everyone's been just great, so now I'm really starting to enjoy it and I'm sad it's going to be over so soon.

*PKM*: So you don't feel like Little Lotta anymore?

**Divine:** No, I feel like Divine. When I walk on the set, fifteen people attack me all of a sudden, doing my hair, my costume, my makeup. And when I finish a scene, someone says, 'a chair for Divine. Where's an umbrella?' That's star treatment, you know. You've got to watch it. You can fall into it quite easily, I think.

*PKM*: Well, you need all that attention with how hard you're working in the sun and the heat and the dust.

**Divine:** I don't think of it as hard work. It's like getting dressed up and going out to play. I mean, I try to be professional by being there on time and being ready when they're ready to roll and knowing what I need to do. But once the camera starts, I like to have a good time.

*PKM*: Did you enjoy the rape scene?

**Divine:** For that scene, they just used a camera on me and all the men come ahhhh at the camera like that. Then the next scene, they're all lying around sleeping with their shirts off. So it's up to you to fill it in.

*PKM*: Were you disappointed there wasn't more interaction?

**Divine:** No, I wasn't. I didn't feel like getting raped so early…I think movies are a bit too explicit now. They don't leave anything to the imagination. This way, you can make it the filthiest rape you ever saw or it could be very Catholic. It all depends on what you're looking for. If you want to see an explicit sex scene, you should go to a hardcore porno movie. I don't think there's any reason to show it all in a regular film.

*PKM*: Well, John Waters gets pretty explicit.

**Divine:** At times, but he draws the line in certain things too.

*PKM*: You've had to do a lot of rolling around in the dirt, too?

**Divine:** Oh, yes. When I did the fight scene with Lainie, we were all over each other. I told her, "Watch it, honey."

Then yesterday Paul said, 'okay, now throw yourself down here and roll. And don't let the parasol go'. I thought, 'my god, that sounds like stunt work to me.' Well, I did it three times. I rolled in the wrong direction one time. But once you get down there and start rolling, you can't tell where you're going.

*PKM*: What about riding the donkey? How was that?

**Divine:** That's the only thing I couldn't do, and it upset me so much. I can get on a horse with five people helping me, but a donkey is built in such a way that you can't wrap your legs around it. Your legs go out like this [stretches arms wide open] so you really have to balance. And I had to hold a parasol in one hand and the donkey with the other. So five people are helping me on this donkey, right, and they said 'the donkey's nervous because you have that parasol'. So I threw down the parasol. Then they said, 'the donkey's nervous because you have that bag'. And I threw that down too. I thought I was going to be nude in about fifteen minutes because the donkey was upset. I was so scared! The other day they said 'your Cadillac's not here yet to take you back to the hotel, do you mind going in the van?' I said. 'I'll go in anything, just don't put me on that donkey!'

*PKM*: So now they just have you leading the donkey in?

**Divine:** Right. And Tab says I look like I'm walking across the desert in fifth position. [laughs] Now there's a wonderful person: Tab Hunter. He gave me a break in this business and believed in me enough to keep me there. I'm sure they could have gotten the money a lot quicker if they used someone else. But Tab said, 'if you're not in it, we're not doing it'.

*PKM*: You did *Polyester* with Tab too, which I loved. I mean, what's not to love when you go to a movie and they hand out scratch-and-sniff cards because it's shot in Odorama? What was it like working with Tab in that?

**Divine:** In *Polyester*, Tab saved me. He would take time out to coach me and help me with my lines, which he still does. I think that was the best performance I ever gave in all those [Waters] movies, and I attribute a lot of that to Tab. He was not only my leading man and co-star; he was almost like my director and acting coach. So when he asked me to do *Lust*, I was thrilled.

*PKM*: You've also embarked on a singing career too. How's that going?

**Divine:** That just happened two years ago. All my life I'd been told I couldn't sing, even though I loved to sing. I was always in the glee club and the choir at church.

**PKM**: What church?

**Divine:** Calvary Baptist. We weren't Southern Baptists; we didn't jump up and scream and roll around. We were the more conservative, high-class Baptists. Quiet. Until you picked up your hymnbook and let it roar, roar, roar. [*sings*] "On a hill far away stood an old rugged cross..." That was my favorite. And "Onward Christian Soldiers" was always a good one to get going.

Anyway, two years ago this record company came to me and said 'we want you to do disco records'. So I spoke to my manager and said 'I think we should tell them no because I'm not a singer and I can't sing'. But they didn't want to take no for an answer. They said, 'listen, if you don't like it we'll shelve it'. So I said to Bernie, 'well, in that case we have nothing to lose and everything to gain. Let's do it'.

***PKM***: You hadn't even been singing in clubs at that point?

**Divine:** No. And I was concerned about my career because movies for me don't pop up every day, I'm not Barbra Streisand, you know. So I needed work, because there were times I had no money and had to depend completely on my friends. Without them, I don't know if I'd be here talking to you.

***PKM***: What happened with that first record?

**Divine:** It was called "Native Love" and I quite liked it. I was shocked because I'm my own worst critic. I said 'it doesn't sound too bad if we could just fix this one little thing.' And they went in there with those machines, and added special sounds on synthesizers and all that. It actually got up to #22 on the charts here. It was on O Records distributed by Vanguard. But Vanguard didn't know what to do with me, so they didn't really promote it and the record just died out.

Then all of a sudden, I got a call from an agent in Holland who said 'I would love to book you over here. Your record's a huge success; you can't go anywhere it's not being played'. So I did another one called "Shoot Your Shot" and went over there and did some shows and was quite successful. Last year I spent ten weeks touring.

Now I have a new record company, Design Communications in London, who fortunately have a lot of money behind them. I'm the only artist they've signed because they think I have great potential. On the charts in England, I'm tied with Boy George popularity-wise for number one, and they want me to open a live show there around Christmas with backup singers and all.

*PKM*: What do you think about Boy George?

**Divine:** I don't think about him very much. [*laughs*] Well, I've met him. He's a fan of mine. I love some of his music, but I have my own career to worry about. His is doing fine.

*PKM*: Do you think people like Boy George, and even Michael Jackson, with his sexual ambiguity, have helped to make you more accessible to the general public?

**Divine:** Oh, definitely. It doesn't scare people so much; they can relate to it easier. Anything like that helps, sure. But the thing with me is that there isn't anyone else who does what I do. I'm alone. Not that I'm complaining. Boy George's is definitely a singing career. He's not an actor. But I try to be all-around. I always want to do everything. That's why it made me so mad I couldn't ride the mule.

*PKM*: David Bowie is another one who's pushed a lot of boundaries. Are you a Bowie fan?

**Divine:** I only met Bowie once. I'm a friend of Elton John's. You just picked the wrong one. David, I don't know very well. I've watched him go through many changes in his career—the bright red hair with all that glitter and lipstick. I think he was one of the first. Well, Jagger, too, wore little girl dresses and mary jane shoes and tapped all the way to the bank. I met him with Jerry Hall a few times, they came to shows I did.

*PKM*: And Elton John came to your shows too?

**Divine:** Oh yes. The first time I met him; he came to my show "Neon Woman" and there was a whole row of people with Elton John jackets so I wasn't sure he was there. But he came backstage afterwards and recited all the lines from my movies. He knew all the dialogue, and I was very impressed. So he took me out to dinner and I told him I'd never heard him sing and didn't own a record. All of a sudden, I owned every record he ever made, and was being flown around first class to his concerts, riding in limousines. It was quite exciting. I did that for a couple months.

*PKM*: Cool! That's really living the high life. Skipping back to your acting career, have you ever worked with Andy Warhol or Holly Woodlawn?

**Divine:** I did play with Holly in "The Neon Woman." We'd done it two and a half years, and she came in the last twelve weeks to replace somebody. I have mixed emotions about that. There's this scene where five girls come out, boom-boom-boom-boom-boom. And I say a line to them and they all have a line one after another. And the last of the five is supposed to be Holly.

Well, four of them are standing there and she's not there. So I said my line to get me offstage, and ran back, and there's Holly. I said 'excuse me, what are you doing?' 'I'm just freshening my makeup'. I said 'well, don't you think you could do that at intermission? You were supposed to be on stage five minutes ago'. Well, she ran past me, ran right on stage, and just started to spill her lines out. They had already gone a scene beyond that by then. I thought, 'I'm glad I'm not on stage right now'. I just did my change and then went back and took it up from there. Holly didn't like to come in a lot, either. Like, 'oh, I can't do the show tonight'.

*PKM*: And Warhol?

**Divine:** Andy gave parties for us when we first opened *Pink Flamingos* in New York, and he's still a friend. Every Christmas I get a big lithograph from him. So I have my own Warhol collection.

*PKM*: Well, that's money in the bank. I understand there are plans to make a video of your song from *Lust*, "These Lips Were Made For Kissing."

**Divine:** Yeah, we talked about it. I think we should have dancing cactuses in it, and make it surrealistic or whatever you want to call it. Because MTV is on twenty-four hours a day and a lot of what I've seen is boring. It's got to just jump off that screen.

*PKM*: Would you do an MTV video with another singing star?

**Divine:** Oh sure. I always wanted to do one with Tina Turner. She's one of my favorites. I think she looks fabulous.

**PKM**: Well, it seems that with *Lust in the Dust*, an MTV video and this record company backing you in England, you could really make a crossover into the heart of the market.

**Divine:** That's part of the reason I wanted to do this movie. Because I thought it wasn't fair to deny all those other people a good laugh. I want to infect them with my humor, too.

I think a lot of people get scared when they see a large man walking around in these dresses, and it takes a little while to break the ice. I had to run into Safeway the other day—without the wig but with the makeup—and the heads were spinning in Safeway! [laughs] But I thought, they'll get over it, I'm not hurting anybody, I'm only trying to make people laugh and have a good time. I think that's what's important.

A good laugh doesn't cost anything, it's free, and it's better than anything. I love to laugh and have a good time. That's what I've based my whole career on: to entertain people.

## PJ Harvey: *Is This Desire?* (Island Records)

**_huH_, October 1998**

REAL ART AND REAL voodoo have the same goal: to produce the desired effect. With supreme artistic confidence, PJ Harvey flaunted that trade secret on 1995's *To Bring You My Love,* growling "it's my voodoo working" while serving as both houngan/priest and mambo/priestess in a ritually choreographed possession during which she was ridden by an entire pantheon of voodoo spirits.

The desired effect is different this time, and so is the corresponding spell. Casting off her brazen-hussy stage drag and *Love*'s levee-breaking hoodoo, Harvey literally wears her mouth on her heart on the cover of *Is This Desire?,* a shockingly intimate album. This isn't *Love*'s ravenous maw. These are lips that whisper secrets written "In the Wind," lay the heart bare in the glare of "Electric Light" and eulogize "No Girl So Sweet"—one of several tracks that erupt like violent action film interjected on an art-house screen. Where *Love* was one huge expressionist canvas, *Desire* is a series of miniatures: sand paintings that constantly reconfigure in a shadow dance with the elements, creating an elliptic self-portrait from the shades of multiple women and the men who love them too much.

Harvey enters the stage on a wing and a prayer as "Angelene," "prettiest mess you've ever seen," with a damaged heart full of hope: "I've heard there's joy untold/Lays open like a road in front of me." By the time "joy" herself appears, soundtracked with the drum-machined desperation of a post-last call dance club, there's "no hope, no faith," just the lingering desire for "hope" (or is that Hope?) to stay. In between we meet "My Beautiful Leah," "who only had nightmares," and covered her tracks too deep for her lover to trail; and the ill-fated Elise, whose "Perfect Day" is recounted by the man who drowned her.

Presiding over it all is Catherine, who first appears unnamed in "The Wind," where Harvey weaves a textured tapestry of pure, angelic song to invoke St. Catherine ("she dreamt of children's voices and torture on the wheel"); her Celtic counterpart Brigid, goddess of keening and whistling; and the corresponding Santeria spirit of Oya, goddess of wind, storm, theater and magic. No wonder that the answer song from her scorned lover in

"Catherine De Barra" concludes its gorgeously chilling litany of what the man envies with "I envy to murderous envy your lover."

But this is no Lilith Fair celebration targeted to wannabe Goddesses; the women contribute actively to their various fates with their own choices, some good, some bad. And the men, though rarely named, emerge as fully-fleshed characters with their own ambiguities. In "The Garden," which like many tracks on this album achieves an unearthly beauty, the Judas kiss is charged with a homoeroticism that anticipated the current "gay Jesus" controversy of Terrance McNally's play *Corpus Christi*. And even boy-girl pairings find tentative redemption marked by true love when they throw their pain in "The River"—emerging, like Mary and Joseph (a.k.a. Dawn and Joe) to contemplate the eternal question *Is This Desire?* on the final track.

PJ Harvey doesn't answer this question, of course. It's just the latest installment of an ongoing dialogue that reconfirms her status as one of the great revelators of our time.

## Lucinda Williams: Live Show Review, Jazz Fest 2007

*OffBeat*, Jazz Fest Redux, July 2007

"I'M FEELING ALL KINDS of spirits here." And homegirl Lucinda Williams called them all down in her first New Orleans appearance since the death of her mother, who lived on Carondelet Street for many years. Fresh from a self-imposed road tour retreat—"I just stayed on the bus for two days, contemplated, and saved all my energy for Jazz Fest"—Williams seized the moment and ran with it. Dancing with the spirits of Jim Morrison and Flannery O'Connor (both of whom she name-checked on stage), she hit every station of the cross, searching for "Joy," pleading for spiritual redemption in "Unsuffer Me" and getting down with her nasty self in the primal ooze of "Righteously" and "Essence." But the most remarkable thing about her performance was the way she shared her feelings with us, every step along the way, confiding in the audience like we were her best friend (which I guess we are).

"With all the tragedy around us, there's always good old-fashioned sex," she reminded us early on, looking sexy as all get-out in a filmy Kelly-green top. Later, she looked tragedy straight in the eye with "Everything Has Changed," an invocation of post-Katrina New Orleans that brought tears to many eyes, including her own. "I knew I wasn't gonna get through this show without breaking down," she said. "That one did it." She paused a moment, then let her eyes take in the sweeping vista of Fest fans before her. "I love all the flags!" she cried. "New Orleans Not War, I like that one. And what's that one say?" "Here!" the flag-bearer shouted, but Williams didn't quite hear it right. "Beer? You know, at the essence of it all we're all primal creatures. We crave sex and beer." Then she broke into "Bleeding Fingers," her paean to sex and beer and rock 'n' roll, and let the spirit of Paul Westerberg carry us all to the other side, with a serious assist from guitarist Doug Pettibone.

"I don't know, I think I had some kind of spiritual enlightenment or something," she said at the end of "Fingers," just before leaving the stage. A tsunami of cheers, whistles, claps, stomps and other human percussion brought her back to "Get Right with God." And oh boy, did she, turning

Gentilly into the Gospel Tent. "Sister Lucinda!" the stage MC cried in the afterglow. "Sister Lucinda!"

Floating out of the Fair Grounds, my head still miles above the clouds, I overheard a guy on a cell phone shouting his review of the show to a friend: "I saw Lucinda Williams. She was good. I think she's on some kind of medication."

No, bro. She just got right with God. Them be God meds.

## Rickie Lee Jones Puts Down Roots in New Orleans

*Intimate Livestream Shows*

*OffBeat*, June 2020

When *OffBeat* asked me to write the April cover story on Rickie Lee Jones for their French Quarter Fest issue, she was scheduled to appear for the first time ever at the two biggest festivals in her adopted hometown of New Orleans: French Quarter Fest and Jazz Fest. Well, we all know how that turned out.

To update the original story for the new abnormal of COVID-19, I interviewed Rickie Lee Jones again, this time via Zoom. The day before we talked, I watched one of the Facebook shows she's been livestreaming from her Marigny living room, and it was her most intimate performance yet. While a river of tiny hearts floated up the screen from fans around the world, Jones wove together songs on guitar and piano with passages from her upcoming memoir, *The Last Chance Texaco*, and off-the-cuff recollections, like the time she and Tom Waits and Chuck E. Weiss stopped at a traffic light in Los Angeles, and every car around them was blasting "Chuck E.'s In Love" on their radios. ("We just looked at each other and laughed!")

Jones invites fans to join her again on Sunday, June 28th, when she'll livestream another episode of "From My Living Room" on her Facebook page at 12 p.m. CDT, with special guest Mike Dillon. More livestream dates will be posted here as she adds them, and are likely to continue for some time; the pandemic lockdown jettisoned nearly all of her 2020 tour dates. (Three Texas shows in late August are still on her schedule as of this writing.) But while she shares that fate with every other touring musician, rather than rail against it, Jones has been embracing the lockdown as a creative boon.

"In a way, this is a dream come true," says Jones. "For years, I'd joke that I would rather play from my house for the whole wide world, than to have to travel to each city. Because it's hard to be sixty-five years old traveling around the world, staying in hotels, going through airports, and dealing with all the drama that's constantly going on in a performance."

Now it's just Rickie Lee Jones and the livestream camera, which she sometimes uses to share other hidden talents. "One of the things I know how to do is draw and write at the same time," says Jones, with a note of pride. In one recent ad hoc video, she demonstrated those skills while sprawled on her floor with a spiral notebook and her playful pup, Jazzy Jones. She was clearly having a ball, as were those of us watching her.

Still, as the weeks drag on, the pandemic has taken its toll. "I think the effect is cumulative," says Jones. "So that finally I just begin to miss doing the regular thing of going to get a coffee and sitting and watching people. But the loss of people, the loss of places to go, this is small potatoes compared to all the other horrible things that are happening."

When Jones and I spoke in early June, the protests that erupted in Minneapolis in the wake of George Floyd's murder by cop had spread to New Orleans and hundreds of cities worldwide, and were weighing heavily on her heart.

"I woke up today just crying," Jones says, with a break in her voice. "My heart hurts so much. Another Black man murdered by the police. When you see that guy with his knee on George Floyd's neck, with his hands in his pockets, that's what I was struck by. Remember at the end of *Psycho*? When Anthony Perkins says, 'I wouldn't hurt a fly? You see how calm I am? I'm not even gonna swat that fly.' And when I see that policeman with his hands in his pockets, he's going, 'I'm not angry, see? I wouldn't hurt anybody; I have my hands in my pockets.' As he kills the guy. And he knows he's being filmed. It's so catastrophic. I'd rather see him foaming at the mouth than having his hands in his pockets."

An acutely observant street poet who holds up a mirror to the world around her, Rickie Lee Jones first wrote about police targeting black men on her second album, *Pirates* (1981). "Skeletons" tells the almost unbearably sad story of a black man stopped by cops while driving his pregnant wife to the hospital to have her baby:

*When he pulled off the road/*
*Step in a waltz of red moonbeams/*
*Said he fit an APB/A robbery nearby/*
*And he go for his wallet/*
*And they thought he was going for a gun/*
*And the cops blew Bird away.*

More than ten years before the current BLM protests, Rickie Lee Jones also recorded "The Gospel of Carlos, Norman and Smith" on *Balm in Gilead* (2009), a heartbreaking song that could have been written yesterday:

*Didn't you hear?/*
*Black is a criminal/*
*White is a crime/*
*Poison is the pen/*
*Writing down this children's nursery rhyme/*
*Didn't you see him standing next to me?/*
*The seeds of change have grown/*
*We don't have to hide anymore.*

"Almost all of my work seems to have relevance about ten years later," says Jones, who can cite numerous examples. "It's uncanny! And if people want to tell a story about what's happening [today], that's a good song to use." So good, in fact, that Jones posted the_YouTube audio of "The Gospel of Carlos, Norman and Smith" on her *Facebook* page with a note saying she hopes "someone can make a compelling video, using available photographs, so that people might finally hear the song."

The song definitely demands a hearing, especially in a world where "it's hard to keep trying to do the right thing," says Jones. "Because we're so pressed upon. And you gotta push it a little further than you're comfortable with." Hopefully, some digitally-savvy fan will answer her call and make a BLM montage using "The Gospel" as the soundtrack. Meanwhile, Jones is looking beyond a still uncertain future to several 2021 benchmarks on her own horizon.

"*Pirates* has its 40th anniversary in 2021 so we'll be celebrating that," says Jones. "I'm also hoping to have a record of new material by next spring, which should be a great time." In early April, 2021, *Grove Atlantic* will release *The Last Chance Texaco,* which will be available for pre-order on Amazon as of July 1, 2020. And when she's finally able to hit the road again, Jones wants to incorporate elements of her livestream shows and "tell the stories of the book in a theatrical setting."

And oh, the tales she has to tell! Rewind to mid-February 2020, when Jones and I got together for a lively in-person interview shortly before the final weekend of Mardi Gras.

### *Pre-Pandemic Flashback*

Dr. John first manifested as Rickie Lee Jones' personal gris-gris man in the summer of 1978, when she was a hot young singer on the Los Angeles club scene and legendary producer Tommy LiPuma dispatched his pal Mac Rebennack to see what all the fuss was about.

"Mac and I went to a bungalow and he started playing weird music, things that didn't belong, and I kept singing," Jones recalls over coffee in a

Bywater Cafe near her home in New Orleans, where she's lived for the past few years. She's just biked over to join me, and looks comfy and relaxed in a baggy orange sweater and jeans embellished with a little hand-stitched embroidery. "He said I passed the audition," she adds, with a sly smile.

Thus, was born a lifelong friendship and professional relationship, which began with Mac's playing on her 1979 self-titled debut; snagged a Grammy for their "Makin' Whoopee" duo on Dr. John's LiPuma-produced *In a Sentimental Mood*; and culminated with Jones singing background vocals on "I Walk On Gilded Splinters" on Mac's final, as yet unreleased, album, shortly before his death. But years before they physically met in Los Angeles, the Night Tripper's debut album *Gris-Gris* cast its spell on a young runaway in 1968.

"I was fourteen years old when I ran away," recalls Jones. "It's a long story, but I was gonna meet up with all these hippies and got a ride to this house in Ontario where everyone was smoking pot and listening to *Gris-Gris* and looking at the cover art. What is this!? It's scary! And 'I Walk on Gilded Splinters' was scary, because I thought he was singing 'Did I murder?, did I murder?, did I murder?'"

Jones breaks into song to demonstrate what "'ti Alberta" sounded like when she first heard the lines that fifty years later, she "put her real spooky thing on," as producer Shane Theriot puts it, while laying down tracks for "Gilded Splinters" on Mac's last album. "Did he murder!? What did he mean!?" wondered the teenage Jones, who reveals all the hairy details of that crazy Ontario afternoon in her forthcoming memoir, *The Last Chance Texaco*. "So that was really scary."

But Rickie Lee Jones has always thrown caution to the wind. So far from hexing her off, that initial gris-gris encounter with Mac was just the first throw of the black cat bones that ultimately led the Duchess of Coolsville to New Orleans, first to live out the fantasy and the second time for real.

In 1981, amped on the meteoric success of her debut album, which earned her a Best New Artist Grammy and sent the single "Chuck E.'s In Love" soaring to *Billboard's* Top 10, Jones dove headfirst into the seamy side of the Quarter with a tribe of swashbuckling outlaws who styled themselves as pirates on lower Decatur Street. Vivid characters like "Cunt-finger Louie" came to life on her second album, *Pirates*, which she recorded while commuting back and forth from her apartment in New York's East Village to the loft she shared with her pirate krewe on Decatur, where she stayed on and off for three years.

"It was a big loft building and it smelled like New Orleans," recalls Jones. "It had that old decaying water smell that I love, like you walked into the pirate ride at Disneyland. And in the bathroom, if you climbed up on the sink, you could look out the window and see the Mississippi River. The roof was made of tin or aluminum siding, so when it rained, it was very romantic. It wasn't a romantic time in my life, but it was a very romantic place."

It was also just a few blocks from where James Booker had a regular weekly gig in the Quarter. "Mac told me about him, so I walked down there and introduced myself and started coming whenever he played, and we became friends" says Jones. "The funny thing is, I didn't know at the time he was taking drugs, and I was taking drugs too then," she adds with a laugh. "I also became friends with Johnny Thomassie, who was Tom Waits' drummer the year we broke up. And Jerry Jumonville, the saxophonist who just passed away; he worked with me on the Pirates tour and was a real calliope of goofiness."

Playing with Mac, Booker and other New Orleans musicians like Thomassie and Jumonville was rooted in seeds planted way back in her childhood. Jones was first schooled in New Orleans music by her father, Richard Jones, a train-hopping singer and actor who inherited the showbiz genes of Jones' vaudevillian grandparents, Peg Leg Jones and Myrtle Lee.

"Louis Armstrong was a big influence on my dad, who lived here for a while," recalls Jones. "I have a picture of him in a top hat with a tuxedo on and a cane, he adopted this whole other persona when he came down here. He'd always been infatuated with New Orleans music, and he taught me 'St. James Infirmary' when I was a little girl. That infirmary song was so heartbreaking to me. I put it on a record I did just before I moved here called *Balm In Gilead*."

But despite her deep New Orleans connections—"not so much to players as to a love of New Orleans music and memories of people that convened in this place"—after the success of *Pirates*, Rickie Lee Jones followed her muse to Paris and eventually returned to California, where she had a rollercoaster relationship with the music business that continued for many years.

### *New Orleans*

As a lifelong improviser, Jones followed her internal creative compass wherever it led her, from successful forays into jazz standards like "Makin' Whoopee" to experiments with electronic music, to an eclectic catalog of covers that showcase the voice of one of the world's great interpretive singers. Working at the crossroads of blues, rock, jazz and folk, she also continued writing vivid tone poems about people in the streets around her, and collaborated with a wide range of artists from Steely Dan to Leo Kottke to Lyle Lovett. She also took long breaks from the business to recharge, returning from semi-retirement with *Duchess of Coolsville*, a three-disc anthology. But at a certain point of hit-or-miss success, she'd had enough.

"What brought me here the first time [in 1981] was to be part of a different scene than the one I was having to live in rock and roll," says Jones. "And that's what brought me here the next time as well. When I returned about six or seven years ago, I was done with L.A. I was almost done with music. I was done. I just wanted to exit. I was thinking of Florida, because I like to be near animals, and they got a lot of animals there. But I had one friend here [in New Orleans], and I opted for the human instead of the animals. I made a really big choice to try to be a human one more time. And it was a great choice, as it turned out."

Slowing down to smell the sweet olive and avoid the potholes gave Jones a chance to re-enter the human race on her own terms in New Orleans and become part of a community.

"For a person like me, who's solitary and reclusive by nature, it was a game changer," says Jones, who initially put down roots in Bywater. "Everywhere I went, people said good morning, hello, how you doing? And everybody, the kid on the bicycle, looks you in the eye. It's the opposite of Los Angeles, where people look away, and even your friends measure your worth by your success. I made a good choice coming here. I've come out. I feel like Boo Radley," she adds with a chuckle. "I finally came out."

Jones is so deeply embedded in the community that the first time I met her she bought one of my Cree-ations at the annual Carnival Costume Bazaar: a one-of-a-kind baby doll bustier with a baby doll pussy, which she proudly sported at that year's St. Anne's Ball. And I was only mildly surprised when she showed up with our mutual friend Lexie Montgomery at a tiny throws meeting for my 'tit Rex krewe, which parades with shoebox floats. Jones was just a couple floats ahead of me in this year's parade, proudly pulling "Jesus Was the First Zombie" through Marigny streets crowded with 'tit Rex fans. She had a ball but was a little trepidatious at first.

"Growing up as a Catholic, it's hard to say stuff like that, even though it's funny," she explains. "You feel like you're bringing poopy shoes into the church. So we get out there and we're pulling a float that says 'Jesus was the first zombie,' and I see all these children and I'm thinking maybe that's a thing they're gonna have to deal with. But then I thought if they're living in New Orleans, they're already seen much more offensive things than that," she adds with a laugh. "No big thing."

## *Desire*

THOUGH SHE'S BEEN ON a creative roll for the last few years, writing and releasing two new albums and going on tour with a small combo, Jones took her time circling back to music when she first arrived. "The way you find your way into New Orleans is, you gotta go slow, and I had lots and lots of hours to just walk about and drive my bike around," she says. "Nowhere to go, nobody to do it with."

Jones began venturing out more on the local music scene after she first bonded with Lexie Montgomery on Halloween 2014. "It was like we were runaway sisters," says Montgomery, who took Jones to see many of the great New Orleans musicians who ended up playing on *The Other Side of Desire* (2015), her first album as a local resident: James Singleton, Jon Cleary, Shane Theriot and David Torkanowsky among them.

Unlike *Pirates*, which mines her French Quarter experiences but was recorded with a stellar roster of New York session musicians, *Desire* is New Orleans to the bone from the opening track, "Jimmy Choos," which puts a jazzy new spin on the old Quarter con "where'd you get dem shoes?" It also travels to Acadiana with the lovely Cajun waltz "Valtz de Mon Pere," while Zachary Richard plays accordion on "J'ai Connais Pas," a Fats Domino tribute that could have been recorded by Cosimo.

While *Desire* was a breakthrough, Jones didn't fully embrace the latest chapter of her life until Montgomery took her to see the vibraphonist and percussionist Mike Dillon at Cafe Istanbul, where he was playing a gig with James Singleton.

"Mike Dillon changed my life," Jones says flatly. "Onstage, he is the most generous musician I've ever worked with. And Mike brought not only a generous heart but the proficiency to execute anywhere I want to go. I'm a real improv artist, and with Mike I don't have any fear. He's so willing, and having that support from one person has helped me raise my head up and find someone to love and live in a town and be part of the world again. And that thing Mike and I have won't get used up. Musicians who've been around at all would never mix romance if they've found that thing—because as wonderful as romance is, romance will get used up."

The feeling is definitely mutual. While Dillon was initially a little star-struck by Jones— "I was like fourteen when she was busting out with 'Chuck E.'s In Love,' and I was like wow, it's the cool chick with the beret!"—they were instantly in synch when he brought his vibes to her house and she sat down at the piano.

"When Rickie and I started playing together, it was really organic," says Dillon. "She doesn't do set lists; she just starts playing and we follow her and just go. And I love that; I'm ADD all over the place. Intuitive telepathic things start happening. Like sometimes on stage, I'll start thinking about 'Coolsville,' and the next thing you know she goes into it. It's like she picks up my thoughts."

That magic carried into Esplanade Studios, where Jones recorded her latest album of covers, *Kicks*, with Dillon and her regular touring band, guitarist Cliff Hines and bassist Robbie Mangano, along with the Naughty Professors Horn section and special guests, including Lost Bayou Ramblers' Louis and Andre Michot. Like the title suggests, it's a real kick and all over the map, from the finger-snapping "Houston" to an exquisite version of the Johnny Ray weeper "Cry" to an Andrews Sisters-style "Nagasaki" for the post-nuclear age (complete with Trumpzilla in the accompanying video).

"Rickie's one of the great songwriters and female voices and iconic singers of our time," says Dillon. "And she's not jaded from the business. She still has a lot of passion for the songs. She's intense and demands that intensity from the band, and that's what I love about her."

While she may be passionate on stage, in her everyday life Jones is as casual as the neighbors on her Marigny block, who she greets by name as she parks her bike by her house. She has a boyfriend of a year's standing with a garden she helps tend, and a young French bulldog named Jazzy Jones, who barrels out to greet us when Jones opens the door to reveal the cluttered hallway of someone still in the moving-in process. (She only recently bought the house after renting it for a year). But the living room is lovely, center-pieced by a piano covered with a sparkly red cloth, which might have been played by Albert Einstein.

"I got it from an old guy across the street in L.A. who died, and he was a physicist with all kinds of memorabilia," she explains. "One was a picture of Albert Einstein standing in the doorway. So, I always like to think Albert might have sat down here and played the keys."

The wall behind the piano is hung with old family photos of her vaudevillian grandparents Peg Leg Jones and Myrtle Lee, who bequeathed Jones the "Lee" in her name, and other showbiz relatives from her highly musical family like Aunt Bea, a jazz singer who "sang with the likes of Tommy Dorsey when he came into town."

But pride of place goes to a great archival photo of Jones jamming with James Booker at the first-ever WWOZ fundraiser, held at Jimmy's Club. "To me, it's the greatest rock action picture ever taken", says Jones. "It shows him up close and the band's right at my feet from behind. It says everything."

One of the best things about New Orleans, as others before Jones have found—from Alex Chilton who went native, to Ray Davies who split after being shot during a mugging—is that most locals treat celebrities like anyone else.

I exchanged pleasantries with John Goodman while we both were buying new glasses, and watched Trent Reznor try out new material in front of a small crowd at the Buddha Belly burger joint across from his then-uptown home. Even Brad Pitt and Angelina Jolie didn't cause much of a stir when they briefly lived in the Quarter. (Nicolas Cage is another story, but that's entirely of his own making.) And Rickie Lee Jones clearly feels at home in New Orleans, where "the soul is being fed," as Montgomery puts it. Backed by Dillon and a band she loves, she expects to be playing out locally a whole lot more when the live-music lockdown finally ends, which is great news for all of us.

"Artists often think they've come to be loved by the audience," says Jones. "And they think what if they don't love me, what if I do something wrong? But they're not looking at the incredible magic of what's happening. The most important thing is, all those people out there: they paid money, they hired babysitters, they drove across town, they went to extreme lengths to come and be loved by you. All you have to do is stand up and give them your love. All you gotta do is love them."

## Rickie Lee Jones: The Duchess of Coolsville is Back

### *Rickie Lee Jones on her new memoir,* Last Chance Texaco

*PleaseKillMe*, April 2021

*Rickie Lee Jones is back in the spotlight with a compelling memoir, Last Chance Texaco, and a fortieth anniversary box set and tour to celebrate her landmark release Pirates, the follow-up to her 1979 debut that put her, and her raspberry beret, on the cultural map, won her a Grammy and kicked off her fascinating career. Over the course of the pandemic year just passed, Cree McCree spoke with Rickie Lee Jones about her hardscrabble childhood, itinerant life, meteoric rise to fame, and the struggles that have tested her innate survival instincts.*

"Some of us are born to live life on an exaggerated scale," writes Rickie Lee Jones in her compulsively readable memoir *Last Chance Texaco: Chronicles of an American Troubadour* (Grove Press), officially released on April 6. Put Jones at the top of that list. The scale of her own epically cinematic life is as deep and wide as the Grand Canyon in her childhood crucible of Arizona, with as many tributaries as the mighty river that runs through it. And her meteoric rise to *Time*-proclaimed 'Duchess of Coolsville' status in 1979, when she rocketed from complete obscurity to raspberry beret ubiquity and reached the pop-culture pinnacles of *Rolling Stone* and *SNL* in less than a year, is but one fascinating chapter in an often-hardscrabble life with enough cliffhangers and whiplash twists to do Charles Dickens proud.

I'd spent a week seeing the world through Rickie Lee Jones' eyes when we met at an outdoor cafe next to the railroad tracks in our adopted hometown of New Orleans, where our conversation was punctuated by loud blasts from passing trains like the ones her dad once hopped. It was almost a year to the day since we'd last met in person during the Deep Gras groove that culminates in Fat Tuesday, when we were both blissfully unaware that Mardi Gras 2020 would soon be maligned as a super-spreader event.

In the interim, my *OffBeat* cover story, which was pegged to Jones' Covid-canceled appearances at French Quarter Fest and Jazz Fest, had morphed into a digital-only version. When we met via Zoom in late May for a pandemic update, nationwide protests were erupting over the murder of George Floyd, which cut her to the quick. "My heart hurts so much," said Jones, who first wrote about murder-by-cop forty years ago in "Skeletons" on *Pirates*. "Another Black man murdered by the police."

Like she did last year, Jones cruised up to our interview on her bike, and joined me at a socially distanced table center-pieced by a crazy eyeball hat I'd made. Like a true New Orleanian, she was making the most of the pandemic-era Mardi Gras by decorating her Marigny front porch with some favorite pieces from past Carnivals. Topping off the ad hoc altar was a three-babydoll bustier, complete with babydoll pussy, which Jones bought from me a couple seasons ago. Later, we'd add my eyeball hat. Now it was time to get down to business. But before we take a deep dive into *Texaco*, Jones wants to flag another landmark 2021 event.

"It's the fortieth anniversary of *Pirates*, arguably my most important release," says Jones. Many critics would concur. The follow-up to her wildly successful debut, which earned her a Best New Artist Grammy and sent the single "Chuck E.'s In Love" soaring to *Billboard's* Top 10, *Pirates* dates back to her first stint in New Orleans, when Jones dived headfirst into the seamy side of the Quarter with a tribe of swashbuckling outlaws. Vivid characters like "cunt-finger Louie" came to life on *Pirates*, which she recorded while commuting back and forth from New York's East Village to the lower Decatur St. loft she shared with her crew of hipster buccaneers.

To celebrate this milestone, Jones is releasing an entire commemorative package in October: *Rickie Lee Jones* (1979), *Pirates* (1981), and a third album of unreleased demos and outtakes. She plans to start touring behind it as early as August and play performing arts centers this fall. "I want to play the Greek," she enthuses. "I haven't been there in twenty-five or thirty years. People can be outside, and I can actually sell tickets! That would be really wonderful, and there's a magical aura that's always surrounded *Pirates*."

"What's the most magical part of *Pirates* for you?" I ask her later in a follow-up text.

"As I place myself in danger again and again and then return from hell over and over it's impossible not to get a whiff of destiny," she shoots back instantly, and that's as good a way as any to summarize her book.

From the moment she was born, to the orphaned son of one-legged vaudevillian Peg-Leg Jones and a mother raised in an orphanage after her grandmother's mad dash across a cornfield failed to save baby Bettye from child protective services, Jones had an inner radar that both courted catastrophe and saved her from its most dire consequences, usually at the eleventh hour. And even during her childhood, in the enchanted desertscape of Arizona, she was constantly on the move, uprooted by her parents, separately or together, honing the survivalist skills she'd need when she struck out on her own and hitched across the country in 1969 at age fourteen.

Like the vivid tone poems Jones creates in her songs, *Last Chance Texaco* is studded with a rogue's gallery of wildly eccentric characters, famous and obscure, and larded with striking images like Alfred's Decapitated Doll Emporium (the mannequin-littered home of her first songwriting partner, Alfred Johnson). The cast includes a host of guardian angels, because "magic never left me," along with oft-unwitting oracles and seers, like the Canadian border guard who warned the bra-less teen she was "in danger of living a lewd and lascivious life."

But what really sucks you in, and lifts you up, is the dazzling magic of her prose. Some of the most lyrical passages are channeled in a fever dream, like her description of her and Tom Waits at the peak of their doomed romance: "Now we were religions, we converted to each other, we inspired each other and we spoke in tongues. He growled; I cooed. He softened; I growled...We were jellyfish, floating from day to night."

Whether you're a longtime Rickie Lee Jones fan, or only vaguely know her name, *Last Chance Texaco* speaks for itself and is one of the most compelling memoirs I've ever read. So I was delighted to explore its revelations with the author in the conversation that follows.

*The following interview has been edited for length and clarity:*

**Rickie Lee Jones**: What did you like about the book? What makes this memoir different than somebody else's memoir?

***PKM***: I feel like I'm living your life, minute by minute, exactly how it happened. You get so deeply inside me that I feel like I am you. And I was savoring it. I was even savoring the trauma, if that makes any sense.

**Rickie Lee Jones**: Oh excellent.

[*RLJ reaches over the table and swats a mosquito away from my head.*]

***PKM***: Oh my god! Thank you! I got vaccinated for Covid, but I didn't get vaccinated against mosquitos! So it was your ability to put me inside Rickie Lee Jones that really made the book come alive for me. Were you keeping any diaries or journals? Or is this all drawn out of your memory?

**Rickie Lee Jones**: If I wanted to, I could almost remember every day. Once memory begins, it's really acute. That story about the horse kicking me in the head would not come to the surface at first. Because it was a feeling more than a memory. I can feel myself hiding in that cupboard. That head injury must have happened just a few minutes before, and it sent me into some other world. And one day I did hide in a cupboard, and I remembered really clearly that I have to come back with handles. And I'm going to use each handle: the corral door, the Volkswagen door, the door to my house. And when I came to the door of my house, I thought I'm back now. Isn't that funny? How do I come back? I use handles. [*laughs*]

*PKM*: That's also a great metaphor. Maybe that traumatic injury sparked something in your brain that helped you access your ability to come back, and to remember so clearly. You always trust your inner radar, and pass that wisdom along to us: "When I sing, you can hear your own tears falling on that window sill."

**Rickie Lee Jones**: When I sing, you're in my room, looking out of my window.

*PKM*: When did you actually start the writing process and say, "OK, this is a memoir"?

**Rickie Lee Jones**: I started writing funny little short stories about my life back in 2001, and I did a live afternoon show at Santa Monica College of reading poems, playing songs and telling personal stories. Then I got an agent, who'd been reading my writing on my website. And when I knew I had a contract, I began working on it seriously about seven years ago. But it took me a few years.

*PKM*. There's a big difference between performing and writing a book. Because when you're writing a book, you're talking to one person. It's very intimate.

**Rickie Lee Jones**: You're right, it's totally different. In the first years of writing it, I'm telling my story. But eventually I'm crafting your journey from here to there. And that took a long time to learn. Because I really want to let them know what color those shoes were! [*laughs*]

*PKM*: But sometimes the color of the shoes is important. Because so many of your details are really striking.

**Rickie Lee Jones**: [*laughs*] That's when Jamie [Dell'Apa] would say, you're taking too much out!

*PKM*: Is Jamie your editor or your agent?

**Rickie Lee Jones**: He's my reader. I have to have a reader, somebody I'm talking to, and Jamie showed up two or three years ago. Finally. I was about to give up. And he said, "it's kind of a mess but you have good stuff here. Let's talk about your themes'. And once we see what themes I gravitate toward, we can craft a book. Magic was one of them. And running away. He said, 'your family's always running away, and so are you."

*PKM*: And it's an incredible story! Do you have any idea how many times your family moved? Either as a unit or you with your father or you with your mother? It seems like it was dozens! How many schools did you go to?

**Rickie Lee Jones**: Eleven by the time I was asked to leave in the eleventh grade. And then I went to three colleges: vocational college, Tacoma College and Santa Monica College. That's a lot of schools, a lot of enrolling. It's a miracle that I'm here.

*PKM*: There were miracles all along the way. But there were also times when you really took charge. Like when you were in Bud Dain's office, and you're totally broke, your employment is running out and he offers you $800.00 a month for writing songs. Which was a lot back then! And you said, 'wait a minute, I have to think about that'.

**Rickie Lee Jones**: No, it's worse than that! They had offered it and I said 'OK, I'll do it'. So I was coming back to sign the contract. And I was about to sign it and I had that feeling of don't do it. If they want you, someone even better will want you. That takes a lot of faith. Not to settle for good and instead go for great.

*PKM*: Yeah! I feel like there was almost an invisible hand stopping you. It gives me chills thinking about some of those moments, when you started becoming Rickie Lee Jones for real. One thing that really holds the book together is the way you organized it: The Back Seat, Riding Shotgun, Driving, The Way Back Seat. Did you come up with that initially?

**Rickie Lee Jones**: Yes.

*PKM*: And the shotgun section's so cool because you were riding shotgun with Dr. John, you were riding shotgun with Lowell George, you were riding shotgun with Tom Waits. You picked your drivers well.

**Rickie Lee Jones**: Well, they were the guys who came along.

*PKM*: I remember you telling that story about Lowell George when you were doing one of your live streams, about floating in the pool while he was singing "Willin'" for you.

**Rickie Lee Jones**: That was a beautiful moment. It's a beautiful song. And he was illuminated from the back, so you couldn't really see him well. That's an image I love so much. And I thought, how can this be happening to me? [*laughs*]

*PKM*: Another through-line in the book is *West Side Story*...It's like a scene out of the musical when you and Tom Waits and whoever else was at the Troubadour that night burst into singing the Jets song.

**Rickie Lee Jones**: There were rumors that Tom Waits hung out there so I had a feeling he might be there. And after the show, everyone was standing in front of the club, pretending like they were in a movie of their own. And someone said, it's like the Jets and the Sharks out here. And somebody sang a line from the song and I answered them: [*sings*] "When you're a Jet you're the swinging-est thing, little boy you're a man, little man you're a king..." I was always singing "when you're a Jet, you're a Jet all the way," and that's how I began to find my people. Because if they know it, they'll answer!

*PKM*: Another one is "Something's Coming." You circle back to that a few times.

**Rickie Lee Jones**: Yeah. So thrilling, so exciting, that moment right before something happens. And sometimes something terrible happens. But before awful things happen, beautiful things happen.

*PKM*: When we finally get to the Way Back Seat, you're at the peak of your meteoric rise, when you appeared on *Saturday Night Live*. And that *Coolsville* trilogy, which was like a twelve-minute video, was playing in record stores across the country. That was so influential, way ahead of its time.

**Rickie Lee Jones**: It was so successful that people went, 'this is the wave of the future'. But by the time they got MTV started, they were going in that cheap direction. [*laughs*]

*PKM***:** You also started seeping into the culture. Everything from Chuck E. Cheese to the beret.

**Rickie Lee Jones**: That's one of the things that's lost all these decades later. People don't remember that. That I had an impact on the culture.

*PKM*: And it happened really quickly.

**Rickie Lee Jones**: It did. The Way Back Seat is the limousine. And I was just thinking, if I read a review that said she doesn't get to the cool part until the end of the book, I wouldn't want to read that book. And I thought how are you going to let people know you're gonna be really glad to read how all these stories unfolded…

**PKM**: You do it in the introduction, which is sort of a preview of coming attractions.

**Rickie Lee Jones**: That's how Jamie helped me. And he was right.

*PKM*: Because people do want to know about Tom Waits and "Chuck E's In Love" and Lowell George, and you drop all that in as teasers. But you don't whip through the book to get to the "good parts." I certainly didn't! I was really compelled by the story of how you somehow managed to survive on the run all those years. With and without your family. But I do want to talk about Tom Waits. Because I was one of those people who thought of you and Tom Waits as the ultimate cool hipster couple.

**Rickie Lee Jones**: How did you know I was with Tom Waits?

*PKM*: You weren't completely on the QT. You made a couple of public appearances together.

**Rickie Lee Jones**: Yeah, he showed up in London. That's where all those pictures came from.

*PKM*: And *Second City* did a skit on TV about you and Tom Waits inventing yourselves inventing yourselves, which I loved.

**Rickie Lee Jones**: That's right. That was incredible.

*PKM*: And you totally stayed in character when you moved in with him and actually set up housekeeping together. That house without air conditioning!? When you both had money!? You were driving around looking for motels to stay in 'cause it was so damn hot. Because Tom liked that down and out image, I guess. He didn't want to be the guy with the air conditioning. [*laughs*]

**Rickie Lee Jones**: Exactly! [*laughs*] But he's got it now!

*PKM*: Have you been in touch with Tom Waits since those days?

**Rickie Lee Jones**: No.

*PKM*: Would you like to reach out to him?

**Rickie Lee Jones**: I think the time has passed.

*PKM*: Yeah, he's kind of settled into a whole new life. He's no longer the Tom Waits character.

**Rickie Lee Jones**: I don't know what he is. Remember the L.A. riots, in the '90s? There was a spirit of 'let's all get back together again', and Waits and Chuck Weiss did a concert so I showed up to bury the hatchet. I'm not going to tell you about what happened…But it had to do with his wife…And at first I said, 'it's like the Yoko syndrome. Fans are mad that she took him away'. But it wasn't…What is the hold that she has over him that he can't even say hello? Can't even look at me? And at that time, it hurt so much.

*PKM*: I used to be a huge Tom Waits fan. Starting with *Blue Valentine.* And I loved the photos on that album, even though I didn't know at the time that was you leaning back against the car.

**Rickie Lee Jones**: He's not real.

*PKM*: You both could have afforded a fabulous place when you moved in together. And it's so Tom Waitsian to opt to get this little un-airconditioned bungalow in a sketchy neighborhood. But I was really shocked at his reaction when you told him you had been using heroin, and he just couldn't handle it. It was painfully honest for you to tell him, but I don't see how you could *not* have told him. How could the person who loves you and is setting up house with you not say, 'hey let's do this together, and get this monkey off your back?'

**Rickie Lee Jones**: You know, he had left the world he created when he created Tom Waits and moved into this house that was more like a house his mom lived in. As close to real as he wanted to come. So he wasn't safe. And all I can think of is maybe people behind the scenes were talking about me, I just don't know. Back then, I might have regretted telling him. But that's how he felt: I don't want anything to do with you. If that's who you are.

*PKM*: I also found it amazing that you were able to stop using heroin on your own. I don't know too many people who have done that. Without having to go to NA and all that stuff.

**Rickie Lee Jones**: That would have destroyed me [*laughs*]

*PKM*: I knew about Mac [Dr. John] shooting you up for the first time, that was in the book. What made you decide you wanted to try heroin?

**Rickie Lee Jones**: I knew Mac was a source because I knew about his past. And at that time, Tom and I were on the outs, the record was coming out, and my father had moved in. These are just little psychological things. And I might have had a romantic picture, that I'd be like Billie Holiday. So I don't know. I tried to supply pictures in the book of why I thought it was possible, like seeing that great movie, *The Man with the Golden Arm*. But I don't know why. I don't know why.

I think there's still a thing that people have about heroin addicts. People are so attracted to it. It will be the first question when I go to talk to people from England. And I think it's so complex why they're attracted to it. But it's just a drug. And when people take it, they just fall asleep all day. That's all there is to it. The moral decrepitude of being addicted is out of date. And there's so many addicts. It's a tragic thing.

*PKM*: Well, it was also romanticized by people like Lou Reed, and Marianne Faithfull, who I interviewed when she was first coming out of her addiction. My god, "Sister Morphine"! That made it very attractive, back in the day. These days, going on heroin is probably a good thing compared to going on fentanyl or all that other crap.

**Rickie Lee Jones**: It's hard to get in and out of that life. I scrambled out as fast as I could. I was gonna die, I was losing my soul. Like I said. I was an addict the way I did everything else. I remember a couple people saying, 'I've never seen anyone as bad as you are'. That's pretty amazing. Thank you! Do I get a ribbon? [*laughs*] But that wasn't true. I've met people who used water out of the sewer to shoot up. I never did that.

*PKM*: But you had to work at getting addicted. It made you throw up a lot but it didn't stop you.

**Rickie Lee Jones**: I know this sounds ridiculous. But you know that movie, *The Man with the Golden Arm* and that doo-da-de-doo-dah, doo-da-de-doo-dah [hums jazzy theme] as Frank walks across the street? And he goes to the man! And it fixes everything! I wanna know what that is, from a young age. So I found out.

*PKM*: Let's jump to the boldface names. You have that encounter with Dylan, where he called you a poet.

**Rickie Lee Jones**: A real poet.

*PKM*: Right. Not just a poet, a *real* poet. That's something to treasure. But other than people we've already mentioned, you don't really talk about many celebrities in your book. You say in passing, oh I could tell more stories about Lou Reed, and Bob Dylan. So I wondered if maybe that's in the second memoir.

**Rickie Lee Jones**: It will be. I'm writing little three- or four-page vignettes about each of them.

*PKM*: Good, good! But what I love, and you even say "wait for it." The one you zero in on is Eddie Money!

**Rickie Lee Jones**: I know! [*laughs*]

*PKM*: That's so hysterical! I literally laughed out loud.

**Rickie Lee Jones**: It's a beautiful story. I was just starting to write *Pirates*, it was summertime, and I was walking on the Upper West Side. Near John Lennon's apartment. I walked by a bar, and I heard somebody call my name. And this guy was standing in front of the bar and he went 'Rickie! It's Eddie Money!' Like I was supposed to know him. "Come on in, I'm with my brother. Come on in and have a drink."

And so we drank and drank and drank. And his brother was a detective with the NYPD. And they were just delightful. And then the bar closed, and they said 'OK, we know a place that stays open'. When I tell this story, I just can't imagine how people can drink as much as we drank! Cause once you take a drink, that's pretty much it, and you can't get any higher than how high you already got. [laughs] Horrible drug. So we drove downtown, and Eddie's brother put the [police] light on top of the car. With the siren. And as we drove, it was if all the lights turned green for us! We went through every light!

*PKM*: And this was in Manhattan, mind you. For me, that was one of the most thrilling scenes in the book.

**Rickie Lee Jones**: Oh my god! We're going to the bar!!!

*PKM*: Because I lived in Manhattan for years, so I know how magical that must have been.

**Rickie Lee Jones**: I love that you know how all these things feel!

*PKM*: Yeah. I've never been to *SNL*, but I have some friends in a band who were on *SNL*, so I know how exciting it is to have that experience. But you didn't live in Manhattan for too long, did you?

**Rickie Lee Jones**: Well, I was an addict when I lived there. I didn't really have an experience of it, other than being an addict. But also, I'd just become rich. And I thought "I have so much money, how can I ever run out? I'm gonna stay in a hotel and spend whatever I want."

*PKM*: So how did you decide when to end the book? Because it ends long before you moved to New Orleans [in 2014].

**Rickie Lee Jones**: Well, from the time my career begins, there's a lot to tell. And by then, I'm already on page three-hundred. And I hadn't even told that much about what came after, and the book is getting long. So even though I really didn't want to end the book after the initial success, that's where it wanted to end. It just delivered itself. And I thought, 'if things go well, I'll find a way to tell how to stay in music', or whatever this story is, in another story.

*PKM*: I think it was a very smart decision. Leave 'em wanting more!

**Rickie Lee Jones**: I wanted to bring it back to family, to deliver you back to family.

*PKM*: I texted you when I finished it, because I was really moved by the ending. After all the ups and downs with your mom and dad, separately and individually, the unconditional love that came through for the family at the end was amazing.

**Rickie Lee Jones**: I wanted to remind people that even though people are neither good nor bad, they're wonderful and terrible, they're your family. And in our case, they may have betrayed you a few times. But in the end, as part of the infrastructure, there's this faith and hope that never leaves.

*PKM*: And I'm sure this wasn't calculated. But for the pandemic, it's great to bring it back to family, when everyone's kind of locked in with their families now. I mean, people aren't running away as much now because it's hard to run away.

**Rickie Lee Jones**: The last thing I added into the book was the bit about my brother, Danny [who lost a leg in an accident as a teen]. I connected with him again about two years ago, when he was in bad straits. And what came out was that memory of trying to get him a membership in a health club. Danny thinks, 'oh good, I'm finally at a club'. 'No you're not, you're out of here'. And I said to the guy, 'hey, you've just broken a law! It's against the law!' [to refuse service to a handicapped person]. And he just didn't care! And that's what it's like to be a handicapped human being every day of your life. That story was good, without being melodramatic. Danny's OK, and life is fucking hard. But we all keep going on. And we're talking to each other in the invisible world. And we keep going.

*PKM*: We keep going...What's the most important thing you want to say about the book?

**Rickie Lee Jones**: It's a memoir like no other. It reads more like fiction.

*PKM*: Because you've had a life that's incredibly cinematic!

**Rickie Lee Jones**: It doesn't shy away from, but it doesn't focus on, celebrity. And by the time it does get to celebrity, I think it's very classy. I don't *not* tell you about lovers, but I'm never salacious. I'm sexy, but not salacious.

*PKM*: Isn't that what that cop said to you when you were trying to cross the border from Canada?

**Rickie Lee Jones**: "You're in danger of living a lewd and lascivious life!"

*PKM*: Right! I would have taken that as a mark of honor myself.

**Rickie Lee Jones**: I didn't really live a lascivious life. But to him, I did! A woman without a bra!

*PKM*: So it's a memoir like no other, which is true. And it reads like fiction, which is certainly true.

**Rickie Lee Jones**: And my reason for writing it was to honor my family. I can hear them saying 'you have to tell our stories'. The orphanage and the running across the cornfield and the one-legged grandfather on stage. Every one of them deserve to have their stories told.

In a hundred years, I want someone to read what life was like for one woman. An extraordinary life, maybe, but maybe other people have lived lives even more extraordinary. So let's tell our story and not shine it up, not hide it, here's what really happened. Here's how brokenhearted I was. Here's how triumphant I was. Here's how egotistical I was. Here's how humble I was. Here's who I am, and here's where I came from. And I cast them into the future, and hope that they grow.

*PKM*: And you leave us with a lovely epilogue, too. Which was very inspiring. Because one working title for my own memoir is *Making It Up As I Go Along*.

**Rickie Lee Jones**: That's good!

*PKM*: You've been very inspiring to me, not only as an artist and a singer. But as a woman and as a writer. It's not a long book, but it's a dense book, it's full of layers. You put us right there, minute by minute. And that's a different type of gift from your songwriting. Because with songs, you also have the music, which helps. But to do that just with prose, on the page, is extraordinary.

**Rickie Lee Jones**: It's a totally different job. Writing the book was so much harder.

*PKM*: Because you're just doing it alone. You and a blank sheet of paper, or a blank screen. Did you write this on a computer?

**Rickie Lee Jones**: Yes. We have other books at home of other versions. Three years or four years ago, I'd written the stories, basically my mother, *SNL*, the attempted rape, some dark things, some good things. So I fly to New York to meet with the editors. And when I came back, they had moved stories around and they were starting my story with *SNL*. And I said 'I'm not gonna publish this. If you start there, there's nowhere to go!' They were so angry! They had already put out a press release.

*PKM*: This was Grove Press?

**Rickie Lee Jones**: Yeah. They were mad, and we didn't talk for a while. But I found my way back to the story of my mother, and I started out with the wonders and experiences of my childhood. And now, when you go back to my mother, you're all right because you already met me as a little kid.

*PKM*: That's what makes it so compelling. I *am* Rickie Lee Jones at age six, I *am* Rickie Lee Jones at age eight.

**Rickie Lee Jones**: In their hands, it would have been just another memoir. People are always trying to make you do what they know how to do. It takes a lot of courage and determination to say no. It takes a lot of guts to say I'm gonna risk it all and do it my way. [sings the chorus of "My Way," Sinatra style] And in this case, it was a good choice. Now my editor [at Grove] loves me. She sends me little notes, "I'm smiling. This is so good!"

## Epilogue: Follow-Up Texts with Rickie Lee Jones

**Rickie Lee Jones**: Yesterday you asked me about the themes of the book. I think one of them was my Will. The strength of one person's will not only to overcome but to see magic everywhere.

This Frank Capra life overtaken by Stanley Kubrick might initially seem like *Forrest Gump* except for the fact that it is real. I actually lived these benchmarks. I lived an idyllic timeless childhood out in the middle of nowhere and I was raised by a loving pack of wolves. I was carried on the shoulders of the big wide world as an itinerant teenager and placed from one on-ramp to the next until I found my way back to King Arthur's Court.

And when I became a mother, I protected the privacy of my family life and my child until she was grown and I could begin to tell the stories. I have been as devoted to family as I have been to music, and now as I start to enter these older last years, I mean to do everything I ever dreamed of doing one more time.

Dreams are my sword and shield. With them there is nothing I can't... Eventually...Manifest

*PKM*: Wow! You're really on a roll with these magical Big Picture texts!

**Rickie Lee Jones:** Good. I like thinking that my job is essential and spiritual and that I can be a comedian and be melodramatic. Isn't that fantastic? I just have to cry mercy, how blessed all that hard stuff that happened was! Like a storm and I was on a boat that simply would not break.

# Rickie Lee Jones: Of Intimacy and American Standards

***DownBeat*, June 2023**

Rickie Lee Jones has a credo that she's lived by all her life: shouting her name out while zigzagging through musical genres and penning a series of idiosyncratic albums that defy categorization.

"Everything you do is an extension of every moment you've lived up to then," she says. "So, own it. You're only here for a little while, so shout your name out everywhere you go."

The self-titled *Rickie Lee Jones* (Warner), her 1979 debut, launched the *Time* magazine-proclaimed "Duchess of Coolsville" from complete obscurity to raspberry beret ubiquity with her hit single "Chuck E.'s In Love." She was awarded the Grammy Award for Best New Artist and scaled the pop-culture pinnacles of Rolling Stone and *SNL* in less than a year. *Pirates* (Warner), her 1981 follow-up, was also a critical and commercial success. Both were produced by Russ Titelman (who has also produced the likes of Randy Newman, George Harrison, Eric Clapton and more), who has now circled back four decades later to produce *Pieces of Treasure* (BMG Modern), a collection of American songbook standards that's one of Jones' most personal, intimate albums to date.

Meeting to discuss *Pieces of Treasure*, Jones continued a conversation that's been going on for several years—ever since she became a fellow New Orleanian. On the last deep dive, Jones had just released her compulsively readable memoir *Last Chance Texaco* (Grove Press UK, 2021).

But *Pieces of Treasure* isn't about her. It's about a series of characters she created to get inside the skin of every song, and the musical framework Titelman gave her to manifest those characters—a framework that includes pianist Rob Mounsey, guitarist Russell Malone, bassist David Wong and drummer Mark McClean.

Titelman, for his part, used the album to showcase "Rickie's artistry in full bloom. Her voice has always sounded a bit younger than it ought to, but on this recording the aging voice sounds even better to me than the youthful one. There's a resonance and warmth in her lower register that wasn't there before. I adore the young Rickie Lee, but I love even more the Old Dame."

The Old Dame arrived at the interview for this article wearing a North Sea Jazz Festival T-shirt, looking very vibrant and youthful, her skin glowing and her face framed by soft waves of blonde hair. At sixty-eight, she makes growing old look good.

*The following conversation has been edited for length and clarity.*

**Cree McCree:** When I first arrived, you told me you'd just listened to the album this morning. What was your reaction to hearing it again?

**Jones:** Usually there's a point where there's a weaker song and you hate it even more as time goes by. But that hasn't happened. The woman who's singing these songs, I don't know where she came from. I mean, she's obviously a development of me, but she feels almost like somebody else. So I can listen to her and enjoy the music. Usually, I'm listening to myself and criticizing it.

**McCree:** Did you realize when you started this project that you were going to be creating a whole other persona who would be actually singing the songs?

**Jones:** No, but I knew I was gonna have to address the issue of age in my voice. Because it's almost like glaucoma, and in the midrange, it wanted to waiver. I could still punch the big notes, and I could go deep, but right here where I like to sing, I was having a little trouble. And that's where so many of these songs are. That's why so much of what happens in this album feels like destiny. Because what I couldn't do the week before, the moment I walked into the studio, I could do it. And some of that power came from the respect of the musicians.

I'm so vulnerable to what people say. And in past studio situations, I can feel defeated before I even start. But these guys came up and said, it's an honor to play with you. That's a word reserved for older people. And I feel like I'm right where I'm supposed to be.

**McCree:** And you completed the whole thing in five days, right?

**Jones:** We did. We actually had days where we did three songs in one day. It was just pow, pow, pow. I knew that I wanted to tell the story, but I didn't care about articulating the words. [*starts to sing*] "When the autumn weather turns the leaves to flame." ...There's a lot of sound in the word "flame."

**McCree:** You can actually hear it flickering.

**Jones:** It's exciting singing every sound, so I did things very differently than I have. And when I'm singing with men who've said this is an honor, we'll receive what you do, I have more courage to be creative. Because when you have men in there looking at their watch, you wouldn't dare throw your beautiful pearls to them.

**McCree:** Let's rewind to the genesis of the project. What brought you and Russ back together again after all these years?

**Jones:** I was coming to New York to do some kind of promotional thing, and we met for lunch. And being with him is like being with the city of New York. He's so engaged and wears a hat and scarf and is always smiling and you're just caught up in all the things that could be when you're talking to Russ Titelman. So I was trying to sound him out to see if he wanted to get involved with the new stuff I was writing, but when I sent him a song, he referred to it as "that funny little song" because he's a traditional guy.

And, he in turn was saying, "I wanna do a jazz record. It's time to do a jazz record." So I said all right, then, that's what we'll do. With players who listen to the singer and can work with a woman.

**McCree:** And he found them. There are so many lovely instrumental solos that you play off. The vibes on "Just In Time" set the tone for the whole album, and that loping bass sucks you right in to start scatting at the end of "One For My Baby."

**Jones:** Frank Sinatra owned that song. And I was looking for a way in, because the one thing I don't want to do is imitate somebody else's spirit. How would I get in? So I went looking and found Ida Lupino, who sang that song in this 1947 film noir [*Road House*]. And it's so contemporary, how she did it. This character in this song has been through it and is kind of rough. So there's my way in.

**McCree:** In your song-by-song analysis, you also said Frank always gives you the strength to go on.

**Jones:** I have this little group of people who, if I don't know what to do, I just become them. What would Miles do here? What would Frank do here? They can't do anything wrong because they own Frank. They own Miles. Everything Miles does by definition is correct because it's an extension of himself. So just be Frank for a minute until you can do me again.

**McCree:** These songs were nowhere near contemporary with you, but you make them sound like you grew up with them.

**Jones:** I got them from my dad and Sinatra and "Moon River," and I have a super ability to remember songs. All I have to do is hear 'em a few times, and they become part of my palette of color. You can teach yourself how to paint with your own language and your own voice.

**McCree:** God, you're so poetic. Just naturally. It blows me away how you come up with these metaphors.

**Jones:** When I read what I've said in a magazine, I go, "Wow, that's pretty smart," but I have no idea I'm saying it at the time. I'm confident enough not to plan—to see what will happen.

**McCree:** So, you didn't have the record mapped out in your mind.

**Jones:** No. It revealed it itself. I had a feeling about the character, and in doing that, I heard the sound of my voice. I was like, "Wow, I can finally hear what I sound like." On so many other records, maybe because I'm competing with other instruments, I can never hear the air and sound of my voice. This is a triumph for that reason that I can hear me. It was made with discipline, and that's what Russ brought.

**McCree:** Toward the end of the album, you get into the songs that are more specifically about aging, like "September Song."

**Jones:** May to December, and automatically you think younger girl, older man. I envisioned an older man in a derby and a long wool coat sitting on a park bench, holding a cane with the winter trees all around him, loving some distant thing that was too beautiful to even touch.

**McCree:** That's very specific.

**Jones:** Yeah. And when I decided to sing it, I wanted to make the person on the bench a woman and give her more reality than the little derby and the cane. The thing I'm singing to is my own youth and the past and how much I love it.

**McCree:** This is an album about aging, but sitting across from me now you look very youthful and vibrant.

**Jones:** I feel at the beginning of something, not at the end of something. I'm excited to be able to keep talking to the world when I'm past my childbearing years.

**McCree:** Every song you sing is so personal. And intimate. There are some very sensual parts.

**Jones:** I just hope it's refreshing and uplifting. Like in the song at the end, "All In The Game." It's not that it's sad, it's just so much delicious feeling that there are no more words and the feeling just takes over.

**McCree:** You literally cry at the end of "All in the Game," which to me is more of a statement that that's just the way it is. What about that song is so devastating to you?

**Jones:** Well, because you don't know. The writer is saying things are hard right now, and the future's looking dim. But you can hang on. You can rise above it. Hold on to yourself. That's hard to do in love. I'm not the only girl who banged on the door late at night. When your future depends on one human being, everything's at risk if they don't call. When I hear my voice that way, I know we're just hanging on.

It's like when my mother saw me on *Saturday Night Live* singing "Chuckie E.'s In Love" and she said, "Oh, my gosh, when you first started the song, I thought you were gonna faint." Only she knew how terrified I was. But I left the sob on at the end because I accepted that there was something happening that was so joyful. There are no words, that's why you get to sob it.

**McCree:** Were there any songs you left out that you wished you had done?

**Jones:** No, I think it's perfect. One of the songs we were gonna do was "It Never Entered My Mind," which I've been doing for about seven years, but in the weird Rickie way. My own weird chords. And so, we ended up doing three versions. One a Rickie, one a band one, and then a mix of both that we cut together. And we almost put on the one with the band because the sound of it was most like the rest. But the fact that it's so dark and sad and a little off would've changed the feeling of the whole record, which I wanted to be uplifting. So there are other great songs, but they don't fit in the record. The Rickie ideas are what led me here. I'm sixty-eight and can do a record of old jazz and feel very proud of it.

# III.

## Sweet Home Louisiana

### *Introduction:*

### *The Heady Hoodoo Brew of New Orleans & Bayou Country*

From the moment I stepped off the plane in New Orleans for the first time ever in 1988, the swampy air caressed me like a lover and made me realize that yes, New Orleans is a woman and the fertile crotch of America, where I am destined to be reborn in my true spiritual home. And, as always, it was the siren call of the music that lured me here, years before I ever set foot in Louisiana.

Dr. John became my main medicine man back in 1968, when "The Night Tripper" festooned himself with feathers and bones, hoodooed me with *Gris-Gris* and mainlined me down to New Orleans, where long before longhairs there was Longhair: the eminent Professor whose legacy he inherited, then reinvented in his own image. Like Papa Legba, vodou guardian of the crossroads, Dr. John (born Mac Rebennack) linked the rich ancestral traditions of New Orleans music with the immediacy of present time, animating the past with the future.

Later, in the late '80s, when he was living in New York's West Village not far from Crossroads, where hoodoo bluesman John Campbell regularly held court, I got to look behind the veil of his stage persona. B.B. St. Roman, who curated every Dr. John performance by making sure the right incense was lit and the proper talismans laid on the altar, became John Campbell's personal manager as well, enabling me to spend some quality time with Mac offstage.

"In New Orleans, all of them Caribbean cultures kind of overlapped—Cuban cats, Jamaican cats, Brazilian cats, plus the African/American Indian mix," he explained to me one night. "The piano players got caught up in the groove of these different rhythms, which go way back. Professor Longhair, and his old style of doing things, was really about percussion. I want you boys to frolic; he used to tell us if we was lagging on a gig."

Dr. John was a major guiding light but only part of the constellation of Louisiana musicians that lit up my New York nights. I spent countless hours on the dancefloor kicking up my heels to Loup Garou, New York's premiere zydeco band. Fronted by Jimmy Macdonnell, who hit the town toting an accordion from his hometown of Lafayette, Louisiana, he dubbed his band of irregulars Loup Garou after the Creole werewolves who howl it up on the Bayou Goula. And he looked a lot like the snap beans that gave zydeco music its name: long, lean and a little bit twisted.

Many lifelong friendships were forged on the dancefloor of sweat-stained Loup Garou marathons at the Rodeo Bar and Tramps, which quickly became Louisiana Central, showcasing everyone from country trail rides zydeco master Boozoo Chavis to Zachary Richard, the "Mick Jagger of the accordion." Our krewe of New York-based Louisiana music devotees soon began making annual pilgrimages to the New Orleans Jazz & Heritage Festival and Festivals Acadiens et Créoles in Lafayette.

The linchpin of our New York City krewe was Sue Thomas, who introduced me to one of the most influential women in my life: Tina Girouard. Born and raised in Cecilia, LA, Tina immigrated to lower Manhattan in the early '70s, where she became a pivotal member of an emerging avant garde scene that included fellow Louisiana artists Robert Rauschenberg and her partner, saxophonist Dickie Landry, a seminal member of the Philip Glass ensemble.

By the time I met Tina in the late '80s, she'd circled back to Louisiana after making a pilgrimage to Haiti, where she got so immersed in the vodou religion that she was formally initiated as a mambo (the name for a high priestess). She also became enamored with the visually stunning sequined flags used in vodou ceremonies, and helped local Haitian artists launch a thriving cottage industry for making and exporting them to the US. She was aided and abetted in this endeavor by Sue Thomas, an American Airlines flight attendant, who managed to slip batches of the flags into cargo when she flew from Port Au Prince to New York City, and brought them down to Louisiana for Tina to sell at Jazz Fest and Festivals Acadiens.

Tina inspired me to take a deep dive into vodou, but I had already begun flirting with it before I even met her. I read Maya Deren's classic *Divine Horsemen* about vodou rites and rituals based on her own Haitian experiences, and devoured several bios of Marie Laveau, the near-mythic Creole free woman of color, herbalist and hairdresser to the wealthy in the French Quarter who offered consultations and presided over a multiracial religious community's ceremonies. So deeply embedded was all the vodou imagery in my unconscious, that I actually had a dream about Sigmund Freud meeting Marie Laveau and wrote a poem about it.

Simultaneously, Louisiana music was casting its spell all over New York City. I caught one of the last performances of ascended zydeco master Clifton Chenier at the Lone Star Cafe, and was introduced to the rollicking, raucous second line sounds of New Orleans brass bands by the legendary Dirty Dozen at the Bottom Line.

Eventually, inevitably, I left New York and moved to the mother lode: New Orleans, where I've now lived for nearly a quarter century. During that time, I've stained countless dancefloors with my sweat, attended every single Jazz Fest, many Festivals Acadiens in Lafayette, and written dozens of articles about how and why the music moves me for the local music magazine OffBeat as well as national outlets like *DownBeat*. But no single piece better summarizes why I came and why I stayed, sometimes against all odds, than "Dancing On Sacred Ground," my High Times report on the first Jazz Fest held in the wake of Hurricane Katrina.

There was a lot riding on the 37th annual New Orleans Jazz and Heritage Festival. Tens of thousands of music lovers converged on sacred ground—the freshly repaired Fair Grounds—to turn the spirit of the city around on the opening weekend of the first Jazz Fest since the post-Katrina federal levee breach devastated my adopted hometown.

The collective healing was a stunning success.

At stage after stage, during three days blessed by the weather gods—rain held off till the gates closed Saturday and let up just in time for a glorious Sunday—artists used the power of music to confront the tragedy and transform it, and colorfully costumed fest-goers exploded with the raucous joy of a jazz funeral second line.

Over in the Gospel Tent, Shades of Praise–three tiers of glowing black, white and brown faces raised in joyful song–provided a blueprint of hope for the future of New Orleans. "Who here lost everything?" the choir leader asked. Several dozen hands shot up. "All right then, turn it around," he shouted and slowly started to spin, gradually speeding up as people throughout the tent rose to perform their own circular exorcisms.

"Turn it around! Turn it around! Turn it around!"

And damn if we didn't banish that evil hurricane eye and put the floodwaters in reverse, bringing the assembled masses to higher ground.

Hurricane season starts June 1st and Jazz Fest can't turn that around if the levees don't hold– or if the leaders we elect on May 20th don't have the vision to restore the city's living culture of marching bands, church choirs, second-line clubs and Mardi Gras Indians. But for a few more fest-filled days—the musical marathon continues this weekend, with 9th Ward survivor Fats Domino closing the show—dancing on sacred ground is just what the Doctor ordered to heal the breaches in our homes and in our hearts.

## Loup Garou: The Godfathers of New York Zydeco

*Downtown Express*, December 1991

BACK IN THE EARLY '80s, when the pans of Manhattan's kitchens had not yet been blackened by the great Cajun cooking attack and the only Buckwheat known to New Yorkers was in 'Our Gang' re-runs, a young Amherst graduate sauntered into Terry Dunne's legendary blues joint, Tramps. His name was Jimmy Macdonell and he was toting an accordion from his hometown of Lafayette, Louisiana. He had a band of irregulars called Loup Garou, the Creole word for folkloric werewolves who howl it up on the Bayou Goula, and he looked a lot like the snap-beans that gave 'zydeco' music its name: long, lean and a little bit twisted.

"I said God, man, I don't know what to do with you but you sure look hungry," recalls Dunne, whose bookings at the newly-expanded Tramps are now dominated by Louisiana bands. "And Jimmy said yeah, man, and I can cook too. I make real good gumbo. All right, I said, let's see—if you can make good gumbo, you got a gig. So, Jimmy threw all kinds of fish heads and junk into a pot and made this amazing gumbo, which we gave out free to everyone in the club. It was a huge success, they became our regular Monday night band, and that was the start of the whole thing. Loup Garou really planted the zydeco seed in New York."

In the back-bayou country of southwest Louisiana, where zydeco music is a family affair, the stomach and the heart are inextricably entwined with the rhythm of dancing feet. So it's fitting that Loup Garou bubbled out of a communal pot of gumbo to become the bayou rulers of New York City, sparking a subcultural explosion: at their Delta 88 basecamp and other area clubs, where they heat up a room of cool urbanites faster than a shot of Tabasco in a Cajun martini; at swanky soirees where black ties are quickly loosened and Scaasi gowns unabashedly stained with sweat; and as de facto house band at Tramps, where they opened the floodgates for the current wave of zydeco imports, from young innovator Terrance Simien to old master Boozoo Chavis.

Beginning with Buckwheat Zydeco and swamp rocker Zachary Richard, many of these Louisiana-based bands have scored record deals in a suddenly-trendy market, where the infectious cross-rhythms of zydeco now pitch everything from Toyotas to toothpaste in TV commercials. But it's yet-unsigned Loup Garou who's kept the home fires burning steadily in New York, simmering up city grit and R&B groove into their own unique brand of zydeco homebrew.

Among their earliest devotees was David Byrne, who most recently tapped Macdonell's accordion for "Don't Fence Me In" on the new *Red, Hot & Blue* Cole Porter compilation. Bryan Ferry saw but one gig before booking the band to open his last American tour. Robert Palmer, the Dead's Bob Weir, and Tom-Tom Clubbers Tina Weymouth and Chris Frantz have all leapt onto the Loup Garou bandstand. And Paul Simon—who invited the band to open his recent Montauk benefit concert and used Macdonell on "Rhythm of the Saints"—has practically become a fixture at Loup Garou shows, where everybody's on the A-List.

No one gawks when Simon straps on the rubboard or spins a two-step across the floor with Melinda Roy, a principal dancer with the New York City Ballet. "Loup Garou changes the energy of an entire room once they start playing," observes Roy, a native Louisianian who made her accordion debut with the band at a Lincoln Center benefit last spring that still has ballet patrons buzzing. "They just crank people out of their seats, and the joy of their music lights up your soul." Social boundaries in caste-conscious Manhattan dissolve on the dance floor, where, onstage, the magic is in the mix.

Tonight, as the moon waxes full over Tramps, drummer George Recile kicks off a swampy bayou jam that gels into "Hey Pocky Way" with the back-beat funk of Jim Gegory's bass. Dreadlocks flying above fishnet stockings, Ronin dons her copper-titted rubboard for "Oh By By," as Loup Garou spins through Slim's Y Ki Ki. Guitarist Mark Dufault cranks up the band's Jimi-meets-Buckwheat bridge into a couple R&B tunes belted out by Ronin, which bleed into some rockin' two-steps recalling the Jay's Lounge era of Clifton Chenier. Nudged across the Texas border by keyboardist Neil Thomas, Macdonell delivers a honky-tonk "Bon Ton Roulez," then straps on his diatonic accordion to re-route us into the way-back-bayou country of Boozoo Chavis. "Shotgun" blasts off a barrage of Loup Garou originals, which interweave voodoo reggae with some achingly sweet ballads and Recile's power-rock vocals on "Somebody".

"Thank you for supporting zydeco music," Macdonell says after the band pushes a "Big Chief" encore over the top. But the crowd keeps shouting for more. Only long after the lights come up does the ad hoc community created on the dancefloor disperse, reluctantly, into the New York night.

"There's two kinds of people in the world: the kind that mix and the kind that don't," observes Loup Garou mix master Jimmy Macdonell.

We're hanging in his Soho loft, which serves as the band's rehearsal hall; as the "zydeco embassy" crash pad for an extended family of Louisiana bands passing through town; and as an orbiting space station for ever-converging constellations of New York musicians. Fourth of July starbursts dance on the computer screen next to an old upright piano; a huge stuffed Marlin dangles dead roses, toe shoes and a faux leopard cap above an assortment of accordions and amps; a man-sized cross festooned for Mardi Gras leans next to a kitschy '50s padded bar, dragged up from a New York dumpster and now plastered with downhome zydeco posters.

Seated across a table cluttered with hot sauce bottles and poetry books is the other key coordinate in the Loup Garou mix: drummer George Recile, who co-writes the band's original tunes. A seasoned player featured on James Brown's last album, Recile recently produced one of Prince's Paisley Park proteges, and hails from New Orleans. We're discussing the partners' separate-but-equal Louisiana roots, often lumped together. The R&B born in New Orleans jazz clubs has a very different feel from the lilting country rhythms of zydeco, whose first percussion instrument was the cross-rhythmic crackle of snap-beans that accompanied Creole slave songs.

"When you mix those different feels, you get Loup Garou," concludes Recile. Then he adds, quite forcefully but with a sideways grin at Macdonell: "This is not a zydeco band. I gotta stress this. It is not a zydeco band."

"I say we are a zydeco band," Macdonell counters, rising to the bait of a longstanding argument. "Let me stress that. We are a zydeco band."

Amidst the ensuing laughter, I flash on the perfect tagline for this debate, borrowed from an ancient "Certs is a candy mint/Certs is a breath mint" TV spot: "Stop! You're both right!"

Recile's right, because Loup Garou's expanding body of original songs creates a new kind of gumbo: a sun splash of reggae, a couple fish heads of funk, a sprinkling of pop, and a stiff shot of R&B are all added to a zydeco stock already steeped in West African rhythms. (It's not surprising cross-cultural cooks David Byrne and Paul Simon were magnetized by this music.)

Macdonell's right, too—and not only because the band's "pure" zydeco numbers are so totally trad in their tributes to Boozoo Chavis. It's also because, as he puts it, "zydeco is as much a sensibility as a style. It's always reached out to popular music. I saw Clifton Chenier play hundreds of times at home, and he was playing the Hit Parade tunes the way he knew how to play them. That's why zydeco can rock and roll."

During Macdonell's Lafayette High years in the '70s, he wasn't just hanging at the Clifton-cum-cockfight gigs of Jay's Lounge; he was blasting David Bowie on his stereo and getting razzed for the New York Dolls T-shirt he sported at basketball practice. (A decade later, he and David Johansen wound up as Tramps softball teammates.) Other Macdonell through-lines converge in the bi-lyrical caresses of "Mon Traitress Marie," which pivots on a startlingly simple image: "If I could just get to my feet, I'd go down on my knees." Here the young boy tutored in French by the Creole women who helped raise him—"I didn't learn from my parents, 'cause when my Daddy spoke French in school, they'd whip him"—meets the Amherst English major.

It's on the common ground of sensibility, of spirit, that the Louisiana core of Loup Garou merges with its other players: bassist Jim Gregory, a respected New York studio vet who, rather appropriately, first crossed Macdonell's path during a Caribbean recording date; guitarist Mark Dufault, a New Englander weaned on the folk music of French-speaking Canucks, whose exiled Acadian ancestors carried it to Louisiana; urban cowboy piano man Neil Thomas, a fellow accordionist whose black hat counterpoints Macdonell's battered grey Stetson; and vocalist/percussionist Ronin, who brings the heart and soul of a Brooklyn cowgirl into what Macdonell calls the band's "spiritual point."

"We're a one-band family," Ronin says, invoking the refrain of their gentle, joyous "Bwana's Garden": "all my children doin' the best they can." Many possible paths converge at Bwana's crossroads—the forest, the shore, the garden itself—but "the road out over the border" is the chosen lot of Loup Garou.

"You've got to commit yourself to something, and we've committed ourselves to this town, to breaking it here," says Recile. I hear "Bayou Ruler"—with its jaunty, two-step segue into pop/gospel harmonies via a totally twisted accordion break - as Loup Garou's spin on "New York, New York": "we're the true believers and we want you to know…the secret on my lips is true, I got my mind made up on you." Then my mind plays call-and-response, and echoing through thickly-ghosted Louisiana fog, I hear another Loup Garou chorus: "I wish it was as simple as that."

Being a New York-based zydeco band has been a double-edged sword. As Macdonell quite accurately puts it, "We're very, very well-known, and we're still very deep underground. There's still people in the industry who don't want to hear a New York zydeco band, simply because they think we're from New York. Which is also why we're never asked to play at the New Orleans Jazz Fest. Because we're considered a New York band." He laughs, and so do Recile and I, over the poetic injustice of it all, then adds, "but Clifton always said there's a reason for everything."

"And there's no way any Louisiana musician—and we're all blessed to be from there, to be inundated with the thickness of that tradition—there's no way we couldn't share that," interjects Recile. "When we walk away from a gig I'm smiling ear to ear. For me, this band is as much fun as you can have in this country without getting arrested."

Jimmy Macdonell lights a cigarette, and watches the drift of smoke form momentary islands that shift and dissolve their boundaries. "A lot of what Loup Garou does is take you out of your region," he muses. "We come from the bayou and play in Manhattan, and it's hopefully an everyman's kind of thing. A lot of people think we have some kind of regional sound, and we do. But the region is the planet."

Then he looks straight at me and adds, "the band is really entering a new creative phase, we're stretching out and tightening up. It's a good time to see the band."

# Francis X. Pavy: Zydeco Picasso

*OffBeat*, January 1992

Swamp pop painter Francis X. Pavy makes art you can dance to. Born on the bayous of southwest Louisiana, his one-man-band of amplified visuals reach out and grab you like the seeing-eye hands of his "Medium Voodoo." In "Drinking Muddy Water"—the seminal piece in a recent series that alludes to the late, great bluesman—colors crackle out of a gumbo of Mississippi mud and spawn a river flow of images: vortexes spin a zydeco two-step across a hoodoo honky-tonk where guitars sprout eyes and you can kiss the lips of a high-heeled shoe.

Like "Live Oak," a metal construction inspired by a monumental tree in his hometown of Lafayette, Pavy's work is rooted in the folkloric soil of Cajun country, with its Creole blend of French, Spanish and Afro-Haitian influences. But the vision that compelled Paul Simon and a host of other celeb collectors—and inspired *Rolling Stone* to dub him the "Picasso of Zydeco"—is uniquely his own.

Mixing metaphors like a mad metaphysician, Pavy combines the four natural elements (earth, air, fire and water) with such local iconography as rubboards, catfish, whiskey bottles, alligators, fighting cocks and backroad telephone poles. The alchemy of this dance, in which the artist becomes the fifth element of motion, creates a magical world of blazing roses and flaming moons, populated by guitar-heads, coffee divas and anthropomorphic accordions.

"It's interesting how you can put the two things together and get something new," muses Pavy outside his Lafayette studio, while his cat plays hide-and-seek under a canvas he's preparing like the Old Masters did it; once the protective coat of rabbit's skin glue dries in the sun, he'll gesso it with white lead paint. "Or sometimes you paint something you think is new and then realize it's an old thing, looked at in a different way."

Slender, supple and as cool as his work is hot, Pavy's muted attire of worn denim and pinstriped T-shirt counterpoints the electric palette of his work. The daemonic muse only surfaces in the studio's blacklight room, where his left eye glows with alien incandescence – a phenomenon I'm not sure is simply the result of a new contact lens. It looks, in fact, exactly like the irradiated ninth eye of the farmer in his "Cultivating Heads," which reflects the polyphrenic cross-pollination of Pavy's own artistic harvest.

"I never lost my ambition to be in a band," admits Pavy, thirty-seven, who only began fulfilling his painterly dreams six years ago and still sits in at dance halls with his guitar and accordion. A master glass-beveller who segued into ceramics, Pavy switched to the more durable medium of canvas and metal after cows trampled a stoneware Telecaster and two life-sized members of a ceramic Cajun band were mysteriously kidnapped. "They're probably plowed over in a potato patch somewhere," he conjectures.

If not, the art thieves could now claim a substantial ransom, for this once-obscure artist has become both highly visible and highly collectible well beyond the boundaries of Louisiana.

Beginning with the New York/Louisiana-based musician and composer Richard Landry, Pavy's work has magnetized a widening circle of notable collectors: Paul Simon, Lorne Michaels, Ron Howard, Edie Brickell, Glenn Frey, Richard Thompson and swamp-rock king Zachary Richard, who commissioned a series of album covers a few years back. The Zachary gig, along with covers for Beausoleil's Michael Doucet and two Rounder anthologies, helped Pavy-ize the marketplace. "People don't necessarily look on the back of album covers to see who I am," he notes, "but when they see the paintings, it's like, oh yeah, that's the guy."

Like the accordion player who wings past the moon in the belly of a gigantic bird in "J'ai Pris Les Chemins"—his poster image for last year's Rencontres Transmusicales, a major music festival in Rennes, France, where he mounted a concurrent one-man show—Pavy's become a frequent flyer.

He's been invited back to France for a one-month residency in ArIes, and will make his New York debut this March at the new SoHo gallery of Arthur Roger, who also shows Pavy's work in New Orleans. And with his stock depleted by his recent success at Houston's McMurtrey Gallery, he'd be hard-pressed to meet demand if he weren't so prolific.

"It's almost like filling in the colors," says Pavy of his ability to work on upwards of a dozen pieces at once. "Except I make up my own numbers. It's like this demands to be painted red so I paint it red." He pauses, then adds, almost wistfully, "The early stuff was very, very simple. What I do now is very complex."

Even the simpler images in Pavy's recent work—like "Stranger in the Full Moon," with its luminous black-brimmed specter—suggest a descent into deeper realms, where zydeco gris-gris crosses into serious mojo country. "(Medium) Voodoo" stares directly out of the darkness through a black-handed veil, and its very title alludes not only to gradations of size and intensity, but to the function of the medium as a channel from the other side.

"I was never really exposed to that as a child, but I knew it was around," says Pavy. "And in the voodoo ceremony, playing the drums in a certain rhythm is meant to call down a certain god to go into one of the dancers. It's a way of achieving a different state of consciousness."

There's a ferocity in this particular painting that calls down the warrior-God Ogun, but much of his other work celebrates the goddess: "Palmetto Venus" rises radiantly out of the bayous on a seashell throne, casting her light on a lone blue man.

Pavy's female-headed serpents imply a yin/yang melding of polarities, while "Small Washed Away" mourns those same elements torn asunder. The two silhouettes in this painting, encoded with stars and hieroglyphics, are cocooned in spirals of energy, which, if merged, would form a double helix: the male is upright, the female is inverted. "It's about being separated," he observes, quietly. "Losing. Washed away."

Then he steers me to "Drinking Muddy Water," one of those crucibles on which an artist is forged.

"It was hell. I was going on a trip and I had to complete it, and I worked like all day and all day and all day in this little tiny room. It was really cold and I had to clear everything out of the kitchen and even that was cold. It got down to nine degrees and the pipes busted. I could only get about this far back from it…"

He suddenly turns and asks, "Do any of these paintings do a physical thing to you?" Yes, Francis, they do. They all do. "Yeah, well I kind of painted it, and there was no guarantee it was gonna turn out okay. But it did turn out very nice."

His whole career is turning out very nice, thank you, and it evolved almost organically, with none of the hype-and-hustle of today's commodities art market. "The business just kind of takes care of itself," says Pavy, who has no agent and seems at ease with handling his own affairs. "I don't think there's anybody who owns a painting of mine I don't like."

His relationship with Arthur Roger is typically symbiotic; when his longtime New Orleans gallery, Simms, closed its doors, Roger fortuitously appeared, and was able to give Pavy simultaneous entree to the tough New York market he'd always wanted to crack but never actively pursued.

"I'm curious as to how New York will receive his work," says Roger, who was attracted to Pavy's ability to "capture a sense of place" while transcending place with a universal language. "All his pieces have a celebratory richness, a narrative feeling that falls within the story-telling traditions of American folk art. My instincts tell me this will be a very powerful show, which will help define the character and image of the gallery."

The potency of Pavy's work also helps define a newfound sense of community among all artistic outcasts who felt estranged from the me-first ethos of the '80s.

"I feel," says Pavy, growing reflective, "that my life is an image that was already put together. Now I'm starting to put it back together again, like a jigsaw puzzle." He pauses, then smiles. "It's like the '90s are the '60s upside-down, only our generation is coming into it with more maturity. I guess it's our time."

## Dr. John Ain't for Turistas

*Downtown Express*, November 1990

DR. JOHN HAS BEEN my medicine man since the '60s, when he hoodooed me with *Gris Gris*. "The Night Tripper" mainlined me down to New Orleans, where long before longhairs there was Longhair: the eminent Professor whose legacy he inherited, then reinvented in his own image.

There's something almost superhuman about Dr. John's left hand, the way it wraps a polyrhythmic bass line around itself, turning the piano into a one-man band punctuated by his swamp-growl vocals. But he's more than a consummate piano-man; and more than the sum of his considerable parts (songwriter, arranger, producer and collaborator with a virtual who's who of jazz greats.) Like Papa Legba, vodou guardian of the crossroads, he links the rich ancestral traditions of New Orleans music with the immediacy of present time, animating the past with the future.

Dr. John, born Mac Rebennack, turns forty-nine on November 20th, when he'll perform at The Lonestar Roadhouse. There's a lot to celebrate: his 1989 Grammy for *In a Sentimental Mood*; his *Bluesiana Triangle* with Fathead Newman and Art Blakey, released just months before Biakey's death; the revitalized dynamics of his new big-hand sound. But when I dropped in for a chat at his West Village pad, such recent milestones were far from his mind. He was busy demo-ing drum tracks for his next Warners album, which is still revealing itself.

**CM**: What is there about New Orleans piano that makes it so unique, that immediately announces itself?

**DJ**: In New Orleans, all of them Caribbean cultures kind of overlapped—Cuban cats, Jamaican cats, Brazilian cats, plus the African/American Indian mix. The piano players got caught up in the groove of these different rhythms, which go way back.

Professor Longhair, and his old style of doing things, was really about percussion. Fess didn't speak about music like no other people did; he painted these great pictures. When I first met him, I said what you call what you're doing with your hands, and he said "Overs and unders." He had his own words for all this shit: "double-crossovers," and "the spew." I want you boys to frolic, he used to tell us, if we was lagging on a gig.

Right before he croaked, he said I wanna record an album with six banjos, two tubas, and some singers and dancers. I said what you gonna use dancers for, on an album? He said, you 're gonna hear their feet move. And he was like real serious. Fess was an original.

**CM**: How did Dr. John evolve out of Mac Rebennack?

**DJ**: It was accidental. Originally, Ronnie Barron, who was the singer in my band, was gonna be Dr. John. But he'd just hooked up with this manager who said Mac, I think that's a bad career move for Ronnie, he should be moving more in the direction of Curtis Mayfield. And I never sang or anything, but when I got the chance to do it, I said fuck, I'm just gonna do it.

We got a break cause Sonny and Cher let us use some studio time. And Atlantic Records—[Atlantic President] Ahmet Ertegun, no matter what he says, didn't want this record—was pissed off about it. But we got in the door, and it happened to come out at the time when all the psychedelical shit was happenin'. Instead of thinking we was a New Orleans voodoo show, people saw all this snake-dancing shit and thought we was psychedelic. That's why we got most of the gigs we got, at be-ins and love-ins and in-ins and out-ins.

**CM**: What about the period when your Night Tripper persona kind of went undercover and you did *Dr. John Plays Mac Rebennack* (1981)?

**DJ**: At the time, I wasn't too up for a solo piano record. I thought, "If this lames out, I'm gonna be stuck in Holiday Inns the rest of my life." I just walked in and winged it, and it did some good for me, it got me some fun gigs when I was working solo a lot. But I'm happy I didn't get caught up in just having to do that kind of thing.

**CM**: And you never got stuck in a Holiday Inn.

**DJ**: Close enough! I have real horrible fears of gigging in some hotel and someone asking me to play "Toot Toot Tootsie" or some shit, and winding up in the penitentiary. I've been through all that, I worked in any kind of joint you can think of. And I ain't a guy who likes to play for turistas.

**CM**: "Right Place, Wrong Time" is one of my favorite Dr. John songs. But now, with the Grammy and having a big band again, does it finally feel like the right place, right time?

**DJ**: I'm always trying to find some other place, some other time. Anytime you get settled in and think this is very safe, I'm covered, all of a sudden somebody pulls the rug out from under you. Then where the hell you at? I'd rather try to look for some other things. 'Cause life is about other things. Things that don't fit into a conversation you can talk about normally. Whatever I do now comes from puttin' different chunks together, just the way I used to put people and songs together, back in New Orleans, where I started bringing songs up to Specialty Records when I was about thirteen. I play piano all right, but I don't sing for shit. But I know how to sell somebody a song. And that's all that it is.

## Jam Today: Boozoo Chavis

*Downtown*, December 1990

It took Terry Dunne two years of wheedling and cajoling, plus some plain old horse-trader's dealmaking, to coax Boozoo Chavis onto the plane that flew him up to Tramps for his New York debut last summer. For though the Louisiana zydeco king routinely levitates entire dancehalls with the bellows of his deceptively-petite diatonic accordion, this was the first time in his sixty years that Boozoo himself was commercially airborne; and one of the few times he'd ventured further beyond his own back bayou turf than nearby New Orleans.

"You don't be wanting to go, but then when you have to, you glad you come," he remarked at the end of that original New York visit, which can only be called triumphal: four straight night of packed houses at Tramps; two glowing reports in the *New York Times*; and courtship by several major labels that resulted in his signing with Elektra/Nonesuch. (See 'Boozoo: The Album' for a review of his deliciously downhome debut disc.) "Hell," he added, "you just get with it and let the good times roll."

Boozoo Chavis will do just that when he returns to Tramps on August 8th and 9th with rollicking, rowdy zydeco that raises temperatures and lowers inhibitions. "Take 'em Off! Throw 'em in the Corner!"—a back home dancehall hit that's emblazoned across the butt of Boozoo briefs you can buy from his wife, Leona—pretty much sums up the spirit of his shows. As he puts it, "once I get going, I'm hard to stop."

A compact hand -grenade of a man known in Louisiana as the "Lake Charles Atomic Bomb," Boozoo's got the stamina of the racetrack horses he both jockeyed and trained during a three-decade hiatus from the recording business. "I know just as much about horses as I d o about music, and they're both the same career: dog eat dog," he notes—and with good reason.

In 1954, the same year his peer Clifton Chenier scored on the airwaves with "Ma 'Tite Fille," Boozoo had his own zydeco hit: the now-classic "Paper in My Shoe." But his contract turned out to be worth no more than the paper that stuffed the worn-out shoes in his song. "I got mad and quit," says Boozoo, never one for halfway measures. He steamed about this classic music-biz burn until the mid-'80s, when he re-emerged on the Maison de Soul label and began playing his current schedule of three-hundred plus shows a year. In the interim, his kids grew up to become Boozoo's built-in band. That's Charles on rubboard; Anthony on drums; and the heavy in shades who looks like a Stallone bodyguard is the family accordion protege, Pancho.

But though his offspring tower above him, there's no mistaking who's the big chief onstage. Sheathed in a plastic apron that protects his accordion from sweat worked up during three-hour sets, Boozoo pumps that little squeeze-box with the down-thrusting, log-sawing strokes unique to him. What comes out of that box has rarely been heard beyond the bayous since the seminal days of Clifton Chenier.

Unlike Rockin' Dopsie and Buckwheat Zydeco—who both invested themselves with crowns upon the death of King Clifton—Boozoo wears a cowboy hat, harking back to the old trail ride Zydeco he continues to play.

Starting with Chenier himself, most contemporary zydeco bands began to incorporate urban R&B, and their own translations of rock and roll, into zydeco's uniquely Creole patois of Cajun, country blues, and Caribbean trade winds. But Boozoo's long hiatus from the marketplace kept him directly tap-rooted into zydeco's earliest origins—not as an archivist but as a totally present-time practitioner. Boozoo sings the blues with a heartbeat grit infused with back bayou seepage from the Mississippi Delta; and his two-steps spin out of old Acadian melodies, whose Celtic roots are as clearly discernible as the West African cross-rhythms that drive them.

Boozoo's subject matter is always downhome (stubborn billy goats; the barking denizens of the local 'Dog Hill'); and sometimes down-and-dirty (his X-rated singles are hotter than July on the crawfish circuit.) But his playing has a complexity belied by the simple joy it inspires: tricky turnarounds that cut across the rhythm with mirror-image riffs; out-of-the-blue notes that startle you with laughter. "You got to flip it like a pancake," is how Boozoo describes his accordion style. "Like you was turnin' over dirt with a spade. You gotta start it, and then you gotta turn it. And you gotta make it rhyme."

Which is exactly what Boozoo's done in his life: made it rhyme, with the dramatic turn-around of his re-born career. If the chips had fallen favorably back in '54, would he be any different today?

"I'd have been in better shape than I was if I'd got me the recognition. Now I got a little wiser," he says, then laughs. "But I be the same guy."

## *BOOZOO: THE ALBUM*

I HAPPENED TO BE RIDING Amtrak when I popped the advance tape of Boozoo's Elektra/Nonesuch debut album into my Walkman. By the time the tape had run its course, I'd let out such a series of whoops, hollers and whistles that my fellow passengers were regarding me with the kind of carefully-averted eyes normal folks reserve for the certifiably insane. Of course, they didn't understand where I actually was: down Lake Charles way, sitting right there in Boozoo's kitchen, the smell of Leona's coffee as palpably fresh as the exuberant pancake-flipping turnarounds of Boozoo's accordion.

Producer Terry Adams of NRBQ—who first shone the spotlight on Boozoo with "Boozoo, That's Who" on NRBQ's 1989 winner, *Wild Weekend*—deserves several gold stars for capturing not only the raw heart and soul of Boozoo's music, but the entire milieu from which it springs. After "Boozoo's Theme" sets the "yeah, you right" tone of the album, a blues-y guitar slides us directly into the bosom of the Chavis family.

"Hey, Leona, put the coffee water on," Boozoo hollers at the beginning of the uproarious "I'm Ready Me," in which he and Leona ("I already done that!") do their zydeco-Bickersons thing while preparing to head out on a trail ride; one by one, their various offspring wander in, each accusing the others of heel-dragging. When the cooler's finally loaded, we're off to the rousingly raucous "Dog Hill." Just about sundown we hit one of the local dancehalls (more likely than not attached to a church) where Boozoo packs 'em in with swampy, snaky, zydeco blues like "Keep Your Dress Tail Down" and such lilting two-steps as "Goin' to La Maison." Along the way, we get the rare treat of hearing Boozoo go head -to-head with "Johnny Billy Goat"—just him, his tapping toes, and his accordion, doubling back and zig-zagging around itself.

It's all essential Boozoo: the voice and accordion call-and-response of "Oh Yae Yae," a zydeco next-of-kin to gospel; the dancehall shuffle of 'Tee Black'; the whistle-baited horse trot through the trail ride of "Zydeco Hee Haw." And it's studded with quintessential Boozoo.

Before the band launches into its rip-roaring re-take of "41 Days"—which dates back to his "Paper in My Shoe" era—Boozoo instructs them thusly: "If it's wrong, do it wrong with me; if I'm wrong, you wrong too. You follow me." An offspring suggests that they "do it like we just done it," but Boozoo ain't having any. "I don't know if we gonna do it like we just done, but it's gonna be done. I can't promise you it's gonna be like it was. But I promise you it's gonna be better."

And mo' better Boozoo's exactly what this album is about. It's a glorious testament to the presence of present time, in which "now" is by its very definition the best that there is. As the zydeco Zen-master sings it, loud and clear, in "Don't Worry About Boozoo":

*Don't worry about Boozoo*
*Cause you know he ain't no fool...*
*Don't worry about Boozoo*
*Cause the music's gonna make you move*

## Bas Clas

*OffBeat*, June 2012

THE BEATLES IN HAMBURG in '61. The Stooges' 1967 Halloween debut at their State Street house in Ann Arbor. The Velvet Underground's living room gigs in Austin, documented on *Live '69*. Certain rock milestones bestow a lifetime of bragging rights on those lucky enough to be there.

For rock fans in Cajun country who danced to the different drummer of Bas Clas—the Cajun term for "low class"—that milestone came in 1978, when the band's first gig at Lafayette's Grant Street Dancehall got them banned from the club.

"All our friends from Mamou and Eunice and Opelousas and the surrounding countryside were so excited we had a gig in a big place," recalls lead guitarist Steve Picou, who co-founded Bas Clas with brothers Donnie and Mike in 1976. "They all showed up wearing porkpie hats and danced on the pool tables and had a ball."

The management was not amused. "He didn't like the look of our crowd or the sound of our band," which channeled Elvis Costello and Talking Heads at a time when most Lafayette artists were rediscovering their two-step roots. "He said, listen, I'm going to pay y'all not to come back. And he gave us $400.00 not to play the next gig."

Bas Clas quickly regrouped at the college dive Mother's Mantle, where overflow crowds proudly flaunted their status in freshly-printed T-shirts: "Banned from Grant Street. We had too much fun."

Thus began a seven-year stint of Monday Night Madness gigs, which migrated from club to club on Lafayette's college strip until the band's self-released single "Serfin' USA" / "Physical World" garnered rave underground music press and national college radio play. Then the oil bust hit and Bas Clas lit out for Atlanta, seeking fame and fortune.

The band came excruciatingly close twice. Initially championed by industry icon John Hammond, whose enthusiasm fell on deaf ears, Bas Clas appeared bound for glory when powerhouse manager/promoter John Scher took up their cause and scored a major EMI publishing contract.

When a corporate takeover sabotaged that deal at the eleventh hour, the band threw in the towel. Donnie stayed in Atlanta and Steve moved to

New Orleans, where he put his guitar on ice for nine years and took a behind-the-scenes job with the Louisiana Music Commission.

During that long hiatus, most people in New Orleans had no idea that a guitar hero lurked inside the mild-mannered state employee who worked with his colorful LMC boss, Bernie Cyrus.

It's no secret anymore. Bas Clas is back with a vengeance. Armed with a new CD, *Big Oak Tree* of freshly recorded songs from Dockside Studios, the band rocked a two-thousand-plus crowd at its first-ever appearance at Festival International in Lafayette this year.

When the Picou brothers took the Scene Malibu stage with bandmates Geoff Thistlewaite (bass) and Ted Cobena (drums), and a bevy of special guests—saxophonist Dickie Landry, accordionist Roddie Romero, Eric Adcock on B3—the prodigal sons were greeted like conquering heroes by Bas Clas survivors and fervently embraced by new converts.

Like their recent live shows, the CD is no nostalgia trip. It captures a band at the height of its power from the opening track, which throws down the gauntlet with "Allons Danser." Driven by Steve's Cajun-inflected guitar riff, which sounds uncannily like a fiddle, the song is spiked with trail-ride "yippee yippee ti yays" and commands you to dance. But "Laissez les Bons Temps Rouler" it's not.

Loosely based on Edgar Allan Poe's "The Masque of the Red Death", the song mocks "them safe behind their castle walls / laughing at the world," along with the clueless dancers who "close their eyes as the band plays more." Penned by resident wordsmith Donnie Picou at the height of the AIDS crisis, it's as relevant today as the gulf between the masses and the gated one percent.

"We want people to have a good time, but we also have something to say," Steve says. "I feel like if you're going to be that loud with all that power and wattage behind you, you really should say something important."

Even the band's gentler songs get under the skin. In "My Louisiane," Bas Clas comes full circle to its Louisiana roots. But though it invokes childhood memories under the "big oak tree," it also mourns the passing of "Maw-Maw," a natural occurrence. It's an elegy for a way of life felled by development, like the dead live oak on the back of the CD cover.

"Back to Work," the final track, is easy to take at face value: A farmer surveys his fallow field after a bad season, and vows to "get back to work!" Bas Clas is doing that now, and hits the studio again in August. "But it's not just about us," says Picou. "It's about getting back to The Garden." Indeed, the song invites listeners to "join us in the fields and dig your hands into the dirt."

I'm in.

# Dr. John Mined Spiritual Connections

*DownBeat*, December 2019

*DownBeat* devised the term "Beyond" to apply to music that defies easy categorization—and no one is a better example of that than Dr. John.

"Yeah, Mac was 'beyond' even when he was still with us," observed guitarist and Grammy award-winning producer Shane Theriot, who produced Dr. John's final gift to the world: the last album he recorded and signed off on before his June 6th death at seventy-seven.

That as-yet unreleased album, which at press time wasn't attached to a label, caps a genre-busting career. Steeped in the funky second-line rhythms of his hometown of New Orleans—where he joined a pantheon of piano greats from Professor Longhair to Fats Domino—Dr. John ranged far beyond his roots, without ever losing that deep connection, collecting six Grammys along the way and earning his rightful place in the Rock & Roll Hall of Fame.

Born Malcolm John Rebennack Jr., he was still a kid when he started channeling Pinetop Perkins on the keys and Lightnin' Hopkins on guitar. As a teen in the mid-'50s, he dove headfirst into the steamy cauldron of R&B boiling over in New Orleans, wrote a couple of regional hits himself, and was touring the South as a guitarist when he sacrificed the tip of one finger to the gods in a Florida motel altercation.

That fortuitous mishap reignited Mac's uncanny ability to "radiate the 88s," as he put it, first as a Bourbon Street strip-joint organist and later as Dr. John The Night Tripper, the bone-and-bead bedecked stage persona he unveiled on his 1968 debut, *Gris-Gris*. Inspired by a Senegalese healer and conjurer who arrived in nineteenth century New Orleans via Haiti, Dr. John soon became inseparable from Mac himself.

"Mac did incantations and chants before the gigs," recalled jazz keyboardist and bandleader David Torkanowsky, who played Hammond B-3 with Dr. John on and off for several decades and accompanied Mac every year to get a New Year's blessing and gris-gris bag from their spiritual mentor, Frank Lastie. "It was sort of a spiritual reset."

"It wasn't a jive thing," noted Theriot, a Neville Brothers veteran who played guitar with Dr. John on before signing on as Mac's producer.

"Everyone would hold hands in a circle, and I always felt different when we got done with that."

Those spiritual resets carried even more weight when Theriot and Torkanowsky were both working on what they sensed would be Mac's swan song. And while some fans might be surprised that the as-yet untitled album invokes the spirit of Hank Williams and other country pioneers, taken in context of Mac's career, it makes perfect sense.

*Ske-Dat-De-Dat: The Spirit Of Satch* (2014), the last studio album Mac released before his death, salutes Louis Armstrong and follows tributes to Duke Ellington and songwriter Johnny Mercer. Now, Williams joins that illustrious list.

"[T]hose songs were dear to his heart," said Theriot, who helped Mac fulfill a dream of following Ray Charles' lead by making his own country album. "This record wasn't intended to be posthumous; that's just the way things happened. It was a cohesive artistic statement Mac put together while he was here."

Like Dr. John's concerts, the forthcoming album has some surprises. Willie Nelson joined in for a joyous rendition of "(Give Me That) Old-Time Religion" and Rickie Lee Jones circled back to put a spell on "I Walk On Gilded Splinters." But even the country standards were "completely Rebennack-ed out," as Torkanowsky put it.

"Mac basically channeled ancestry, which is what great jazz players do," Torkanowsky said. "Every time you played music with him, you were speaking to several of his ancestral griots at the same time. That's why his music was so deep. It was informed by history and a deep reverence for those who came before him."

## Dancing on Sacred Ground

*The joyous spirit of Jazz Fest helps the City of New Orleans heal*

*HighTimes.com*, May 2006

THERE WAS A LOT riding on the thirty-seventh annual New Orleans Jazz and Heritage Festival. Tens of thousands of music lovers converged on sacred ground—the freshly repaired Fair Grounds—to turn the spirit of the city around on the opening weekend of the first Jazz Fest since the post-Katrina levee breaches devastated my adopted hometown.

The collective healing was a stunning success.

At stage after stage, during three days blessed by the weather gods—rain held off till the gates closed Saturday and let up just in time for a glorious Sunday—artists used the power of music to confront the tragedy and transform it, and colorfully costumed fest-goers exploded with the raucous joy of a jazz funeral second line.

The visiting big guns delivered, bigtime. First-day headliner Bob Dylan, wearing a white cowboy hat and a grin wide as the Mississippi, let his songs speak for themselves in a spirited set that invoked "High Waters" and closed with a Cat 5 "All Along the Watchtower." Elvis Costello unleashed the furies with "The River in Reverse," the title track of his locally-recorded album with New Orleans legend Allen Toussaint, moving many to tears with an invocation of the darkest post-K chaos ("they're counting widows/ crosses in splinters"). And closing act Bruce Springsteen delivered a full-bore rock and roll revival with his rollicking Seeger Sessions Band hours after touring flooded-out Lakeview and what's left of the 9th Ward.

"The criminal ineptitude makes you furious," said Springsteen, who wrote new lyrics for the Depression-era song he dedicated to President Bystander: "How Can a Poor Man Stand Such Times and Live." A sea of hands and a swell of voices answered his call to "rise up!" and rebuild "My City of Ruins" before The Boss brought it home with "When the Saints Go Marching In," delivered not as a rabble-rouser but as a quiet acoustic prayer.

But it was the other ninety percent of the lineup—local Louisiana musicians, many of them homeless returning evacuees—who infused the festival with its lifeblood, from the Mardi Gras Indians to the gospel choirs to headliners like Dr. John and The Meters, whose Church of Funk was in full swing across the Fair Grounds from Springsteen's band.

"The only thing holding my bones together is my imagination," quipped Cajun country singer D. L. Menard, whose furniture shop in rural Erath, Louisiana, was trashed by Katrina's evil twin Rita. The same could be said of all the local Jazz Fest artists, who responded to the job at hand by drawing deep on their own creative wellsprings.

For Irvin Mayfield, that meant playing "Amazing Grace" for his father, who died in Katrina's aftermath. For Cowboy Mouth's Fred LeBlanc, that meant tempting the gods with the pre-K anthem "Hurricane Party," then soldiering on when the power failed, hurricane-style, with an acapella version of "Over the Rainbow." For Johnny Sketch and the Dirty Notes, that meant leading the crowd in a heartfelt singalong of "Sweet Chalmette" ("that's in St. Bernard, y'all"), a paean to frozen fish sticks, mac & cheese and "Friday nights at the Daiquiris and Cream"—which, like most of St. Bernard, ain't dere no more. For the hip-hop brass band Soul Rebels, back in town after scattering to Houston and beyond, that meant a massive call and response to banish the evacuee blues: "No place like home! No place like home! No place like home!"

And for fest-goers throughout the Fair Grounds—whether they were in the Juvenile or Dave Matthews throngs, hoisting umbrellas in a second line, or sucking crawfish heads—it meant marveling that post-Katrina Jazz Fest felt just like pre-Katrina Jazz Fest, minus a couple stages but with bursting with more heart and soul than ever.

Over in the Gospel Tent, Shades of Praise—three tiers of glowing black, white and brown faces raised in joyful song—provided a blueprint of hope for the future of New Orleans. "Who here lost everything?" the choir leader asked. Several dozen hands shot up. "All right then, turn it around," he shouted and slowly started to spin, gradually speeding up as people throughout the tent rose to perform their own circular exorcisms.

"Turn it around! Turn it around! Turn it around!"

And damn if we didn't banish that evil hurricane eye and put the floodwaters in reverse, bringing the assembled masses to higher ground.

Hurricane season starts June 1st, and Jazz Fest can't turn that around if the levees don't hold—or if the leaders we elect on May 20th don't have the vision to restore the city's living culture of marching bands, church choirs, second-line clubs and Mardi Gras Indians. But for a few more fest-filled days—the musical marathon continues this weekend, with 9th Ward survivor Fats Domino closing the show—dancing on sacred ground is just what the Doctor ordered to heal the breaches in our homes and our hearts.

## Smith Diaries: Back in New Orleans

April 2006

### *Chapter 2:* Life on the Strip in the New Normal

MARDI GRAS HAS COME and gone, along with the St. Patrick's Day parade (both Uptown and Downtown versions), the Italian parade, the Irish-Italian parade, the towering food altars of St. Joseph's Day, and a scaled-down version of the Mardi Gras Indians' annual St. Joseph walkabout. So, for a brief period between now and the big French Quarter Fest that immediately precedes Jazz Fest, things are pretty much back to (ab)normal in New Orleans, or the New Normal, as *Times-Picayune* columnist and rising national media star Chris Rose calls it.

For me, the New Normal is life on The Island (as Chris calls it), which I like to call The Strip: the high and dry band of land right next to the Mississippi River, stretching from the far reaches of the Bywater and Marigny through the Quarter and all the way Uptown, which for the most part escaped major flooding and remains more or less intact.

Less is the operative word, even in The Strip: Home mail delivery happens once or twice a week if you're lucky (and no magazines at all in the still-forbidden 701 zip zones of Orleans Parish). Garbage pick-up (maybe) once a week if you're very lucky. No recycling until probably forever (and it still feels weird throwing bottles and cans and papers away with the boiled shrimp shells). Lots of traffic lights are still out, replaced by the ubiquitous four-way stops where distracted drivers glued to their insurance adjusters on mobiles bump and grind their way to meetings with their contractors. Stores and restaurants are open but with limited hours, scaled-back menus, and skeleton staff. Translation: you can't make a 10 p.m. beer run to Sav-A-Center, or get a pizza delivered from Rocky's, or pay for breakfast with plastic at Slim's.

But these are minor inconveniences. Our place, House of Boo (named for the cats that rule our roost) was only grazed by Katrina's winds and not victimized by the Army Corps of Bunglers, whose man-made levee breaches flooded most of the town. We didn't even have to toss out a moldy refrigerator to fester in the streets, thanks to the foresight of my husband,

Donald—who may be the *only* person in New Orleans who emptied the fridge of food before evacuating. (Donald also put "Terrorist Target" high on his list of reasons to leave New York City for New Orleans, where we moved into our house on August 11th, 2001. But that's another story.)

When we came back home after two months of post-K exile in Asheville, North Carolina (which ain't exactly the Superdome), most of the plants we'd dragged inside were dead. But our lucky "money" plant was still alive. And, more importantly, so was Tig—the outdoor cat we'd left behind, who reappeared miraculously right after I stopped searching for him online at PetFinder.com. ("Moron!" he meowed. "I'm out here, on the deck!") Everything else was exactly the way we'd left it—not a speck of mold besmirched our artwork or Donald's extensive collection of avant books and records or my stock of vintage clothes and costumes—which would soon help me spawn my most successful season ever as a Mardi Gras costumer.

So am I wracked with survivor guilt? You bet; though I swore off Calvinism years ago, there's still an inner Methodist that says I don't deserve my good fortune. But I also know that what Donald and I do—make music, make art, and keep the underground economy bubbling with flea markets and community sales—is a vital part of the recovery process. I also believe that those of us who don't have to spend our energy gutting our houses have that much more to give to a city that's given so much to us.

What's astonishing is that people who *are* gutting their houses are right there in the trenches with us. The vast majority of my friends and fellow artists, even those who lost everything, are back in town and rebuilding their lives. There's Brett, who made a harrowing escape from Mid-City at the height of the shoot-and-loot insanity and not only lived to tell the tale but is making it into poetry. Wendy, a UNO communications prof who salvaged nothing from her Lakeview home and is staying sane by teaching a meta-class in post-K narratives and baking up a storm in her Uptown rental. Jimmy and Sue Ford, who gutted the first two floors of their flooded house to accommodate a home elevator for their two wheelchair-bound teenage sons, who suffer from muscular dystrophy—and didn't let the heavy labor slow them down. Sue still rocked the Muses parade as the leader of the all-girl Mardi Gras band Pink Slip, Jimmy still served as Grand Marshal for the Lyons Marching Club, and the Fords still hosted a Mardi Gras bash for out-of-town friends in their new, vastly improved digs. That's the thing about rebuilding; as long as you gotta do it, you might as well do it right.

# The Chance Music of New Orleans' Kidd Jordan

*DownBeat*, June 2020

Master improvisers can turn on a dime. So, when keyboardist Darrell Lavigne called Kidd Jordan in early March to set up a recording session while he was in New Orleans, the elder saxophonist sprang into action.

Joined by Jordan's son Marlon on trumpet, Mark Lomax on drums and Eddie Bayard on saxophone, the quintet convened at McDonogh 35 Senior High School to record *Last Trane To New Orleans*, an epic live throwdown that's due out digitally on June 15th, and on CD and LP on July 15th.

Immediately after the session—which was produced by Jordan's daughter, Rachel Jordan—the city was shut down because of the pandemic. But the resulting career-capping masterwork marks Jordan's eighty-fifth birthday, finding the saxophonist laser-focused on an uncompromising vision after helping to raise seven children and educating thousands of young musicians in schools and colleges, as well as the Louis Armstrong Jazz Camp, where he serves as artistic director.

Jordan has performed with a slew of jazz greats, too, from Cannonball Adderley and Ornette Coleman to Cecil Taylor and Lena Horne, and passed the torch to students like Branford Marsalis, Donald Harrison, Trombone Shorty and Jon Batiste.

A Hurricane Katrina survivor—who lost his house and most of his instruments in the ensuing 2005 flood—Jordan spoke to *DownBeat* via Zoom from his daughter Rachel's house, just around the corner from his own home in New Orleans.

*The following has been edited for length and clarity.*

**Last Trane To New Orleans is a great album title for the patriarch of free-jazz improv in a trad-jazz town.**

Yeah, well the whole trip for me, I'm playing the song in my head. I don't work off charts, I'm not playing changes. And when [John Coltrane] came out, man, that changed things. When I first heard Trane play, I felt like I was getting ready to shout and get out of my body. Even today, when you put late Coltrane on, people start walking out like crazy.

**Just like people used to do at the New Orleans Jazz & Heritage Festival, when I first started seeing you play there.**

And the more we emptied the room, the more we'd play! That happened with everybody. Ornette Coleman was like that. He really stretched into some advanced stuff; I mean, it was all over. I loved Ornette's music from the first time I heard it, back when he was playing with an R&B act. He was living down here for a while, and then he went on and did what he had to do to do what he did.

**So did you. And now you're the "Lion In Winter," the opening track of the album. What were you like as a cub?**

When I was young, I was always with an older crowd. Now, I'm the oldest kid in the crowd! When I was coming up, I played a lot of baritone, but I was also listening to everyone else. And when Charlie Parker came to town and I heard him play at [The Municipal] Auditorium, I thought I met Jesus! Afterward, me and [clarinetist] Alvin Batiste were talking to him, and when his road manager said it was time to take a cab, Bird said, "No, man, I'm talking to some friends." Being called a friend of Bird's made me a little legit. And that same night, I met my wife. That was a humdinger, that night.

**You also listened to avant-garde composers like Karlheinz Stockhausen, who came to one of your shows in Berlin.**

I listen to all types of music that moves me. One night, I saw John Cage at Tulane [University] and then went downtown to see Louis Armstrong's last show in New Orleans. Louis Armstrong broke all kinds of rules; he did some wild things when he was young—like Ornette and Trane. And Albert Ayler. I dedicated this album to Albert, because he didn't really get his due when he was playing. Albert kept this thing going in a different direction.

**It's a very spiritual album. "Holy Ghost Suite" invokes Ayler in its very title and segues into "The Revival Suite," which your frequent collaborator, bassist William Parker, said was about the "history and the mystery of New Orleans."**

I don't know about that. After the music is played, you can come up with all kinds of descriptions. But at the time, I'm hearing what's going on inside the harmonic things. And the music really comes out of the church. When you hear the "hallelujahs," you just gotta go. Jazz is chance music; you don't know what's gonna come out. You may have one thing in mind, and then you go someplace you never thought about before.

**What's the thing that keeps you going as an improviser?**

Well, I don't care what people say. And I knew when I started, I wasn't going to get rich playing this music. I taught school and played with a lot of bands in other genres to raise my family. So, in my leisure time, why should I not do what I want to do? Even if nobody likes it, I like it. And that's the thing.

## Shuttered SideBar in New Orleans Continues to Provide Creative Outlets

*DownBeat*, July 2021

"Behold! The sky's a shining shell!"

Gazing out at the socially distanced crowd gathered at the open-air Broadside Theatre in New Orleans, where the moon was rising behind him in a purple-streaked twilight sky, the Seattle-based saxophonist Skerik took a moment to drink it all in at. It was mid-April 2021, and for his first event in front of "real live individuals" since the pandemic started, he traveled from Seattle to play with two frequent co-conspirators: New Orleans-based cellist Helen Gillet and Portuguese percussionist Pedro Segundo. The three hit the stage like long-lost siblings, and proceeded to create a kaleidoscopic forcefield of sonic invocations and improvisations that levitated the players and audience alike. Which often happens at a Scatterjazz/SideBar show.

The Broadside show was the latest incarnation of SideBar, the little venue that could. Originally housed in a way-off-the-beaten-track watering hole, where lawyers from the nearby Orleans Parish Criminal Court once talked shop in the shadow of Orleans Parish Prison, SideBar became a nexus for a far-flung network of creative musicians, from local stalwarts like New Orleans free-jazz founding father Kidd Jordan, James Singleton and Simon Berz to visiting artists like Hamid Drake, Mars Williams and Simon Lott. It also spawned multi-day events like SideFest, held during Jazz Fest season, where Gillet was scheduled to play her annual set of duos with Skerik and saxophonist Jeff Coffin in 2020 before the lockdown led to its cancellation.

"SideBar grew into an incredibly important place for the fertile exploration and advancement of music," said Gillet, who was an integral part of that scene from its earliest days. "And New Orlean musicians need that. All these players who are great at making people move their butts and party are extremely talented musicians, and they need an outlet for their active, creative minds." And though the physical venue closed last August, SideBar has continued to provide that outlet.

Just days after the pandemic killed live music, when most venues across the country were struggling to adjust, SideBar founder/owner Keith

Magruder started streaming high-quality shows from the shuttered venue. Last fall, those streams migrated to Magruder's own SidePorch, a block away from the old SideBar, where he hosted the 2021 SideFest in Exile, complete with crawfish boil. Together with his Scatterjazz partner Andy Durta, a longtime curator of creative music in New Orleans, he took it to the next level by producing a regular Wednesday Scatterjazz/SideBar series at the Broadside, which also hosts special SJ/SB events. So far from shrinking SideBar's reach, the pandemic has actually expanded it.

"Keith jumped on [streaming] right away," Gillet recalled. "Those first few weeks of the pandemic, when we were all losing our minds, I was just holding it together watching those SideBar streams. And while we were sad to see the SideBar go, it's the people not the place, and now we have the Broadside. It's gone from this tiny venue to this giant outdoor movie theater stage. The Broadside is a celebration of what the SideBar was."

What did the original venue offer? SideBar patriarch Jordan, eighty-six, a 2021 United States Artists Fellow, summed it up succinctly: "We got to do what we do," the saxophonist said. Which was by design.

"We want everybody to do what they do," said Durta, who hopes to lure Jordan to the Broadside soon. "But Kidd, especially. It was a great honor to have him there so often, almost always in a setting he hadn't been in before."

Drawn by the freedom to explore their creativity in an intimate venue, world-class musicians came from all over to play in a tiny room where the sound ricocheted off weird trapezoidal angles in unpredictable ways.

"Musicians loved that sound," Durta recalled. "Before the pandemic hit, we had a jazz educators conference, we had Instigator Fest, we had the great Dave Leibman. And when [Netherlands-based percussionist] Michael Vatcher came to town for the first time, we had Vatcher-Vest, a pun on 'fest.' Five nights of Michael playing with Phil Mitman, Audrey Chin and all kinds of great people."

Vatcher-Vest was just one of countless highlights in a room where Gillet's new duo project with Coffin was born, and Jordan traded road stories and riffs with fellow elder-statesman saxophonist Dickie Landry and rising star Aurora Nealand. And now that SideBar has metastasized into the Broadside, with an ever-growing livestream archive, it's opening the ears of larger audiences in New Orleans and around the world.

"If we can secure funding, fingers crossed, we can get SideBar back up and running," said Magruder, who's applied for a Shuttered Venue Operators Grant specifically created for small venues. "At a new, bigger and better location. Meanwhile, we've got the Broadside and Side-Porch, which my neighbors really enjoy."

In whatever form it takes, SideBar may be just what the doctor ordered coming out of the pandemic.

"I feel like accepting how difficult this time has been can truly be felt through improvised music," said Gillet, who was on deck to play a Scatterjazz/SideBar show at the Broadside with Coffin and preeminent New Orleans drummer Johnny Vidacovich when we spoke. "I know for a fact that my audiences have been responding to the grittiness and visceral qualities in the music. The discomfort, met with resolution at times. It feels familiar to people right now, so I think it's an important art form."

# All You Need is Roux: A Personal Jazz Fest Retrospective

*OffBeat Jazz Fest Bible*, 2022

Jazz Fest popped my cherry in 1988, when I hit the mud running and instantly went native, gatoring in the Blues Tent (still on the infield then), joining in tribal rituals like the watermelon sacrifice, and melding my sweat-slicked body with a dizzying succession of partners to the mesmerizing beats of the greatest live-music jukebox in the world.

Little Freddie King or Lost Bayou Ramblers? Irma Thomas or Beausoleil? Galactic or The Soul Rebels? With a dozen stages and tents spread out over one-hundred-and-forty-five acres at the Fair Grounds, charting your course involves intricate calculations to hit your personal sweet spot on any given day of the seven-day musical marathon. And despite the Fest's ever-slicker corporate trappings, the sheer power of the music always breaks through, sometimes against all odds, the way the sun pierces the clouds after a torrential downpour, creating one of the event's signature elements: mud.

Mud is the roux of Jazz Fest that binds all the disparate parts together at (almost) every New Orleans Jazz and Heritage Festival, which has stayed surprisingly true to its "heritage" legacy since its 1973 inception in Armstrong Park. Out-of-town headliners may generate the bulk of the revenue, but local culture bearers remain a vital part of the mix, from the sacred chants of Mardi Gras Indians to the joyous second lines snaking their way around the Fair Grounds.

The following time capsules capture two critical years of Jazz Fest history: 2004, when beloved Fester Daniel Breaux was murdered near the festival site; and 2006, the first Jazz Fest after the levee breaches devastated my adopted hometown in the aftermath of Hurricane Katrina. Both distill why Jazz Fest matters: the healing power of music, and the essential social aid that social aid and pleasure clubs provide.

Which brings us to Jazz Fest 2022, which weathered three cancellations during a pandemic that took a heavy toll on New Orleans in the years leading to this long-awaited resurrection.

## *Jazz Fest 2004*

Muddied by rain and shadowed by a senseless killing, the thirty-fifth annual Jazz Fest called down the power of music to celebrate life—and ten years of freedom in South Africa.

The New Orleans Jazz and Heritage Festival has weathered a few storms that caused it to close its gates, as it did in 2004 when torrential rains washed out the second Friday. But in thirty-five years, it had never been struck by violence. The killing of Daniel Breaux, a local artist and beloved Jazz Fester who was shot after leaving the Fair Grounds in a botched street mugging, ended an age of innocence. But it also testified to the power of music to bring people together. And on the last Sunday of Jazz Fest, the day after he died, Breaux's spirit was everywhere.

In Economy Hall, trumpeter Gregg Stafford played a jazz funeral dirge near a shrine friends built around Breaux's dancing clogs. Over at the Fais Do Do Stage, the Jazz Fest tribe held a traditional "watermelon sacrifice" in his honor, carving "Daniel" into a melon that was massaged by dozens of hands before being cracked wide open and eaten off the muddy ground. Steve Riley and the Mamou Playboys dedicated "Bon Reve" to Breaux as the late-day sun broke through the clouds. Next door at Congo Square, the stage was bathed in golden light as Hugh Masekela and other South African stars raised their voices in song to their own "beautiful dream": ten years of freedom from apartheid in South Africa. It was a stirring finale to Jazz Fest '04, which celebrated South Africa's liberation and offered a rich mix of soulful artists, on and off the Fair Grounds, who make "music about struggle, pain, and joys," as Masekela put it.

## *Jazz Fest 2006*

There was a lot riding on the thirty-seventh annual New Orleans Jazz and Heritage Festival. Tens of thousands of music lovers converged on sacred ground—the freshly repaired Fair Grounds—to turn the spirit of the city around on the opening weekend of the first Jazz Fest, nearly six months after the levee breaches devastated vast stretches of New Orleans.

The collective healing was a stunning success.

At stage after stage, for three days blessed by the weather gods—rain held off till the gates closed Saturday and let up just in time for a glorious Sunday—artists used the power of music to confront the tragedy and transform it with the raucous joy of a jazz funeral second line.

The visiting big guns delivered. Bob Dylan, wearing a white cowboy hat and a grin as wide as the Mississippi, delivered a spirited set that invoked "High Waters" and closed with a Cat 5 "All Along the Watchtower."

Elvis Costello unleashed the furies with "The River in Reverse," the title track of his locally recorded album with New Orleans legend Allen Toussaint, moving many to tears with an invocation of the darkest post-Katrina chaos ("they're counting widows/crosses in splinters"). And just hours after touring flooded-out Lakeview and what's left of the 9th Ward, Bruce Springsteen delivered a full-bore rock and roll revival where a swell of voices answered his call to "Rise up!" and rebuild "My City of Ruins."

But it was the other ninety percent of the lineup—local Louisiana musicians, many of them homeless returning evacuees—who infused the festival with its lifeblood, from the Mardi Gras Indians to the gospel choirs to headliners like Dr. John and The Meters, whose Church of Funk was in full swing across the Fair Grounds from Springsteen's band.

"The only thing holding my bones together is my imagination," quipped Cajun country singer D.L. Menard, whose furniture shop in rural Erath, Louisiana, was trashed by Katrina's evil twin Rita. The same could be said of all the local Jazz Fest artists, who responded to the job at hand by drawing deep from their own creative wellsprings.

### *Jazz Fest 2022*

THERE'S ALSO A LOT riding on the fifty-first annual Jazz Fest, though the circumstances are not analogous to 2006. The levee breaches were a gaping wound that still hasn't fully healed, not the often isolating, sometimes paralyzing quicksand of COVID we've all been living through. But after weathering three cancellations during a pandemic that took a heavy toll on New Orleans—and particularly the music community—we can finally breathe a huge sigh of relief—even if (perhaps because) it rains.

Dancing on sacred ground is just what the doctor ordered to heal the breaches in our homes and our hearts the pandemic brought to the Jazz Fest community. But with jazz funerals and tributes celebrating all the giants we lost—Ellis Marsalis, Art and Charles Neville, Dr. John, Dave Bartholomew, Little Buck Sinegal, Jazz Fest founding father George Wein—and every artist on every stage celebrating their own pandemic liberation, there's no doubt among the faithful that the collective healing of 2022 will be a stunning success.

# Wendell Brunious Named First Musical Director of Preservation Hall

*DownBeat*, **October 2023**

When you enter Preservation Hall in New Orleans, it's like stepping back in time. The small no-frills room looks pretty much like it did when Allan and Sandra Jaffe first opened the now-legendary French Quarter venue on St. Peter Street in 1961. Bare unvarnished floors serve as the stage, surrounded by wooden chairs where the audience sits—until, as often happens, they are moved to get up and march around with a band that celebrates the living past of New Orleans jazz.

At the center of all the action is master trumpeter Wendell Brunious, the band's exuberant long-time leader, who's just been named Preservation Hall's first-ever musical director. A tall, sharply dressed gentleman, his domain extends far beyond the walls of this tiny "hall." As Pres Hall's ambassador to the world, he brings the joyful spirit of New Orleans music to far-flung countries around the world. He's also a born storyteller who lards his tales with pithy one-liners, as he did for an interview on his home turf.

Spiffy as ever, in a cream-colored suit and elegant brown-and-white spectator shoes, he was accompanied by Caroline Brunious, his Swedish wife of twenty-three years, who blows a sizzling hot clarinet in the Preservation Hall All-Stars. The scion of legendary trumpeter John "Picky" Brunious—who, like his son, was educated at Juilliard as well as by the brass bands of New Orleans—he's also the brother of the late John Brunious Jr., who preceded him as Pres Hall's bandleader.

Our interview ranged from his boyhood memories of Louis Armstrong to close encounters with jazz masters like Dizzy Gillespie, as well as the vitality of the music he passes on to future generations.

**Cree McCree:** I've been to Preservation Hall performances, but I've never been back to this room. It feels like a sacred space.

**Wendell Brunious:** It's called the Library and it's got a lot of beautiful old things, like the largest collection of miniature tubas in the world.

New Orleans is a living library of music and rhythms, and just being born here is a great advantage. Because you grew up with the music.

**McCree:** You picked up the trumpet when you were eleven, right?

**Brunious:** That's when I got serious. But before that I would just take the mouthpiece and make these little duck-call sounds. Sounds kind of like a kazoo. [*Grabs a mouthpiece and starts to blow.*]

**McCree:** Wow! That's even better than a kazoo.

**Brunious:** Then, when I was ten, Louis Armstrong came to town and my dad took us all out to the airport. About a hundred musicians had gone there to meet him, and Louie was one of the last ones off the plane. We thought maybe he missed it. Then, suddenly, there he was. The air got thick enough you could cut it with a butter knife, and the whole gang started playing "When The Saints Go Marching In." That was magic. God put him here for a specific purpose to teach and influence all of us. If you're a guitar player, you think you don't owe something to Louis Armstrong, think again. He revolutionized the whole art of music, especially American music.

**McCree:** What a thrill that must have been for a kid just starting out on the trumpet. Did your dad give you any specific tips about the trumpet?

**Brunious:** Not really, because he was always working. He played on Bourbon Street at night, and during the day he worked as a truant officer at Milne's Boys Home. But on Sunday, when my dad was off, he'd tell everybody go get your horn. There were eight brothers and sisters in our family, and though just me and my older brother John got to the level of playing professionally, everybody played. Dad would say you hit this note, you hit that note, and it'd be this real crazy chord. And he'd say, see, that's the kind of stuff I like. It was wonderful growing up with that.

**McCree:** You were still pretty young when you joined Preservation Hall.

**Brunious:** Yep, twenty-three. I was the youngest person ever to be on the payroll, and it was strange how I came to play here. One night I was playing around the corner on Bourbon Street, blowing my brains off for $88.00, and my car was parked here. So, as I came down the street, I passed right by the gate. I'd never been inside, but it wasn't but $1.00 to get in, and when I went inside there was nobody playing trumpet. I said, "You need a trumpet player?" And the drummer said, "Man, we don't let people sit in." I said, "I'm not sitting in, I come to play, man." And I took my horn out and played a couple of songs. Allan Jaffe was there, and Kid Thomas [Valentine], and they came up front to see who the heck was playing that trumpet. Kid Thomas had this scowl on his face, and I felt like, "Oh, my God, I had violated something." But he wasn't angry, that's just the way he looked. Then Kid put his hands together and the whole audience started clapping. And I sat down next to him and played the rest of the night.

But I was still playing on Bourbon and barely squeaking out a living. Then one morning my phone rang. It was the great trumpet player Wallace Davenport, who said, "I got a gig for you playing with Lionel Hampton. They need an extra trumpet player tonight." I must have done OK because after that gig, I went up to New York and joined the Lionel Hampton Band for a while.

**McCree:** Is that where you met Dizzy Gillespie?

**Brunious:** No, that was when Dizzy played the New Orleans Jazz Fest. There's a picture of Dizzy, Mahalia Jackson and Duke Ellington outside Municipal Auditorium. I wasn't in the picture, but I was sitting there, and Dizzy was holding court. He said, "Man, Charlie Parker told me, keep one foot in the future and keep one foot in the blues." And I've continued to spread that message. Because the blues is not one, four and five or one, four, two, five, one. You could wake up with a flat tire or a headache this morning, that's the blues, man. When you hear Charlie Parker playing "Laura," that's not a blues. But you hear the blues all through there, that's what makes your individual voice.

**McCree:** Circling back to Preservation Hall, I was very surprised to learn you weren't just the youngest musical director but the first musical director. Why was there never a musical director before?

**Brunious:** The world has gotten more complicated. A lot of our older people have passed on, so I'm gonna help channel the music in the right direction. Kids have so many options today that we gotta bring their focus back to where they need to be to play this kind of music. Back in the 1990s, Ellis Marsalis called me up one day, said, "Would you come teach 'em how to play?" So, I made up a class, forty forms of the blues. Hey, man, you really know how to play the saxophone, but are you delivering the message I want to hear?

**McCree:** And what is the message you want to hear?

**Brunious:** You want to speak to someone's heart, not just befuddle their brain. 'Cause there are enough things that do that, anyway.

## Harrison's "Passion" Mixes Hard Swing, Trap Hip-Hop

*DownBeat*, **April 2024**

"IF YOU DON'T LIVE it, it won't come out of your horn." That sage advice from Charlie Parker became Big Chief Donald Harrison's lodestar, even though Parker passed away before Harrison was even born.

"I realized that was the path I should be on," recalled the New Orleans-born saxophonist and composer, the scion of Big Chief Donald Harrison Sr. "I was already part of the roots culture of New Orleans music and Congo Square. So, I went on a mission to play with as many masters of jazz as I could and see where that would take me."

His trajectory flew fast and far. At age nineteen, he started playing with Roy Haynes and introduced Big Apple jazzbos to New Orleans brass bands with New York Second Line. Miles Davis became an early mentor, as did Art Blakey, and Harrison's quest to explore the musical omniverse soon took him to Africa, South America, the Caribbean and beyond. Closer to home, he gleaned material from the radio and The Notorious BIG, his Brooklyn neighbor. But it wasn't until 2005, when he released *3D* (Fromp), that the NEA Jazz Master began recording a single song in several mix-and-match genres.

*The Art Of Passion* (Ropeadope), his new three-track EP, premiered January 11th at New York's Town Hall with guest stars ranging from DJ Logic and Vernon Reid to Charles Tolliver and Arturo O'Farrill. Shortly afterward, Harrison sat down to discuss his musical journey and *Passion*'s mix of hard swing, trap hip-hop and jazz.

**Cree McCree:** I love the title, *The Art Of Passion.*

**Donald Harrison:** Yeah, passion comes in many forms. The recording shows a mirror image of two styles of music: hard swing that greats like what Coltrane and Miles Davis were doing in the '60s and the modern trap hip-hop young people came up with. Those two bookends merge in the middle track, so you can see the whole journey if you listen to the music.

**McCree:** And you were living that journey, just like Bird advised. You were mentored by Miles and actually lived near Biggie Smalls in Brooklyn.

**Harrison:** That's the part I'm always pinching myself about, being around some of the greatest people in the world. Biggie would come to my house every day to work on music and became the king of East Coast rap. If you type in "Notorious BIG quotes," you'll see all these messages of hope to young people hidden underneath his music. That if you work hard, you can achieve anything.

**McCree:** You also learned a lot from the quantum physicist Stefon Alexander. How did that connection come about?

**Harrison:** After I did a recording called *Quantum Leap*, I emailed him to ask about the idea of multiverses: that if they exist, each one would be different, but they would contain the same elements. We've stayed in touch and it's been a great marriage. Sometimes when we're talking, we come up with the same ideas. It's a little bit scary, but wonderful. Einstein was a violinist, Max Planck was also a musician and Stefon Alexander plays saxophone.

**McCree:** Bingo.

**Harrison:** Music fueled their finding new ways to look at science. In the universe, everything goes to its natural conclusion. If you see a tree blowing in the wind, it moves naturally because of the wind. Music is the same way. The great bassist Bill Lee, Spike Lee's father, would always say, be true to yourself. Be natural. When John Coltrane and Sonny Rollins were playing together, each stayed true to his realm.

**McCree:** Why did you choose Ropeadope to continue your journey?

**Harrison:** Because it embraces the totality of music that's out right now. It's open to new ideas. I've been trying to get other labels to look at releasing multi-genre music since my early days on Impulse. And they always looked at it from a marketing point of view: We're not gonna spend that much money to put all these songs into all these different marketplaces. But Ropeadope embraced the idea wholeheartedly.

**McCree:** What do you hope listeners will take away from *The Art Of Passion*?

**Harrison:** Well, I hope they enjoy all the music. That people who may not normally listen to hip-hop realize, OK, this is actually good music.

And that people who mostly listen to hip-hop get a taste of jazz and see that jazz is something that they should add to their list of musical styles.

**McCree:** How does New Orleans fit into your musical equation?

**Harrison:** New Orleans is a root incubator for the world's music and the cultural home of jazz. Because if you play our traditional songs like "Handa Wanda," everyone from a two-year-old to an eighty-year-old knows those songs. All the social and economic strata, all of the races. The music and the culture ties us together as one. We all enjoy it and love it together."

## New Orleans Jazz & Heritage Festival: A Bounteous Banquet

*DownBeat*, May 2025

The New Orleans Jazz & Heritage Festival is a bounteous banquet of music, from local New Orleans and Louisiana bayou artists to guest headliners like Lenny Kravitz and Santana, so it's easy to get overwhelmed. And even if you focus primarily on the lineups in the WWOZ Jazz Tent, over the course of two four-day weekends it's impossible to see everyone on your short list.

Among the acts I was especially sorry to miss: Nicholas Payton; George Wein Centennial, featuring Randy Brecker; Adonis Rose & the New Orleans Jazz Orchestra; and Kermit Ruffins' Tribute to Louis Armstrong. The good news? The three artists I did get to see delivered in spades, and I was able to catch their entire sets, not just a few numbers.

Branford Marsalis' Jazz Fest appearance at the WWOZ Jazz Tent was also a homecoming for the eldest scion of the Marsalis jazz dynasty, who recently returned to New Orleans to take over as artistic director at the Ellis Marsalis Center.

Currently touring in support of his new album, *Belonging* (Blue Note), a reimagining of pianist Keith Jarrett's groundbreaking 1974 release that he recorded at the Marsalis Center in March 2024, Marsalis revisited that album with his longtime chamber ensemble: pianist Joey Calderazzo, bassist Eric Revis and drummer Justin Faulkner. But he also reached back a century to cover Fred Fisher's "There Ain't No Sweet Man That's Worth The Salt In My Tears," and reconceptualized Jimmy McHugh's "On The Sunny Side Of The Street" (1930) with a delightfully laid-back version.

Switching from soprano to tenor saxophone, Marsalis frequently stepped out of the spotlight to groove on what his ensemble was playing, including Calderazzo's beautifully elegiac "Conversation Among The Ruins." And the audience was right there with him, nodding their heads to "Sunny Side" and clapping along to his jazzed-up version of the honky-tonk tune "My Bucket's Got A Hole In It," which segued into a surprise guest appearance by Dr. Michael White.

Watching those two giants play together, bridging trad and modern jazz, brought the final WWOZ Jazz Tent performance of Jazz Fest's first weekend to a pitch-perfect conclusion.

Joshua Redman Group featuring Gabrielle Cavassa received a standing ovation for their sultry rendition of "Hotel California" at the WWOZ Jazz Tent on the second Friday of the fest. "This is one of the great musical festivals of all time," the saxophonist said, "and being here is coming full circle, since my current project began in New Orleans in 2022."

That's when he hooked up with New Orleans native Cavassa and combined forces for *Where We Are*, their first Blue Note release. An intensely physical player, Redman also showcased his ensemble: bassist Philip Norris, drummer Nazir Ebo and pianist Paul Cornish, whose keyboard solos were especially mesmerizing. Soaring above it all were Cavassa's lilting vocals, as cool and fresh as an ocean breeze.

"We couldn't *not* play this next one," Redman announced at the end of the set before launching into the Louis Armstrong classic "Do You Know What It Means To Miss New Orleans?" Cavassa introduced the song, which segued into a duo with Redman before the band joined in, then brought it home with her super-fine scatting.

"I've traveled all over the world, and this is still my favorite festival," said New Orleans native Terence Blanchard after dazzling the overflow crowd at the start of his set at the WWOZ Jazz Tent on the fest's second Sunday. Blanchard traveled back in time to revisit his 2005 album *Flow*, produced by his mentor Herbie Hancock, regaling us with stories about its production along the way. "Toward the end, I told Herbie I was running out of music, and he said, 'All jazz musicians should run out of music,'" he added, to appreciative laughs. Joined by his E-Collective band—guitarist Charles Altura, drummer Oscar Seaton, bassist David "DJ" Ginyard and keyboardist Julian Pollack—he propelled extended versions of *Flow* compositions with his trumpet, leaving ample space for the collective to embroider. Altura's lyrical guitar was especially compelling; so was guest vocalist Michael Mayo, a world-class scatter.

"This last tune is a new one, possibly for a new project, based on your reaction," Blanchard announced. "'Prism' refracts different colors, and right now this country needs more of that." Judging from the reaction of the crowd, who rose to their feet with a long ovation after letting it wash over them, "Prism" is a keeper.

# IV.

## Droppin' Some NYC: The '90s Jam Band Scene

### *Introduction: My Life as a Teenage Boy*

In the summer of '91, when I turned forty-four, I was on the road with Blues Traveler, with pit stops on the east coast and throughout Colorado, en route to their very first Red Rocks gig–twice as old as the band members and even older than many young fans, some of whom were still in high school. But you wouldn't have known it to look at me, casually clad in my '90s jam band attire: faded flannel shirt with artfully ripped-off fringed sleeves topped by my requisite two-pocket vest to stash my smokes and my mini-theme books for scribbling notes on the dance floor.

Inside the rental car I'd maxed out my credit card to secure for the BT tour was a journal I used as a diary to record everything I was experiencing. Because the first volume of this journal had been stolen from under a bar stool at Dan Lynch's, two doors down from the Nightingale, I listed my home address so the finder could return it: 612 E. 6th St., New York City. That was just a short few blocks from ground zero at the 'Gale, where first Blues Traveler and then Spin Doctors created a collective forcefield during epic gigs that ran well past the wee hours. Yet more proof that geography is destiny.

Inside the front cover, I filled in the Class Program. School: Life. Class: R&R Alchemy. In which Crystal Flame and Lady Kerosene go on the road with Blues Traveler, Spin Doctors, and Cree comes along for the ride.

*Excerpts from that journal follow:*

## *8/10/91. Boston: The Big Rip/Road Warriors*

DAWN, MOTEL PARKING LOT. Grant goes to check on the equipment truck and it's all gone: all the info stored on midi, Popper's twelve-string, Chan's Chard-customized guitars. Have to rent gear for gig and play on schlocky equipment.

Some kid jumps onstage, Rob throws him off, hard, Popper gets on mic to say please go easy on the crew cause we've just been ripped off, and a few Bostonians start taunting the crew.

Bobby throws his bass down & storms offstage. But they do come back for an encore cause ninety-nine percent of the audience is with them. Then things start up again & when Chan stage dives at the end of "Johnny B. Goode," so does Tim Vega (who's onstage because he got all his merch ripped off). Bottles start flying and it turns into a BT brawl for a few more broken-glass minutes. Timmy's still got a bandage on his hand from his war wound.

Bobby tells me later it was one of the best gigs they ever played!

## *9/16-9/30/91. After Red Rocks weekend*

THE SCALE OF BT's growth echoes off those vast, timeless rocks, stained deep with sunset colors. Washes of light across the crowd illuminate crystal flames. Crystal Flame, I'll do anything you say. Speak to me in tongues and I will answer you.

Gearing into serious Traveler tour mode, Red Rocks photos recharged my batteries and now I've got the old BT itch to just give it up on the dance floor.

BT rocks Hollywood & Vine, Palace Theatre levitates. Nicki calls, she's just cabbed it up from San Diego with DG [David Graham] after acid-tripping thru the night–a cool two-hundred bucks but they make it in time for the big A&M confab.

"Love & Greed" opens kickass Palace show. (Bobby: "I didn't wake up till about the third song.") Bras on ears! Ear bras! Post-show paparazzi party. They schmooze; I shoot.

What I missed: Dave P [Precheur] pulling a Jim Morrison, dangling eleven stories above Hollywood Blvd. from a hotel window. Big bad behavior.

Big Sur coast drive with Widespread to the luxury stop of the tour. No more back seats and frat house couches, stylin' at the Seacliff: psychedelic fish pool w/ turtles, coffee machines, patio porches, sweet pool & jacuzzi. Serious male bonding between Widespread Dave & Chan, who's gonna play Widespread guitar tonight cause Mike's old lady got sick and he's outta here.

Fast forward to Warfield in San Francisco. Popper dedicates the whole set to Miles, who just died, and specifically "Sweet Pain."

Image: Chan & Popper holding bouquets aloft, soaking in the Warfield's storied history and thanking San Fran. These boys know they are blessed, and they're blessing us back, bigtime.

Golden Gate Park: Tibetan monks hovering onstage during BT set. Afterwards, head honcho tells Popper he especially liked the dancing ("very Tibetan dance"). Also loves the harps so Popper gives him one from his bandolier and the monk slips it inside his robes.

And the band plays on, to a meadow blanketed with the warm press of human flesh as the fog rolls in and drapes us inside the clouds. Sixty-five-thousand strong.

### *Summer of '92. Back in New York City.*

LAST NIGHT I REDISCOVERED THE BOOK (yes, Ron Kinchla, there is a book). My Life As a Teenage Boy is only a chapter (albeit a hefty one) or maybe not a chapter at all but a superannuated subtext. And the essential impetus that made me start to write was The Breaking of the Glass

What immense exhilaration I felt when I pitched that beer mug–a heavy mother, too, no mere dime store tumbler–against the wall at the Continental in New York's East Village. It hit right on target, a glorious fracturing of light against dark, and my arm felt as strong as Dwight Gooden's. I was one of the boys for real, that moment in time, right on the roll with Chan & Bobby, whose birthday gave us license to kill.

Even before the moment of impact, I set that mug flying with a whole set of complexly interconnected muscles, nerves, ligaments, fascia, etc.–which had never coordinated their efforts in quite this way before. Lordy, how it flew! It wasn't so much that I set it in motion, but more like I facilitated the trajectory of the motion, and let that mug hurl itself against the wall because that was exactly what the mug wanted to do. To shatter itself on the altar of the spirit, and release the shards of all my yesterdays and maybe tomorrows into one glorious, right-on target. YES. YES. YES.

This moment: the shattering of the glass is a glyph for the shattering of all preconceptions, all carefully composed outlines and plans, which are essentially goal-oriented. The shattering of the glass is the moment everything in my entire life led up to. A totally unanticipated moment in time that existed outside the very history that was shattered at the moment of impact.

The instant that glass splintered, I realized I wasn't just a fellow traveler like BT's horde of fans. I'd become a de facto working member of the band and its official scribe, writing numerous articles like the ones collected here, and doing due diligence for the book Chan's dad Ron Kinchla always encouraged me to write, tracking the heady early days of bands clearly destined to become world famous.

Though I didn't tour as heavily with the Spin Doctors, I documented them thoroughly with photos and even wrote the liner notes for *Pocket Full of Kryptonite* (as well as its twentieth anniversary edition). I also witnessed the inception of the John Popper-named H.O.R.D.E tour ["Horizons of Rock Developing Everywhere"], in which BT and the Doctors banded together with their brother jam bands Widespread Panic and Phish.

I hit the road with the first H.O.R.D.E. tour armed with a prototype of a magazine called Tangle, which had a Psychner (Steve Eichner) shot cover of John Popper, Chris Barron and Trey Anastacio from Phish. We sold a promotional T-shirt that said "Get Tangled In the Web" before the internet really existed, and came *that close* to getting the magazine funded.

And, just like I predicted, both Blues Traveler and Spin Doctors had huge early successes.

It didn't hurt that David Graham, son of famous rock impresario Bill Graham, became an instant BT convert after catching them play a Columbia frat house gig, while BT's fellow Princeton, New Jersey high school classmate, Chris Barron, got a boost from opening BT gigs before going on to form Spin Doctors. But it was their ever-growing throng of young live-show fans that made them an easy sell (A&M signed Traveler while Epic snagged the Doctors).

Traveler was first out of the gate with their radio hit, "But Anyway," which reached #8 on *Billboard*, spent nearly one year on the charts, won the Grammy Award for Best Rock Performance and helped the album *Four* go platinum. And the Spin Doctors, who were much poppier than Traveler, made the cover of *Rolling Stone* after *Kryptonite*'s first two singles, "Little Miss Can't Be Wrong" and "Two Princes" hit #1 and #3 on the *Billboard* charts and made that album go platinum, too.

And then.... suddenly, it was over.

Once Nirvana hit in 1991 with *Smells Like Teen Spirit,* Seattle grunge-rock, with its far bleaker take on life became the dominant musical phenom, aided and abetted by the suicide of Kurt Cobain, and jam bands were yesterday's news.

The first Lollapalooza in '91 (which I actually attended with Chan Kinchla and BT artist Darren Greene), quickly eclipsed H.O.R.D.E. and harder-edged bands like my personal favorite, Jane's Addiction. Fronted by the manic Perry Ferrell, the band reached deep inside my groin with their gospel "Nothing's Shocking," and rocked me so hard I blasted them at full volume during countless road trips, started climbing the charts. The rise of cooler-than-thou indie bands, and the juggernaut of hip-hop and rap also helped dethrone jam bands from their pop cultural peak.

But like the true road warriors they've always been, Blues Traveler continues to hit the highway, spawning new generations of fellow travelers. After the untimely death of Bobby Sheehan (in my current hometown of New Orleans, where we almost became neighbors), Chan's brother Tad Kinchla stepped in on bass and BT added a permanent keyboardist (Ben Wilson), as Sheehan had often urged. That band of brothers solidified way back in 2000, and continues to draw enthusiastic fans on their road tours which includes (as always) their annual July 4th throwdown at Red Rocks.

Spin Doctors also regrouped after founding guitarist Eric Schenkman left the band, which he later rejoined, and original bassist Mark White left for good. They cycled through a couple replacements before Barron, Schenkman and founding drummer Aaron Comess bonded with bassist Jack Daley, who went into the studio with them to record *Face Full of Cake*, their first album in twelve years, released on Capitol Records.

The two Nightingale brother bands reunited for a massive '90 reunion tour with the Gin Blossoms, which kicked off at Red Rocks on July 4th, 2025, and continued until mid-September. Far from being a pop culture footnote, they're back baby, big time!

I still stay in touch with Popper and Chan on social media, where I've been enjoying Chan's kickin' new side project, w4rhors3. I also interviewed founding drummer Brendan Hill for Celeb Stoner about his artfully curated legal marijuana dispensary Paper & Leaf on Bainbridge Island, shortly before BT made a trip to the 2022 Grammys, where *Traveler's Blues* was nominated for a Best Traditional Blue Grammy. Far from resting on their laurels, they followed that up with *Traveler's Soul* (Round Hill Records, 2023), and put their own mark on soulful classics like "I Can't Stand The Rain."

Meanwhile, the old Nightingale gang continues to convene periodically for ad hoc reunions, most recently at the 2024 Sleepy Hollow Music Festival, headlined by the Nightingale All-Stars: Jono Manson, Craig Dreyer, John Popper, and Joan Osborne.

At the beginning of the pandemic in 2020, the entire BT/Doctors family came together to help save Bar Chord, the live music bar in Brooklyn founded by Christie and Jonny Sheehan, the late Bobby Sheehan's younger brother. During a virtual live performance featuring multiple Nightingale alumni, we auctioned off prime pieces of old school scene memorabilia and raised nearly $10,000.00. We're still family after all these years, and I still believe in the Traveler mantra: "Trust in Trust."

Because "to my sweet surprise it does work out that way."

## Blues Traveler: Blues for the Road

***Details*, February 1990**

It's 3:00 a.m.at the Wetlands, where the collective force field created by New York's reigning jam band, Blues Traveler, has reached critical mass. "We're gonna do 'Johnny B. Goode' on speed," announces front man John Popper, a bear of a guy who stashes his arsenal of harps in a bush-camp bandolier. "And when we hit the floor, you hit the floor."

The band dive-bombs off a cliff of psychedelic hardcore, and ka-boom! collapses in unison with a couple hundred sweat-drenched dancers. We sprawl in postcoital bliss while B.T. plays a literally laid-back encore of their signature song, "Dropping Some NYC." Then bassist Bob Sheehan signals an ad hoc coda, and Popper shifts into a half-lotus position: "We'll do another tune if you all sit Indian-style with us." Quick as an acid flashback, the room is filled with cross-legged happy campers, and you don't have to be eighteen to know that somethin's happenin' here.

Blues Traveler inspired me to renew my long-lapsed subscription to the Sixties, which they update as a Nineties credo: "Tune in, turn on and kick some ass!" Months before their recent ascension via master impresario Bill Graham—who's booking them with everyone from Youssou N'Dour to George Thorogood and the Neville Brothers—they were magnetizing exuberant young "fellow travelers" with original harp-driven astral projections, aptly described by guitarist Chan Kinchla: "You rock their brains out and leave body parts against the wall."

Strong melodic hooks glue those body parts back together, and what makes their music so damn fun to dance to is the push/pull dynamic between familiar ground and uncharted territory.

Though Blues Traveler was born in a Princeton, NJ basement, this is not your standard-issue garage band. Popper is a jazz-trophy winner who was dubbed the "Eddie Van Halen of the harmonica" by MTV's Dweezil Zappa; Sheehan and drummer Brendan Hill ran their respective Dead and Led Zep licks through the same New School jazz program that nurtured Popper; Kinchla copped his chops laying Jimmy Page riffs over TV commercials and pushed the group over the edge of the stoned jam.

Wordman Popper scat-sings lyrics that are often cleverly ironic and sometimes keep-the-faith earnest ("the truth will set you free is what I hear them say, and to my sweet surprise it does work out that way"). "Brother John" addresses Sheehan's real-life sibling—a now reformed crackhead who's become a frontline boogie-er—and is emblematic of B.T.'s extended-family ethos. When Bill Graham signed the band, he got a package deal: Four support-system comrades share equal status with the musicians.

"Blues Traveler is simply the best young band I've seen in New York—they're fresh, they rattle their bones and they make you feel good," says Graham, who immediately booked them at last fall's Housing Now march with Tracy Chapman, Jefferson Airplane and Stevie Wonder. And that feeling was confirmed when one-hundred-and-fifty-thousand fans reacted in the same jubilant manner.

Graham was led to Blues Traveler by his son, David, who caught them at a Columbia frat house gig and is now helping oversee A&M contract negotiations. Popper says the sudden leap from bar band to big biz is "strange. But even stranger is finding you have the capacity to deal with it." After all, B.T.'s ultimate goal is to shoot the moon.

"I wanna play weightless," says Kinchla. "The moving shuttle gig," adds Popper. "We want to be the first band in space," sums up Sheehan. "And you have to be a pretty big band to do that."

## It's OK to Be Happy

*Downtown Express*, October 1990

***Two Bands are Converting a New Generation to Rock and Roll.***

Every once in a while, the human heart colludes with the cosmos in a conspiracy of hope. When that conspiracy takes the form of music–as when the trance-dance reign of New Orleans voodoo queen Marie Laveau and the juke-joint blues of the rural South joined at the hip to spawn the divine, two headed monster known as rock and roll–it enters the realm of magic.

For the past couple years, a black cat's been stalking the bars of lower Manhattan in the guise of a band called Blues Traveler. Together with their brother band, Spin Doctors, who only emerged last May, they've created the most cohesive live music scene to magnetize a mostly young (fifteen—twenty-five), mostly white New York population since the hardcore heyday of the early '80s.

But hardcore was a kind of ecstatic rage. This music reinvents the communal spirit of the '60s with voices as original and fresh as the '90s, and has a much wider embrace: the ecstatic transformation of rage into joy, or what Blues Traveler bassist Bobby Sheehan calls "a fabulous festival of fun." It's a concept so antithetical to the ironic distance cultivated by New York trend mongers that, while inspiring a full-fledged phenomenon, it's been totally missed by the media. It has not, however, been ignored by the music industry.

"The world is their oyster right now," says A&M's Patrick Clifford, the A&R exec who signed Blues Traveler after being "literally devastated" by gigs at such downtown clubs as Mondo Cane, Nightingale's and the Wetlands. "They're reinventing a tradition of incredible live music that connects with people, and people want to be part of it. They already have a strong clan network around the country, and when they play with Spin Doctors, you get five hours of nonstop music that's totally outrageous. They're gonna make a lotta, lotta people happy for a lotta, lotta years."

Young "fellow travelers" now look back nostalgically on Blues Traveler gigs of just last year, when their ranks numbered in the dozens, rather than thousands. "The last 'Gale gig, the night they got signed, was so hard," recalls Parsons' student Kelli Stevens, who was there from day one, when you hugged every person in the room and the band announced your entry from the stage. "I was crying because I was so incredibly proud, but also because it was the end of our Blues Traveler. Now they're everybody's."

It was, of course, the messianic fervor of fans like Kelli that helped make the scene grow as fast and furious as one of the Traveler's blues/speed jams. "Both bands snowballed really quickly, partly because of this tribal loyalty," says Tom Hosier, manager of Nightingale's, the downtown dive that was Blues Traveler's basecamp before they outgrew its confines. (You can still catch the more recently formed Spin Doctors there, but not for long.) Older bands like the Worms and the Surreal McCoys, who did the seminal spadework for the Nightingale's scene, are somewhat bemused by all the hoopla.

"We gave these young'uns gigs opening for us," recalls the Worms' Jono Manson, thirty, whose work-the-crowd energy inspired both bands. "Now we're lucky if we can get a gig opening for them. But bottom line, I'm really happy they caught that wave."

The swelling wave is the kids, says Hosier, "who will go see Blues Traveler or Spin Doctors six or seven nights a week. They'll follow them to New Haven and Philadelphia, even California. The obvious comparison is to the Grateful Dead scene."

There's a definite cross-pollination from the recent influx of youth into the ranks of old-guard Deadheads; a small army of them shot straight from last month's Madison Square Garden show over to the Traveler's Marquee gig. "The Dead aren't gonna be around forever," as one young Deadhead observes. "The Travelers are like my age. They don't sound like the Dead, but it's a similar vibe, and this is like *our* music, *our* band."

Blues Traveler blossomed concurrently with the '60s revival at the Wetlands, which can no longer advertise what was once their house band. At a recent gig, five-hundred kids waited in the rain hoping to get into an already over-packed house, while the trendy dance club Quick! languished for lack of customers next door. Earlier that night, I caught Rudolf, the infamous club impresario who'd just washed his hands of Quick!, fleeting by like a black-clad ghost. "I haven't had a thought in years," he said with a thin-lipped smile when asked to opine about the tie-dyed encampment outside Wetlands. "But, yeah, definitely, there's a comeback of live music."

Rudolf's former employee Walter Durkacz, who made his name as a DJ on the old Mudd Club/Danceteria circuit and now books Wetlands bands, is more emphatic. "A lot of the old club people don't understand this is history in the making. These kids are doing the '60s in their own way, for the '90s, and it's like nothing that ever happened before. It's a thing in itself. Blues Traveler is not a retro band in any respect, and neither is Spin Doctors, who are definitely the next link on this chain."

Nor are they alone. Though no other contenders have yet incited the familial zeal of the Traveler/Doctor scene, '60s-vibe bands like Phish and Widespread Panic are kindred spirits. "We've come to realize," says the Traveler's John Popper, "we're part of something that's happening all over the place."

The rapid ascent of Blues Traveler, who just released their A&M debut album, has something to do with Bill Graham, who signed them last year and began booking them to open arena acts like the recent Allman Brothers tour. But the momentum came from the scene itself. Graham was hipped to the band by his son David, a Columbia student, who's now hands-on manager with peer Tom Gruber. And the family babysitter inspired manager David Sonnenberg (who put Meatloaf and Jimmy Cliff on the charts) to check out Spin Doctors.

"It was an extremely easy sell," says Sonnenberg, who signed them to CBS/Epic Associated within a month. (An EP's due this Christmas, with an album to follow.) "I brought record people downtown to these little bars, packed with passionately excited fans who knew every word to every song with no record out. We really had our pick of labels."

It's time now to speak of the source of all this passionate excitement: the music. Blues Traveler, observes Darren Greene–creator of the ubiquitous black cat logo, and now Spin Doctors' artist/merchandiser "is not your average, MTV-ready band. You got a huge fat guy who looks like a combination of John Belushi and Elvis playing the harmonica." But, oh, how that fat guy can play.

John Popper, twenty-three, approached harmonica the way Hendrix did the guitar, as a vehicle more than an instrument-in-itself, lifting the blues harp to the demonically celestial realms of Charlie Parker. "That guy's got the groove in his back pocket," said jazz maestro Chico Hamilton upon hearing him play.

"The ferociousness of the harp grabbed me instantly," recalls Frans Westra, an original fellow traveler known as the Vibe Tribe captain. "And the entire band had this very fluid jam going. What I saw from the beginning was this whole fervor feeling that it's actually okay to be happy."

Over the past years, goosed by nonstop gigging and arena dates that earned them encores opening for Jerry Garcia and the Allman Brothers, the band, always good, has melded into greatness. Chan Kinchla, twenty-one (guitar); Bobby Sheehan, twenty-two (bass); and Brendon Hill, 20 (drums) weave effortlessly in and out of the Traveler's canon of original songs, incorporating whatever occurs to them onstage. (Like wrapping "Sweet Talking Hippie" around the Stones' "Miss You" and "Bad to the Bone.") Complex chord collisions come out of nowhere, time compresses space, then slingshots back to "hit you right between the eyes," as Traveler soundman/Panfish producer Richard Vink puts it. "If you don't wanna get hit, you'd better duck."

Of course, that's why you're there: to get hit, to get the rush that inevitably happens when "G-L-O-R-I-A" pops up anthemically, the purest moment of sheer exaltation in this cosmic revival meeting of trance-dance possession. "There is," says Traveler artist Tim Vega, summing it up perfectly, "no separation between you and the band."

What "Gloria" is to Blues Traveler, "House" is to Spin Doctors. We're still in the house of the Lord, but this is a throw-the-Pharisees-out-of-the-temple kind of Lord. Poet laureate/vocalist Chris Barron, twenty-two, composes adhoc verses on the spot, but the chorus, joined loudly by the crowd, remains the same: "This is my house, if you don't like it just get outta, get outta, get outta." Barron, a rubber-band performer with a limber tongue, believes, like Popper, "life is a work of art you create yourself. At my best, I serve as an example that you can build your own house. I think the world created us, the scene made the clay, and maybe we're just shaping it."

The Doctors–who include Eric Schenkman, twenty-six (guitar); Mark White, twenty-eight (bass); and Aaron Comess, twenty-two (drums)—have a back-beat funk, and an almost hip-hop edginess to their tunes that's very different from the Traveler's blues/rock/jazz collisions. (And which some observers feel may ultimately make them more mainstream radio-ready.) What they share is monster musicianship in which every member of the band has equal weight; a complete commitment to the endless boogie and present time (neither band follows setlists); the jazz-savvy dictums of The New School (where all but Kinchla and White improvised); and, believe it or not, Princeton, New Jersey.

It's my theory that aliens landed in button-down, ivied Princeton, where all the Travelers, their road manager and the Doctors' Chris Barron were high school buddies. Barron has another explanation: "Princeton was like the wall we were banging our heads against; it gave me fuel to show those uptight bastards I could do really well."

The blood-brother bonding cemented among these rebels-with-a-cause became the root of their extended family ethos, which empowers the music with an open heart.

"I was an outcast, like a lot of us," says private school student Sasha Krienik, an original fellow traveler. "Nobody's taken at face value in this scene; people want to know who you are." Adds scene newcomer Jennifer Lipman, "You don't feel like an outsider coming in. You see people who didn't know where they fit, and made their own place to fit." And if someone's hurting, help is on the way. When Bobby Sheehan's brother, John, was crash burning on drugs, Blues Traveler tossed him a collective lifeline called "Brother John," which remains a rousing crowd sing-along."

"That song was my rehab," says John, who recovered to become one of the most boundlessly energetic presences at gigs. "The band has the power to change a life, and that's a big, big thing."

It's also a recurring theme. "The band writing 'Gina' basically changed my life," says Gina, an original fellow traveler immortalized on their album who's now employed as "Fan Relations" liaison. Merchandising chief Tim Vega–who together with Darren Greene created the visual explosion of poster, T-shirt, and mural art integral to the scene's proliferation–echoes this sentiment: "Blues Traveler basically changed my life."

The Traveler's entire workforce, which now numbers an even dozen, are all familial fans; like Spin Doctors' road manager/troubleshooter Jason Richardson, they began as volunteer equipment-schleppers and flyer-mongers. "We're just a new extension of an old family," believes flutist Roger Fox, who sits in regularly with both bands and is, at thirty, their elder statesman. "The family's been around for thousands of years."

Like any family, old or new, it's also had its downside. "When the family was its strongest, all of us, except Blues Traveler, who had night jobs, were blowing off our lives in a big way," recalls Sasha, who's now cracking the books to catch up to her college aspirations. "But some nights were blessed. I appreciate all the life lessons."

And the Traveler's mounting success has brought an inevitable dilution of the old intimacy with what Sasha calls "superficial pseudo-hippieness."

"There's always a trade-off," agrees Popper. "Soon it will become schlocky like the last scene that was here in the '60s, and then another scene will happen. But I think the heart's gonna last a very long time 'cause there's a genuine need for good music."

During a Traveler/Doctors outdoor show in Greenwich, time warped amid twenty-five-hundred fans half my age, I had a revelation: it's all in the segue, which these guys have made into an art form, seamlessly from band to band so the music never stops. Maybe this whole '60s/'90s thing is just a twenty-year segue. "Always stretch a segue," laughs Popper when I advance this theory. And Chris Barron—who was conceived in 1968 on a boat carrying his father to a Pearl Harbor stopover en route to Vietnam—spins it out to the stars and back.

"All of us born at that time have got to have the '60s in our subconscious, and there was a lot of genius going on in the '60s. Genius isn't a personal thing. When you write a poem about the moon, the moon has a share in it, and all the poets before you, and everything you ever heard and ever saw. It's not the individual, it's the artistic-tide that's important.

We have to be careful that people like Dan Quayle don't turn the '60s into just tie-dyed T-shirts. It's got to be more than dye in a bucket. There has to be a tie."

## Jam Today: And the Lord Said Reclaim Rock 'n' Roll (And They Did)

*Downtown*, June 1991

Several eons ago, back in the spring of '89, I decided I was outta here. Oh-so-cool New York, with its velvet-roped prisons posing as palaces and its sad pseudo scene of jerk-off "art" rock and jackhammer noise bands, was clearly no place for a hot boogie queen whose spirit was withering from the lack of Real Music. So I said screw this town, I'm moving to New Orleans.

Then two things happened, almost simultaneously, that not only changed my mind, but fundamentally changed my life.

The first was called John Campbell, and the wholly unholy holy spirits he was raising on his 1934 National Steel guitar, over in the corner of a little Vietnamese restaurant called Monsoon, revealed the deepest, most secret recesses of the blues to my own body and soul.

The second was a young jam band called Blues Traveler, who rocked me so far out and rolled me so far in—over at this funky little place called Nightingale where they played like there was no tomorrow—that I was bathed in an aura of radiant light.

John Campbell taught me that the blues song is a victory. Blues Traveler taught me to trust in trust. And lo and behold, miracles began to happen in New York City.

Just this week, in the span of a single day, I toasted John Campbell's publishing deal while the final mixes from his Elektra debut album raised the hair on my neck; listened to rough cuts from Blues Traveler's second A&M disc, *Travelers and Thieves*, which is a monster in the making; got word that, starting this Monday, Joe Flood's fabulous "Miss Fabulous"—the unofficial anthem of the whole bar-band scene—goes national as HBO's summer-season theme; and watched the Dreyer Brothers resurrect the spirit of the old Lonestar Cafe.

So, here's to all the true believers, the Real Music people of New York City, those who came before and those who followed. You know who you are.

But this one's for Blues Traveler, who started a revolution when they reclaimed rock 'n' roll.

As any fellow traveler can tell you—and there's thousands of us now, all across the country—when you really hook into Blues Traveler you sign on for De Tour, and half the fun of De Tour is getting there. For just like their music, it invariably involves all manner of sidetracks, backtracks and loop-de-loops, near-fatal crashes and roadside epiphanies.

So trust me, we will actually get there, to Suntan Lake, where Blues Traveler kicked off their summer tour season headlining an outdoor show with Steppenwolf and the Marshall Tucker Band that put real meat on the bones of that stoned-dude stock superlative: Totally Awesome. But this particular chapter of De Tour story begins at home, in New York City, up at RPM studios, where the band's *Travelers and Thieves* is currently being mixed.

"This may be totally off the wall," says Blues Traveler bass man Bob Sheehan, punctuating a notion that just popped into his head with a what-me-worry laugh, in much the same way that he automatic-pilots the band's space-shuttle orbits of ever-transiting segues. "But I was just wondering, since we have this gig coming up and we haven't played out for a while...do you think we should maybe, like, actually rehearse?"

There's a moment of stunned silence from all of the band members, convened here for a studio confab. Then Bobby cracks up, along with guitarist Chan Kinchla, while drummer Brendan Hill beams enigmatically. Finally, after mulling it over while his harp slingshots "Optimistic Thought" over the playback of today's mix, harmonica guru John Popper speaks.

"Nah," he concludes. "If we rehearse, we'll just start bummin' if we sound too sloppy, 'cause we won't have any energy coming back from a crowd. Let's just dive right into the gig." A roar of consensus echoes back from the Traveler team of championship divers. "What I'm gonna do," he adds, "is take a long walk, and that'll be my rehearsal."

John Popper did take that walk, a long walking-blues walk, and it was one helluva warm-up. Because he took it onstage with Gregg Allman, fresh from their studio sessions, where Gregg arrived wearing a Blues Traveler T-shirt to lay down some Hammond organ and vocal tracks on Traveler's "Mountain Cry." This walk occurred, serendipitously, at the Lonestar Roadhouse, after Rick Danko pulled a disappearing act for the entire second set at what was nominally his gig.

Danko's abdication was a gift from God. Because what we got, those of us fortunate enough to witness it, was some very serious blues from two cats who speak the same language, a heart-to-heart dialogue between two very old souls. By the time "Stormy Monday" brought Popper to his knees, his harp was whirling-dervish dancing so deep inside the sonorous chords of Gregg's moon-howling Hammond, they'd become one instrument. Then Gregg strapped on the guitar and Popper just kept wailing, the hellhounds hot on their trail as they turned "Rock Me Baby" inside out.

Not so coincidentally, my ride-hook to Suntan Lake, warrior chieftain T.J. Can-do, also bore witness to this quintessential segue into total Traveler turf. So, by the time we rev up the rental van, loaded with fellow travelers including Freddy the stuffed bear, proudly sporting his B.T. colors, we're so fuckin' psyched, and jonesin' so hard for Traveler after their six-week studio hiatus, we damn near teleport to the gig, where the mise-en-scene is gloriously surreal.

Suntan Lake is a kind of raging-hormones day camp, deep in the heart of Bon Jovi country, where some local tits and butts are fulsomely displayed on the diving board of an Olympic-sized wading pool that's flanked by a stable of motorcycles. But the main actions on a vast expanse of grass, where the assembled multitudes, four-thousand strong, have just been raucously "Born to Be Wild" with John Kay and Steppenwolf, and are jonesin' harder than ever for that ecstatic, epiphanic rush only the Traveler can provide.

So, for that matter, is the band—who lives and breathes to play live—though the backstage vibe is very en-famille mellow: Chan Kinchla's dad, Ron, gamely doing The Wave, flanked by Chan, Bobby and Popper; Traveler road honcho Grant cruising B.T. baby Cassady around in his stroller; and all the lovely ladies, flushed by the sun, their bodies glistening with swim-dew.

Then at last it comes, the dive-right-in moment when you buckle up your seat belts and get ready to ride the groove, a knee bone's-connected-to-the-thigh-bone kind of groove that shoots straight up the spine to the epicenter of the Blues Traveler experience—which is, of course, the rush: that arterial swell of life force that pulses through the collective entity the Traveler creates right here, right now, in this particular moment of time.

Today they hit hard with "Ivory Tusk," an I-am-you-and-you-are-me centrifugal forcefield centerpiece on the new album. And midway through, right at the juncture of that killer slow change, the first serious rush sweeps over the crowd, who lets out a long, collective cry of release. And it feels just like the Man says: "like rain fallin' down, washing every-thing away..."

Then Chan's guitar begins to climb, spinning a sitar mantra into outer space that boomerangs, growling and snarling, deep into the bowels of the earth, getting way, way down with "Gotta Get Mean." And fuck me if Bobby's bass doesn't goose that sucker straight into "Brother John," and suddenly Joan Osborne's up onstage for the a cappella chorus of skewed harmonies the Traveler has raised to an artform. And soaring above it all, as we swell into the hook of "Gloria," is that phenomenon of nature that is John Popper's harp, knock-knock-knocking on heaven's door, which opens ferociously back into "Mean" while Brendan drives it home with the heartbeat throb of his drums, staying the course.

And it's Nightingale's all over again, all these old songs segued together, but Nightingale's magnified to the nth power, for the Traveler keeps rising to meet its own challenges. (Not for nothing did they put in their time at The New School of Jazz, mentored by godfather Amie Lawrence.) The new "Sweet Pain" is precisely that, gently rising off Popper's acoustic guitar and gradually flaming into the hellfire heaven of Chan's final, out-of-left-field satanic solo, the one that etches him forever into the ranks of the heavyweights.

While Blues Traveler segues "Mulling it Over" into The Hit—"But Anyway," off the first album—I survey the crowd from a nearby hill. They appear to be a vast undulating wheatfield of color and light, or one gigantic organism composed of flesh and blood, born of the flash of the spirit that is the music and the moment.

Later, much later, after T.J. Can-do shotguns us back to the city, steering our wildly careening designated driver and our van-load of post-orgasmic Traveler-heads safely home; after we've wound down twice, first at Wetlands with a Traveler-inspired band called the Gooneybirds, then at Nightingale's for the late-night hang; I find myself downing some brews with Bob Sheehan, directly across from the old Fillmore East.

"You know," Bobby says, apropos of nothing, "we never really thought about what we were doing. We just went ahead and did it. And look what happened."

## Jam Today

### *Nightingale: Hot and Getting Hotter*

***Downtown*, June 1991**

*People who come to Nightingale are very obsessed with music. I don't blame them; I'm from North Africa so strong rhythm always moves me. Some are crazy, some are really beautiful people, all searching for beauty and something good.*
—**Sadig**, 13th St. Deli (The Nightingale Annex)

*I've probably played here with more different bands than any other musicians in New York. How many gigs? Shit...God...from day one? Thousands. Literally. Thousands. I wore a hole on the stage.*
—**Bassman Jerry Dugger**, one of the Founding Fathers

*Anything can happen at Nightingale. I've been there when people appeared to be having sex on the pool table. Anything goes, you can just let loose.*
—**Steve Eichner**, House Photographer

*I just try to keep myself entertained.*
—**Tom Hosier**, Temple Guard

As far as billiard-balling goes, you'll have to take Steve Eichner's word for it, though I can testify that tranced-out dancers have been known to mount the Nightingale jukebox. But it's the kind of thing that could have happened at any point during the eight-year existence of this Second Avenue spot, a Downtown legend even before it evolved into Scene Central, after Blues Traveler and Spin Doctors rocked the house so hard that all these crazy music-obsessed kids started coming in droves and even the industry suits took notice.

It's here that the Traveler popped champagne corks when they signed to A&M; here that CBS/Epic threw its in-house launch for the Doctors, making Nightingale's history with catered hors d'oeuvres; here that A&R types now routinely brave the beer-and-sweat soaked environs, scouting the Next Big Thing. The past five years of all its roof-raising history are documented in Eichner's retrospective photo show, which opened on Monday and will continue hanging on the walls of the 'Gale until probably forever.

Though the hole Jerry Dugger wore in the three-inch plywood riser that passes for a stage has since been covered by a mangy piece of carpet dragged in from Second Avenue; and the street front window where The Worms once held forth was long ago bricked over after neighbors complained about rock 'n' roll racket; the rest of the 'Gale's decor remains pretty much unchanged and stolidly ungentrified.

Grimy glass globes chandeliered on aging metallic limbs—one of which was permanently bent by flutist Roger Fox's head when it spun into free-fall during a fellow artist's bar-top performance—date back to a previous incarnation as a hamburger joint. A requisite nude hangs over the bar; defunct condom machines are enshrined in the bathrooms; and a dime store disco ball dangles above the black-and-white checked dance floor, which amounts to the entire house since the sole extant table is Tom's Table, up by the door.

Tom Hosier is the Temple Guard of Nightingale, where his job description reads: manager slash booker slash doorman slash pinch-hitting soundman slash wry-and-bemused observer of it all. And should anyone doubt that this bespectacled Charles Manson buff is one of the great unsung heroes of New York City, check this out. Right now, we're supposed to be doing an interview. But life has intervened, and instead he's air-dancing on the catwalk of my fifth-floor fire escape, trying to liberate the apartment I've been locked out of during the eighteen hours since the bag containing my Entire Life was summarily stolen.

"Bravo!" I cry, exultantly, after Tom spots the hidden barriers in the casings of my tiny bathroom window, opens it full up, and somehow manages to snake his long, lanky body through a space that would give a six-year-old pause. Not only has he rescued a damsel in distress; he's provided the perfect metaphor. Because what Nightingale has become during Hosier's three-year regime—and what was implicit since its inception—is a small, but highly effective, window of opportunity that's allowed some great New York bands to shimmy their way into the marketplace by creating a music-never-stops, no-holds-barred Scene that often spills exuberantly into the streets.

Tonight, as summer casts its sultry spell over 2nd Avenue and 13th Street, it takes me a good hour to actually work my way inside—where The Authority's driving a packed house into oblivion—because everyone's out, brown-bagging beers from the nearby deli, shooting the shit and networking on the kind bud circuit. Not that Hosier actively encourages the street action; he's already had to answer to one disorderly premises citation and isn't courting another. But he's savvy enough to recognize the Scene has long since taken on its own momentum, and that the Nightingale tradition of laissez-faire-is-more is part of the momentum.

What drives that momentum is, of course, the music, which created the Scene in the first place. And from its earliest incarnation as the house built by those legends-in-their-own-slime, The Worms; through the neo-psychedelic era of Dreamspeak, which conjuncted with the early stirrings of the anti-folk movement and segued into the jam-band launch pad for Blues Traveler, Spin Doctors, and their successors; Nightingale has been the kind of musical melting pot where sitting in is practically proforma. Thanks in part to its symbiotic relationship with the equally legendary blues bar Dan Lynch, just a couple doors down, any and all permutations are possible.

Though there have been a few 'star' drop-ins—the Allman Brothers' Warren Haynes, New Bohemians' Kenny Withrow and John Bush—it's our own New York all-star team that provides most of the action. And it really doesn't matter that the sound system consists of cast-off speakers (the bar only recently acquired more-or-less monitors, bequeathed by saxman Craig Dreyer); or that the bands' amps are lodged in upended barstools. Because it's state-of-the-art music issuing forth from Jono Manson's guitar or John Popper's harmonica or Joan Osborne's remarkable vocal cords—to name but the barest few—at whomever's actual gig it happens to be.

"It ain't Carnegie Hall, you know," observes Hosier, who religiously listens to new bands' tapes and even takes copious notes. "Droning alternative rock...dreary...terrible synth funk" are among his withering putdowns, but if you catch his ear, he'll definitely give you a shot. A bone-dry realist, Hosier also notes that "while a couple of bands have made it here, a lot more haven't and have broken up or whatever. It's a Darwinian process." And though, far from being a horn-tooter, he will, if pressed, concede that his own role in nurturing the life-force spirit that's been surging through the 'Gale is not entirely inconsequential.

"Well, of course," he says, with a minimal smile. "It's my show."

The beauty of that show is that it also belongs to all of us: to the musicians who make the 'Gale their home-away-from-home, dropping in on off-nights to enliven the late-night-stretch; to the ever-growing crowds who don't need a schedule to know that Real Music is almost invariably on the menu; to the street people, like the Tree Man, who sports a thriving bush on his head and is very much part of the Scene; to the guys at the 13th Street Deli, a.k.a. The Deli of Life, who not only have watched their business boom, but have become an integral pan of it all, proudly wearing the colors of their favorite bands and mixing it up on the dance floor.

As Sadig of the laughing eyes puts it, quite eloquently: "We're here in this deli four years now, and I never expected it to be this way. We've made so many friends, and all the things we were looking for, we finally got. A beauty that I've been searching for all my life."

## Jam Today: My First Dead Show

*Downtown*, July 1991

So, IT TOOK ME a couple of decades, but I finally caught up with the Grateful Dead. Or maybe the Dead caught up with me. In any case, a conjunction occurred on the space-time continuum of Giants Stadium, where a "Picasso Moon" rose over sixty-thousand Deadheads and this neophyte initiate, who was totally under-whelmed-and-thoroughly-overwhelmed-by the once-in-a-lifetime experience called My First Dead Show.

Ever since they separated from the epochal pack of San Francisco '60s rock bands to become a Phenomenon—first by simply surviving, then by building their mighty empire with its nomadic community of camp followers—The Grateful Dead have served as a kind of countercultural crucible, forging both Deadheads and Dead-dissers alike. Finally, after years of straddling the some-of-my-best-friends-are-Deadheads fence while Dead-dissers hissed in my ear, I decided it was high time to shit and get on the pot.

So, I hooked myself a trip-tick from Captain Hook himself, T.J. Can-do, who's riding serious shotgun while Bro Witt steers us out to Jersey, three hours behind schedule but right on time.

En route, my tour guides, now entering their third Dead decade, hip me to the Entire Situation: this isn't just a concert, it's an environment, a petting zoo, a dog-and-pony show. They also regale me with tales from the "Dark Star" dark side that make me glad I've worn my combat boots: the Bear Lake tear gassings back in '72; the kid who, just last year, was unceremoniously dumped to his death off a bridge by security thugs; the determined Deadhead who, undeterred by security-inflicted stab wounds, bled through an entire show and then stayed on tour. By the time we swing past the Midway of Jerryworld's GD Village, with its thriving common market of hippie hawkers and tailgate trippers, I'm expecting just about anything. including the Apocalypse.

As it turns out, we're blessed by the gods tonight, who not only cancel their scheduled thunderstorm, but radar us to the perfect parking spot, then waive the standard Dead show rules of Waiting and Standing. We cruise straight up to will-call, where our ticket packet miraculously contains an extra pair—instantly donated to the Mighty Sweetones' Jono Manson, who appears, serendipitously, at precisely the right moment. Then it's into the vast, ominously stark shell of Giants Stadium, where Little Feat has long since come and gone and the anticipatory buzz from the rainbow bedecked-and-bedazzled crowd is beginning to swell.

Stadium shows are *not* my métier; I haven't been on a playing field since Shea, when I went thrice in one week (but hey, that was for the Rolling fuckin' Stones, who have been, and will always be, My Band.) So there's the usual crowd-claustrophobe disorientation, tempered by a vibe that can only be called mellow (no tear-down-the-fences scenarios tonight). Then the band materialize on stage, gigantic video screens roll down, multicolored lights begin flashing to the strains of "Picasso Moon" and the entire stadium starts coming on to its Dead dose instantly.

Me, I wait so patiently, a stranger in a strange land. Everyone else goes nuts when they pull "Bertha" out of the hat, but I don't know the material, the codes, the familial signals—and, worst of all, I'm not getting off. The visuals seem to be overpowering the band, the music ain't getting inside my body. There's no vibrations I can seriously groove to, it all seems like so much psychedelic mood music, scattered to the winds. Then along comes "Red Rooster," which gives me some bearings, and even though I'm wishing it was Clapton or Mick. instead of Bob Weir, the blues inevitably draws me right up to the stage, where things begin to change.

Up close and personal, the Dead are grittier, the sound waves more compelling as the acoustics begin to crystallize, and they seem to read my mind, spinning me through "Candyman," "Memphis Blues," "Stagger Lee," tunes I can almost stomp to, amidst all these hippies. Now the music's inside my skin, big first step, but it hasn't yet raised my demons. "Blues Traveler!" the kid beside me yells, spotting my New York City home-team T-shirt, while I compare-and-contrast, still analyzing.

That's one reason I'm here, the Traveler/Dead connection, looped together not only by Bill Graham but by the sizable number of young Deadheads among Traveler fans. Both a boon and a curse, it lays the Traveler wide open to Dead-dissers, who've probably never heard either band's music. And though there's a similar communal jam vibe, the M.O.'s are radically different, despite the mainline connection between the Dead's Phil Lesh and Traveler bass man Bob Sheehan. The Traveler's about concrete cliff-dwellers scaling passed peaks, the Dead is more hills and valleys—less intense, more sinuous than sensual.

Now that I think I've got it, I'm ready to get into it. And come second set, I do, lured into a seductive web as the molten silver of Jerry's guitar insinuates itself into the keyboard tapestries of Bruce Hornsby and Vince

Welnick, their voices melding seamlessly as "Jackstraw" nestles inside the velvety-thick cocoon of Phil Lesh's bass. I get a serious buzz somewhere amidst "Crazy Fingers" and "China Cat," and suddenly I'm totally OFF, no longer at close range but at middle distance, where the synthesis of visuals and sound can wash over me.

It's an epic musical journey, the hills higher, the valleys deeper, crazy as the marching bears kaleidoscoping on the screens; as vividly close to the bone as the grinning skulls; as subtly saturated with color tonality as the scrims that flank the stage, like unfurled sails of a Chinese junk, melting images together in a Rauschenbergian kinesis of shadow and light. We land together gloriously with "I Know You Rider," and suddenly it's just us and the band again, Jerry's white hair flying behind him like angel wings. All of us singing "the sun's gonna shine in my back door again" like it was the Hallelujah Chorus.

An expectant hush falls over the crowd as Mickey Hart and Bill Kreutzmann begin a drum dialogue, amplified by video illusions in which they appear to be drumming their own, as well as each other's, bodies. Everyone else knows what's coming, but I have no idea; I just think it's a far-out drum duet until suddenly we're right in the center of the heartbeat of the Mother, Mickey Hart invoking her on his panoply of singing and soaring percussion instruments and gongs while Kreutzmann takes the tribal pulse of the Amazon rainforest that's appearing before our eyes.

The entire stadium's sitting down now—at a rock concert—because we're all in this kind of cosmic amphitheater. And though the guided meditation stumbles a bit when it segues live-action shots of unspoiled nature into the rainforest's devastation (the visual team could take a hint from the more menacing lyricism of Godfrey Reggio's *Koyaanisqatsi* here), still I catch my breath as a giant tree is felled upon us. Then gradually, almost imperceptibly, we're being transited out of the earth's gravitational pull, via Jerry's guitar, into "Space," a prolonged sense-surround meditation in which the silence between the notes defines their movement while the jet-propelled images tunnel me so far inside my own solar system I start to slip through the black hole.

Then—whoosh!—we're all up on our feet and back on terra firma, and there's this really terrific bar-band onstage, and Bob Weir's rousing my spirit so lustily with "I Need a Miracle" that it seems totally insane that I ever wished, even for an instant, that he was anyone other than Bob Weir.

I'm so far gone by now that the details begin to blur inside the overall feeling of being assimilated into the sinews of the music, into the inner mechanisms of the Entire Situation. But I do recall "Not Fade Away," how the band dematerialized and how the crowd kept the groove going, and going, and aging, like a super-animated version of the Traveler's "Sweet Talking Hippie"; and also my disappointment that, when they finally rematerialized, they didn't pick right up the groove, which I fully expected them to do (Travelerhead that I am), and polish off "Fade Away" before hitting with the encore. But hey, maybe next time.

And there will be a next time. I'm not gonna rearrange my life to go on Dead tour, but I now understand what it's like to be inside the Dead's head, and I like it in there, inside all those cranial crevices of multisensory perception. As for the trappings of Deadheadism—the dog-and-pony show of the parking lot scene—it's a great time-warp and a lotta fun, but it's so much window-dressing.

Because what matters to me most, as always, is that the music reaches me. Deeply. And the Grateful Dead finally reached me. Deeply. Period. The end.

## The Iliad and the Mosh Pit: New York City Jam Bands Hit Lollapalooza

*Downtown*, August 1991

THE SUMMER OF '91 was more than a little pregnant. Even before Lollapalooza lanced the crepuscular boil of the Reagan/Bush era, boundaries were beginning to bleed, blotting out the '80s like some Rorschach rabbit test. Raging hormones came home to roost, not only in Seattle, but in New York City, where the space/time continuum bent under the weight of rampant wish fulfillment, in the form of Blues Traveler, Spin Doctors and their hyper-attenuated families of hot hippie kids and Byronic boho rockers.

Most of that long hot summer, The Bands—as we still referred to them en famille—labored in the road tour trenches, unleashing '60s libido into America's frat-brat/mall-rat bloodstream. But one sticky August morning, sometime after noon, in the Doctor's now-defunct East Village crash pad, several horsemen of this Apocalyptic Renaissance made ready to test their mettle at Lollapalooza—armed not with their trusty laminates, or even backstage silks, but only their own sweet insouciance.

"Potassium sky juice, people?"

Chris Barron grins at the assembled company, his lips glistening with the froth of the banana 'shroom milkshake that will psychoactive our journey to the fields of Waterloo in Stanhope, NJ, where Lollapalooza is encamped. Fresh from a shower that purged the sweat of two back-to-back shows on the Wetlands stage, Spin Doctors' poet laureate looks quite natty in a nerdy sort of way: a pristine straw fedora tops a spanking white T-shirt tucked into sensible walking shorts. ("I'm practicing to be an old Jewish man," quips Chris, who has, in truth, just bid a lingering farewell to his brief-but-hectic career as a rock and roll slut.)

"Twist my arm, dude," laughs Blues Traveler guitarist Chan Kinchla, grabbing the sky juice with a massive hand that dwarfs the blender as he downs a hefty hit. Bare-chested, sun-burnished and freshly laid, our resident Hippie Hunk sports Air Jesus sandals as eminently unsuitable for the mosh-pit as Chris Barron's whites. Tattooed on Chan's bicep is the Traveler's joint-smoking black cat mascot, brainchild of Darren Greene, also known as D. Spin/Traveler artist and perpetual prodigal son, D's the

Jane's Addicted organizer of the Lollapalooza foray; designated den mutha is Mama Luke, the Doctors' road-seasoned drum tech and today's acting polestar, whose six-and-a-half-feet make him easy to spot.

Representing Gaia in this rather incestuous group is the radiant Kalista, a young woman of many gifts. Soul sister to Chris Barron, whose lit-crit citations she can match one for one, Kalista once bested the Traveler A-Team in the brutal drinking game of quarters (no small feat). I'm aboard as the tribe scribe, and though a woman of a certain age, my operative script of the moment is My Life As A Teenage Boy. This whole trip is kind of a Boy Thing, a sly commando raid with a rite-of-passage subtext, inspired in no small part by the siren call of our host, Perry Farrell, who's been looping on the Doctors' tour bus for the past few months.

"The first time D and I heard Jane's Addiction was in a Dunkin Donuts somewhere outside Chicago," Chris recalls as we pull into Waterloo Village, our windshield wipers clicking merrily (and inexplicably) away under a cloudless blue sky. "The tune 'Summertime Rolls.' It sounded like weather or foam on the ocean or reeds in the wind, something God would do offhandedly. I felt like I sometimes do after making love to a woman—standing in Dunkin Donuts, eating some fuckin honey-dipped donuts and just listening to that song."

Weaving our way through the honey-dipped flesh of suntanned hippies, and the far more predominant permutations of sunburnt vampires, we make a low-key entrance into the concert grounds, lingering by the beer stand to get our bearings. Traveler fans and Spinheads periodically materialize, offering joints and sometimes seeking counsel. "If you call yourself something that comes up in everyday conversation," Chris advises one fledgling rock band, "you'll already be a household word." "Yeah," concurs Chan. "It's amazing how often Traveler pops up."

Things start to go ballistic when the Butthole Surfers attack the stage with their Texas chain saw massacre, scattering our forces and setting off a three-beer alarm in my bladder. I'm jockeying for position in the Porta-San line when a strange apparition lurches into my peripheral sightline: a towering human phallus teeters above the crowd on the side of the field, a tiny hat perched on its tip–holy shit, it's Chris! For an instant I think he's shroomed his way up. Then my eyes travel down the shaft and I recognize D, who's shouldering Chris and, sure enough, there's Chan, rooting the whole erection.

"We busted a triple!" D shouts triumphantly, minutes or hour later (sometime after Kalista and I lace our cokes with mescaline), giving me a quick high five as he hurtles toward the pit. Nine Inch Nails just hit. Fuck it. Enough lolly-gagging on the sidelines like some friggin mosh-pit virgin (which, in truth, I am.) I'm going *IN*.

My eyes fixed on Mama Luke, who's standing tall in the center of the fray, I enter the molecular structure of the mosh-pit, notebook in hand, scribbling WAVE-FORM PHYSICS and GLOBAL PLATE TECTONICS as I make my way over, under around and through shape-shifting nuclei and free-floating electrons that collide, merge, and boomerang like billiard balls careening off the left ban of the Body Electric. I'm thinking Life against Death, I'm thinking Norman O. Brown, when I reach my 'hood, my own particular microcosmic air pocket. Where a hardcore hoedown's in full swing.

Yes, folks, Little Miss' Mister "she holds the shotgun while you do-si-do" Chris Barron is cuttin' some barnyard rug. Swing your partner 'round and 'round, Chris and Chan and D, breaking the set with the rules of the game. Serious sidebar, comic relief! Segue into three-quarter time, Blue Danube country and (footnote for Spinheads) 'Gunsmith's Waltz,' all danced to the thrash of Nine Inch Nails. Who at this point splinters a cheap guitar, hurling the detritus into the madding crowd. D, on a roll, snags the neck in mid-flight. Bingo! And on this trophy is written: "Played by NIN."

I'm thinking, whoa, ANAIS NIN!? Fancy meeting you here, you high-toned boho whore! Is this Henry Miller's schlong? Can we suck him back to life? I'm thinking Henry and June, I'm even thinking Uma Thurman. (Those lips!) The last thing I see, before I offer myself to Living Colour, surfing on the sweat of strangers' souls, is Chris Barron's battered straw hat bobbing up and down on the Sea of Flesh like the grin of the Cheshire cat.

I don't have to tell you about Jane's. Or maybe I do, now that it's ancient history. POW! Smack in the Soul Kiss kisser. Blood Wedding. Cheap red wine. Dionysian dialectics, doggie-style. (Arf!) Pyrrhic polytechnics, Porta-San purges in Perry's vomitorium. Pure polymorphous perversity. Lair of the White Worm. Intimation of Immor(t)ality. Sympathy for the She-Devil, fiddling while Nero burns. Crush of breasts, buttocks and dicks, none of them (all of them) mine. Group (safe) sex, the mosh-pit as the ultimate condom. Or maybe not. Up against the fence, a skinhead is humping a skanker chick, his butt cheeks pumping out a punchline channeled by Papa Legba and his high holy fool, Perry Farrell. Nothing's Shocking, sex is violent, thank you boys.

"It was a fuckin pisser, goddamit," raves our family photographer Psychner after the smoke settles and the lights come up. "I got fuckin moshed and squashed and fuckin half-laid by a freakin hot bitch, it was fuckin CRAZY." I've lost my sweat shirt, Kalista's lost her money and keys, and we've all long since lost our minds. But Chris has hung on to his hat, his trusty mosh-pit mojo, which is rupturing straw like Dorothy's scarecrow; mangled and muddied by dust and sweat, his T-shirt's turned into a toga and he looks like Marc Antony on the way to Oz.

"I've been Lollapalooza-ed!" Chris proclaims, brandishing his hat in testament as we lurch, hobble and limp our way back to the van, fueled by enough endorphins to stagger an elephant. "We had some pride in there, buddy!" D crows, stabbing the sky with his captured NIN neck. "I've been totally brutalized," Chan exults, beaming down at his own war trophies: bloodied and battered feet that braved the pit in his Air Jesus sandals, surviving toe-to-toe combat with countless Doc Martens. "My body hurts so bad and that feels so GOOD," sums up Kalista as we straggle into the parking lot, where we stumble into a comic opera right next to our van.

Seems early this afternoon, in a stoner fuckup worthy of Wayne and Garth, the members of a local funk band called Gangway Fathead–which Chris promptly rechristens Gangway Knucklehead–managed not only to lock the keys in their car, but to leave them in the ignition with the engine running. Nor did they notice this oversight. They simply headed for the concert, which means a good ten hours of juice has been draining from the car's poor battery while its owner got Lollapalooza-ed. We watch with sympathetic bemusement while a succession of Knuckleheads probe for possible points of entry, all to no avail, until Chan can no longer restrain himself from stating the obvious.

"Bust a window!" he shouts, and then, as if on cue, we all take up the cry. "Bust a WIN-dow (clap, clap), bust a WIN-dow (stomp, stomp)" we chant, getting a mean groove going and banging on the hood of the van as we build to a crescendo: "BUST A FUCKIN WIN-DOW!!!"

We wait for the climactic crash of splintering glass that surely must follow. But NO. The car's owner—a drummer, no less—stubbornly refuses to smash his way in. By this time, we're the last two vehicles left in the lot, and everyone's chilled to the bone. Still, we can't leave the Knuckleheads and it's Mama Luke to the rescue. Taking charge, he strides directly to the hatchback with his drum tech kit, and performs some sleight-of-hand magic that pops the lock open. "If that hadn't happened," he confides when we finally drive off, our good deed done, "I was fully gonna bust a fuckin window!"

Cruising back to the city, totally spent and still adrenalin-rushing, we compare notes. "I was like fondling this fuckin hot chick, she was all over me," D reports, gloating. "Did you see when Perry French-kissed the guitarist?" asks Chan, still pretty impressed. "They've been doing that for years," Kalista says, dismissively. "What I want to know is, what were those two women doing onstage? All I could see was a butt going up once in a while." "They did more than that," Chan grins. "They were like nothing's shocking. They were doing each other doggie style; that's the funny part."

So, just for the record, what's it all about boys?

"You're fuckin crammed in front of the stage, totally surrounded by people crushing your chest, sharing each other's sweat, sharing each other's breath, trying to become one," is Chan's response. "And it's like Perry said, where are you all trying to go? I dunno Perry. Same place you are. I feel like I've cut all the strings, like I'm gonna just give myself to the crowd and see what happens."

"In terms of the press of flesh, it was a lot like the battle of the Iliad," muses Chris, who's been dipping into Homer for his light summer reading. "All those guys pushing each other apart so they could fuckin get a sword between each other's ribs. 'The screams of the dying mingled with the vaunts of their destroyers.' Think of the horror! And Zeus is releasing the dogs of war and panic and strife on the field.'"

Yikes! Heady thoughts. Which takes a Homer erotic turn as we cruise back into town through Hell's Kitchen, where the working girls and drag queens look radiantly fetching tonight. "I want to see a man's lipstick on my dick," Chris says suddenly, not entirely in jest. To which Kalista rejoins "go for it Chris!" The boys laugh it off as just Chris being cute and the moment passes, just another roadside attraction.

In truth, the closest Chris comes to actually having kinky sex is a late-night snack threesome, back at his pad: "Cap'n Crunch, the milk and me." But it's the kind of remark Perry would have loved and, after all, it's the thought that counts.

"For me, Lollapalooza was a good boost to the ineffable," Chris concludes, polishing off the Cap'n Crunch and chasing it with a sardine sandwich. "Getting up on a little step ladder to try to get your fist full of heaven. Even though you physically can't, knowing that in your dreams, when you do, it's true."

## Rolling with the Spin Doctors

*High Times* cover story, October 1991

### *THE DOCTORS R IN...ARMED WITH A NEW ALBUM FEATURING THE POT ANTHEM, "MARY JANE," NEW YORK'S SPIN DOCTORS TOOK THEIR SHOW ON THE ROAD THIS SUMMER TO WOODSTOCK AND BEYOND...*

"WELCOME TO THE THIRD act, people!"

With a deft flick of his wrist, as if conjuring white rabbits out of the high-hat of Aaron Comess's drum kit, Spin Doctors' singer Chris Barron greets the late-show audience at New York's Bottom Line—the band's last pit-stop before a major world tour with Cracker and Gin Blossoms that includes Woodstock '94 and opening several Rolling Stones dates. For two nights running, the Doctors have been loosening the seams of this normally staid industry showcase to christen *Turn It Upside Down* (Epic), the long-awaited follow-up to their multiplatinum studio debut, *Pocket Full of Kryptonite*. Now they bust the joint wide open.

As the band launches the spiral trajectory of "Uranium Century"—the B-side of the new album's jazzy first single, "Cleopatra's Cat"—an overflow crowd of old and new faithful spills exuberantly into the aisles. "I'd like to know which mushroom it will be," sings Barron, stretching his elastic tenor around the radioactive riffs of guitarist Eric Schenkman, the phat undertow of Mark White's rainbow-colored bass and the hypnoerotic pulse of Comess' drums. "The lightning shows…the uranium century...?" It's the same question posed by psychoactive futurist Terence McKenna, and tonight the menacing mushroom cloud is clearly eclipsed by the metaphoric magic of 'shrooms. The moon is in groove; the crowd's up for grabs and the Doctors are playing a GIG.

Doors of perception fly open in the rabble-rousing "House," inviting all comers to the temple of present time. Celebrants wing their partners 'round when the sweetly goofy "Mary Jane" rolls us all up in a home-grown hoedown. By the time Blues Traveler harmonica man John Popper teleports into the encore—planting his girth firmly amidst the delicate lyricism of "How Could You Want Him (When You Know You Could Have

Me?)"—the room's become one huge Cheshire cat grin, and the weight of the light is palpable. As Barron says later, still somewhat in awe: "It felt like something momentous was happening."

Indeed. And the collective forcefield of that momentous "third act"—which Comess calls "the really true essence of Spin Doctors"—was also the perfect segue into the Doctors' own Act Ill. Acts I and II being, by my reckoning, "Killer New York Bar Band Hits the Road" and "Heavyweight Hitmeisters Bust It Bigtime." Act Ill is a work-in-progress. This is, as Comess notes, less with trepidation than anticipatory glee, "a very mysterious time for the band." Still, some predictions can be made.

"I have a hunch," says Schenkman, sitting cross-legged on the floor of his down-town Manhattan loft, "that with the new record out, we can get back into what we used to do. Because the audience will be that much more familiar with our material." One of several gospelizers on a compilation disc now in heavy rotation chez Schenkman, the superbly nuanced tones of Marion William are born aloft by a new sound system cobbled together from the guitarist's own aural history: the same Dynakit tuner assembled by his father in the '60s, picked up for a song second-hand; a Canadian-made amplifier; custom monitor speakers gleaned from the *Upside Down* sessions.

Passing a joint, Schenkman goes on to delineate the Doctors' Act II learning curve: "When you're playing for thousands of people who've never seen you before, and maybe only know one song because you've moved into that hit radio shit, it's more effective to play basically the same set, referencing the record. *Soul Asylum* was kicking our ass for the first part of the [1993 MTV Alternative Nation] tour before we figured that out, and turned it around. Now I think we can take a step back and be more intimate—which for us means playing the evening and the room, as opposed to 'the show.'"

Spin Doctors' old Act I intimacy was born in New York City on the cusp of the '90s, when the band played marathon, mix-it-up gigs eight nights a week and their ever-growing following of fans cohered into an ad hoc family. But you needn't have been there to be there. Encoded in the tracks of *Turn It Upside Down*—recorded in New York City during a freak March blizzard that yielded a fistful of first-take wonders—is an aural/oral history of Spin Doctors. "It's got layers to it," Schenkman notes. "You can peel it back, like an onion."

You can, for instance, follow the tail of "Cleopatra's Cat" back to the band's inception and subsequent transformation.

Set the wayback machine to 1989. Chris Barron has just been liberated from his pizza-parlor roost in Princeton, NJ by his high school buddies

Blues Traveler, who've dragged him into the heart of their own exploding neo-hippie scene. Amidst the communal chaos of the Traveler's Bergen St. Brooklyn pad—a greasy breakfast-special era immortalized on "Hungry Hamed's"—Barron starts pounding out lyrics for "Cleopatra's Cat" and other tunes on the kitchen table. He also tags along with Popper to Arnie Lawrence's New School of Social Research jazz class, where Torontonian Schenkman and Texan Comess are among an elite subculture of rockers being initiated by enlightened jazz masters.

After preliminary head-butts with Schenkman over some long-forgotten territorial pissings, Barron bonds with him and Comess. The drummer recruits his Queens-bred bassist bandmate White from their funk band, Spade. White just happens to have this upbeat bassline that meshes with "Cleo's Cat."

While Spin Doctors are busy being born, Barron ventures onstage with Blues Traveler as a solo acoustic act, where "Cleo" becomes his signature segue into the Traveler's second set. The song soon becomes a staple of the now-solidified Spin Doctors shows, which quickly take on a life of their own during the Mondo Cane/Nightingale epoch of late-night madness celebrated on "Laraby's Gang." Semi-retired from active duty during the post-Epic signing "red van period"—when the Doctors hit the highway with a ferocity invoked by "Bag of Dirt"—"Cleo" resurfaces as a crowd-pleasing segue into their mega-hit "Little Miss Can't Be Wrong" on last summer's Alternative Nation tour.

Fast forward to early '94. Fresh from a series of New York City improv gigs under the moniker Wasabi with Popper and Lawrence ("Invasion of the Jam Bands," June '94 HT)—which bequeaths the out-of-the-blue(s) "Beast in the Woods"—Schenkman, White and Comess converge on Barron's newly-acquired "little red farmhouse" in rural Washington state. There, amidst blackberry thickets and crowing roosters, they throw everything into the pot. Goosed by what Schenkman calls "that dance thing," the scatty, swingin' "Cleo" makes the pre-production A-list, and eventually emerges in the studio as the world's most unlikely rock single. "We're the Spin Doctors," shrugs Comess. "We always do things upside down."

During the video shoot in the Temple of Dendur in the Metropolitan Museum's Egyptian wing—"Egypt came to us," quips Barron—a final transformation occurs. "The coolest part was we were jammin' between takes," recalls Schenkman, "and it started to feel like a gig. The Temple turned into a club."

Talk about coming full circle. Kind of like the way Schenkman's paramour Linda Kelly turned a bummed-out afternoon as a ski-slope widow into the imagistic poetry of "Indifference," which became a hauntingly beautiful ballad after she slipped her lyrics into Schenkman's guitar case. Or the way "You Let Your Heart Go Too Fast" was miraculously reborn out of the foul rag-and-bone shop of moldering rejects to become a country-honk hit. But the most alchemical twist of all pivots on "Mary Jane," which metamorphosed from a manic-depressive ditty into what Barron describes as "a love song to pot."

"Mary Jane" dates back to Fun Bunnies, an early Spin Doctors' side-project featuring Barron and partner Ben Lewis as a kind of literate, latter-day Everly Brothers. "Chris had written a similar song called 'The Other Day' with really mean-spirited lyrics," recalls Lewis at the record release party at The Cooler where, in a very backstage-with-Spin-Doctors scenario, he's playing chess with Barron's brother Jeremy (a.k.a. "The Prophet").

"It was a very harsh, but kind of entertaining song about a girl who killed herself," says Barron, who picks up the story on a buttery leather sofa just outside the velvet curtains of the chess-game room, looking very neo-Renaissance in a soft paisley shirt that reflects the reddish-gold highlights in his beard. "But it was really too harsh for my sensibilities, so I never played it. Then one day Ben and I decided we should write a really cool song about pot because there aren't many good ones. And Ben said let's write it to the music of 'The Other Day.' So we did. We were laughing our heads off the whole time."

"Mary Jane" is a good time gal for sure. And long before Fun Bunnies, she was kicking up her heels on the grassy hillside slope right next to the Toronto junior high where Schenkman first got stoned. "I felt this immense wave of happiness," he flashes back, grinning at the memory of his pot initiation under the startled eye of a cow he once stalked with his camera in pre-dawn Canadian fields. "I couldn't stop laughing. Maybe that's why I smoke pot. To remember the child inside."

And, in keeping with the spirit of *Upside Down*, Schenkman approached the new record from a fresh point of view. "I played totally straight in the studio. I wanted to appreciate the psychoacoustic effects of listening to it later-stoned out of my mind."

It's a good way to listen to Spin Doctors, especially when they're painting aural landscapes like "More Than Meets the Ear," whose sonic textures and lyrics recall "Forty or Fifty" from *Kryptonite*. "It's great to be handed a guitar line," Schenkman says of the "More" riff Comess came up with. "There's a beautiful interchange, because the person who hands it to you also gets something back. Like, I originally gave Mark the bassline of 'Hungry Hamed's.' And it's a fuckin' joy to me every time he plays it, because he brings his whole sensibility to it."

White's sensibility is considerable. The simmered-in-phat "Biscuit Head"—White's own colorful metaphor for butthead—was inspired by the Doctors' communal history of stoopid road tour disses, and reflects the "Yo Mama's a Pajama" funky tradition. "I had this really silly bassline," White says about "Biscuit Head," which crystallized at the farm house sessions. (True to form, he commuted daily from a Seattle hotel because "I don't like no farms, and I knew I'd be miserable if I stayed there.") "I gave this goofy bassline to Chris. Goofy and Chris kind of go together."

So do pot and Chris, a bong-hit man whose experiential spectrum ranges from mild paranoia to "pleasant diversion" to "major inspiration." "Pot kind of takes the lid off things," he observes, pun fully intended. "And you never know what's under that lid. It's up to her. The Goddess decides." Eric prefers joints, which stand in for smokes when he's trying to kick tobacco—at least until his system backfires. "I can't get high all the time," he notes, "because there's no reference point." Non-smoker White is all reference point: "Pot should be legal. That's all I have to say." And, as a former pot· head turned abstainer—"I stopped smoking one night at Nightingale when I suddenly found myself too high to play"—Comess intersects with both arcs of the loop.

"I can't deny pot's been an influence on my musical life," Comess says, leaning his long, tall Texas frame against a parked car outside The Cooler in Manhattan's meat-packing district. "I love jazz, I love improvisational music, I love the Grateful Dead. There's no denying that that's drug-induced music. My classic early pot experience was listening to 'Dark Side of the Moon.' So if Chris and Eric are stoned I can really relate to their state of mind. But I don't have to smoke to get that now."

"What's cool," notes Schenkman, "is that we're dealing with two different mindsets and we can still play together." In fact, the band's sliding-scale quotient of THC—push-pull coordinates of space and time that punctuate their music with black holes and white lightning—is part of what makes the Doctors spin. Whether or not anyone's actually high, there's an implicit alchemy: Comess and White hold a safety net under the burning building from which Schenkman and Barron leap (and are as likely to bounce them back to the roof as plant them on terra firma). Offstage, the Doctors present a united front on the subject of legalization.

"People have the right to choose," White says flatly. "I've never once seen pot hurt anybody, or seen anybody who was high hurt anybody else," notes Comess. "So it seems a shame for someone to spend even one night in prison [for a pot bust]."

"Sending people to jail is taking an element of society that could be a productive, creative one and turning it into a destructive and degenerate one," laments Barron—who has a pretty clear vision of what revenue taxes should bankroll if Mary Jane ever gets the official government nod.

"Education, man. You get in there with those kids and show them some books. Get them literate and teach them a little Aristotelian logic, so no one can get over on them. Teach them a couple of classical virtues, some aesthetics, and art. Get them to sing a few songs and draw a few pictures and buy some crayons for the kids." Schenkman is more succinct: "I think it's stupid that pot's illegal."

But music, after all, remains the medium of the Spin Doctors' message, which is inherently psychoactive: turning shit into gold, and picking up gold where you find it—whether it's the shinbone alleys of "At This Hour" or the future freeways of "Someday All This Will Be Road."

Throughout this quixotic quest, the Doctors keep intersecting with what Barron calls "the lattice of coincidence." How else to explain the fact they landed in London for their first overseas tour on the eve of the Gulf War, armed with What Time Is Its "damned jihad" prophecy? Or the cosmic convergence of the signing of the Arab/Israeli peace pact in Cairo with the "Cleopatra's Cat" shoot in an ancient Egyptian temple? "We sort of deliver images like the milkman delivers milk," says Barron by way of explanation. "It's our job."

Act Ill is the job at hand. With an album that seeps inside your brain instead of hitting you over the head, Spin Doctors are primed to ambush the road with the old Act I sneak attack. They can also reference Act II, when they slipped through the cracks of the suddenly-mainstream, doomed-rock-star syndrome while selling six million copies of *Pocket Full of Kryptonite* worldwide. How did they pull it off?

"We've been sort of intelligently stubborn about trying to make our show work whenever we hit the next step," opines Schenkman. "That—coupled with the fact that nobody's a heroin addict, nobody's a coke addict, nobody's an alcoholic and nobody's dead—enabled us to stay grounded. We rode out the storm in a pretty respectable fashion, and we've grown a lot as a brotherhood. I see *Turn It Upside Down* as a transformation, a way of trying to make our lives reasonable in context of what's been going on for the last five years."

Walking over to the funky baby grand, he starts noodling around on the keyboard, framed by the scanning eye of a massive flower peering at him from a Cezanne print, which basks in the sunset glow of a nearby window.

"We've just walked along the road and tried to figure out what's happening now," Schenkman concludes, as visiting werewolf Jimmy Macdonell from Loup Garou slides onto the piano bench and picks up the top end of an ad hoc duet. "So far, that's worked."

## Live Rounds: Jono Manson Band, Nightingale, New York City

*huH*, May 1996

EVERY MUSIC SCENE HAS magic when it's busy being born. But to recapture that glorious, ephemeral moment when all things seem possible precisely because they're improbable—what it felt like, say, to be smack in the middle of Berkeley's Gilman St. scene when Rancid and Green Day were just a couple of local punk bands—can only be achieved through a kind of reverse alchemy that transmutes gold and platinum records into the original rock from which they were extracted.

Which is exactly what happened when the Jono Manson Band played Nightingale, New York City's equivalent of Gilman St. for such rock & roll revivalists as Blues Traveler, Spin Doctors and Joan Osborne. All of whom are graduates of the Jono Manson school of bar-band epiphanies, and two of whom—Blues Traveler's Chan Kinchla and Bob Sheehan—are working members of his band.

So it's fitting that ten years after Manson played his first-ever gig at the 'Gale—and five years after he split the scene for Santa Fe—the band should christen its A&M debut disc, *Almost Home*, in the House That Jono Built. And though the tour will be officially launched three days hence at Irving Plaza, with Blues Traveler's John Popper blowing harp, this is the gig Popper is still kicking himself for missing.

Hours before the Manson Band hits at the traditional 'Gale's headliner time of midnight (meaning one a.m.-ish), the overflow crowd is mouthing the same mantra above the suitably demented wails of Mike Parrish's Drug-Sniffing Dogs: "It's just like the old days!" The old days being the cusp of the '90s, with Blues Traveler on epic Monday nights when you routinely blew off Tuesday to "drop a little New York City" and anything could happen—like, say, Joan Osborne discovering she could sing—and the answer to Spin Doctors' "What Time Is It?" was the forever after-hours "4:30 a.m.!" ("It's not late, no, it's just early, early, early!")

Tonight, it's back-to-the-future time when, over a year after his acrimonious rift with Spin Doctors, guitarist Eric Schenkman unveils Chrysalids, his burnin' new trio with bassist JP Fitting and drummer Peter McNeal.

"It means survival," grins Schenkman, who's in fine fettle indeed as he whips out a series of tunes crackling with sassy hooks and drenched in churning psychedelia that recalls the pre-pop Doctors' era of "Refrigerator Car."

Then, sporting a star-emblazoned shirt that dates back to the old days, the master Rolling Rocker takes stage with an incantatory "Wheee!!!!" that unleashes the deep 'Gale's groove of "The First One's Free." "But the last one will hurt you bad," taunts the gravelly-voiced Manson, who attacks the high art of low-rent songcraft with a paid assassin's precision. Santa Fe drummer Mark Clark and a tightly-rehearsed Kinchla and Sheehan prove themselves worthy by nailing the vintage Worms tune "Hanging Out For You Love," provide impeccably timed whoo-ees on Joe Flood's forever-fabulous "Miss Fabulous," and underscore Craig Dreyer's classic sax line in a classic rendition of Manson's classic drifter's paean "Move Along," still the most-played single on the Nightingale jukebox.

Then out of the blue comes Traveler's "Crash Burn: and I scrawl "this is a holy nite" in my beer-stained notebook while dancing on the barstools along with half the house. By the time Sheehan's bass chases "Sad, Sad State of Affairs" down a labyrinthian rabbit hole, we've become a collective forcefield that sticks to every syllable when Manson belts out "Big Daddy Blues." "ABCDEFGH/I'm tired of paying these dues/on these 123456789 to 5 big daddy blues." Not that anyone's, like, really going to work tomorrow.

Even the set-break was monumental. Only in the presence of Jono the Healer would Eric Schenkman and his ex-Spin Doctors partner Chris Barron have actually shaken hands after a year of refusing to speak. Capping this reconciliation, Manson's own once-estranged Worms partner Simon Chardiet joined the band for the second set—as did Barron, who gave the kids a history lesson: "This was just an omelet joint before Jono and Simon played here."

Somewhere between the ensuing singalong of Blues Traveler's "Brother John" and an "I'll Take You There" that would have shot through the roof if the roof still remained, I stopped taking notes. I do know that when I looked at the clock it read 3:45 a.m. when I was sure it was maybe around two. And that was way before the double encore, when Manson testified to the power of love in "Days and Nights Together," and Kinchla bent some totally twisted notes while Barron and the rest of us born-again scenesters confessed "I'm a winner/I'm a sinner" to whatever guardian angels works overtime shift at the 'Gale. Just like the old days.

## In the Limelight: The Visual Ecstasy of New York City Nightlife in the '90s

*PleaseKillMe*, October 2020

STEVE EICHNER WAS THE *photo king of New York City mega-clubs. He is also a chameleon who moved seamlessly through the multiverse of colliding worlds that was New York City nightlife in the 1990s. Cree McCree talked with the photographer about his career and a handsome new book collection of his work for PKM.*

Long before Instagram made all the world a stage for smartphone-wielding celebs and wannabes, photographer Steve Eichner aimed his camera at the proto Insta Influencers of the phantasmagorical '90s club scene in New York City, where outrageously dressed Club Kids vied for the spotlight with the A-Listers that mega-club impresario Peter Gatien hired Eichner to shoot.

*In the Limelight: The Visual Ecstasy of NYC Nightlight in the 90s*, a lavishly produced Prestel book compiled with photography editor Gabriel Sanchez, out October 20th, gives you a ringside seat for all the action. Ranging far and wide throughout Gatien's domain—Limelight, the Tunnel, the Palladium and Club USA—Eichner also club-hopped to other hotspots, from the Roxy and Glamourama to Club Expo and Reins, and turned his lens on the "outlaw parties" that could pop up anywhere in oft-dangerous dark corners of the city. Packed with flesh-on-flesh bodies cramming the dancefloors and converging in VIP rooms of multitiered pleasure palaces, the book is the perfect wish-fulfillment fantasy for these dark pandemic times, when we're all craving to be in the limelight instead of stuck inside at home.

"I didn't plan it this way, or shop it around with that in mind," says Eichner of a project that was years in the making and involved countless hours of digging through vast archives of negatives, photos and slides. "But people now are just so longing to be in a crowd, because when you don't have something, you want it so much more." And whether you were just a kid in the '90s, or actually lived through that era in New York City and wax nostalgic about those times, *In the Limelight* teleports you inside the bubble of an ecstatic fever dream that could probably never happen again.

"All these clubs were the breeding ground for a cultural revolution," says Eichner, who was always "looking for the best party" on his nightly mission to document it all. "It was a petri dish, a primordial slime of musicians and designers and artists and LBGTQ. There were no cellphones, there was no social media. You couldn't be part of it on your phone from your basement. You had to show up. The only way to build your following was to get out in the clubs. That's how I built my photography career. I would hand out business cards in the clubs, I would give people photos." And thanks to Eichner's sharp eye, and his party-hound's instincts, his old-school self-promotion worked like a charm.

Eichner also lucked out when he set up his first photo studio on 27th St. at 11th Avenue after moving to New York from Long Beach, Long Island in 1987. Auspiciously located just blocks away from the Roxy on West 18th St., it put him within shooting distance of one of the hottest clubs in town. His career initially took off when Roxy owner Gene DiNino rolled out the red carpet and gave Eichner access to every VIP nook and cranny. And it went into overdrive when Peter Gatien handed him the keys to his four-club kingdom. "The fact that I was willing to get beeped in the middle of the night and run to any club to get the shot was a big selling point," recalls Eichner, who was on call 24/7 so he wouldn't miss a single *Page Six*-worthy moment, like Julia Roberts making a surprise 2:00 a.m. entrance on the dance floor at Club USA.

"My job for Peter Gatien was to capture celebrities to get publicity for the clubs by selling the photos to newspapers or magazines," explains Eichner. And he delivered in spades. He snapped Tommy Lee and Pamela Anderson canoodling in a dark corner of Limelight, caught Mickey Rourke goofing around backstage at the Palladium with House of Pain, and scored a stupendous close-up of Brendan Fraser giving a big, fat finger to the lens at Tunnel, where he also shot Boy George striking a Christ-like pose in Tunnel's famous ball-pit. All these and other boldface '90s New York City scenesters, including Donald Trump in full predator mode scanning Club USA for chicks, are sprinkled throughout the book. But *In the Limelight* is also a labor of love, where the wildly creative Club Kids, colorfully-clad cigarette & candy girls, imperious clipboard-wielding door people, hefty bouncers and regular old club-goers all take center stage.

"80 percent of the photos in the book are the photos that I shot for myself," says Eichner, who was free to roam around freely once he met his celebrity quota. "Either artistically, or to document the era. Those are the unpublished photos that I really want to share. The Club Kids all got dressed up for the cameras, so I was their window on the world, I was the social media. When I rolled in with my camera, I was like a rock star. Everyone would pose for me." It was all pretty head-spinning for a twenty-something photographer, who came out of the tour-centric jam band world of Grateful Dead psychedelia and landed smack in the middle of the Gatien ground zero of mega-clubs. "I was new to New York City, I was new to the club scene, so to have all of this…it was like Halloween on acid," Eichner recalls with a laugh. "The photos in this book are really an expression of a young photographer finding his voice and having great subject matter."

In his alter ego of Psychner, Eichner was also deeply immersed in the young jam-band scene spearheaded by Blues Traveler and Spin Doctors in the late '80s and early '90s, which was exploding downtown everywhere from tiny dive bars like Nightingale to the neo-hippie mecca of Wetlands. And he never abandoned that. In fact, he continued to immerse himself in both scenes simultaneously, toggling back and forth between the gritty black-and-white world of bar bands and the flashy technicolor stage sets of the Club Kids' domain.

I know, because I was right there with him, crammed up against the bands on the Nightingale floor, while he was shooting and I was scribbling notes on the dancefloor for several downtown rags. As semi-official BT family historians, we became quite the dynamic duo, often going on the road with the bands as they grew. And we circled back to those years together during the pandemic this summer, when Steve started posting archival photos of that crazy Nightingale/Wetlands era. His ongoing Big Scan project also unearthed other random gems, like a shot of Hunter S. Thompson arriving to speak at Columbia's druggy Delta Phi, and a meet-your-hero moment with famous African wildlife photographer Peter Beard, who borrowed a roll of film from Eichner at Club USA.

So, when *PleaseKillMe* assigned me to cover *In the Limelight*, and the photographer who shot all those stunning photos, I jumped at the chance. During the course of multiple conversations via Zoom, phone, email and texts, we discussed everything from Steve's growing up in a family with his younger half-brother Billy Eichner, the comedic genius behind Funny or Die's *Billy on the Street*, to his sunrise epiphany as a photographer during an epic Grateful Dead tour, to his take on Club Kid ringleader Michael Alig's gruesome murder and dismemberment of Angel Melendez, an Altamount-style death knell that heralded the demise of the Club Kids' scene and Gatien's clubs themselves. (With typical Eichner luck, Steve himself had already made the transition to his nearly two-decade stint as a staff photographer for *Women's Wear Daily* and New York Fashion Week shutterbug before time ran out on the Gatien clock.) We also talked about the infamous riots in Tompkins Square Park, not far from the 11th St. studio where we often worked together, and much, much more.

But before we set the wayback machine to the '90s, I want to circle back to the process of creating *In the Limelight* and Eichner's serendipitous connection with former *BuzzFeed* photo editor Gabriel Sanchez, twenty-four years his junior, without whom the book may never have come about.

*PKM*: You and Gabriel Sanchez getting together seems like real kismet.

**STEVE EICHNER:** It was. Gabriel was too young to have done what I did, but apparently he became enthralled with that period. He was doing a *BuzzFeed* story about the craziest photos of 1990s club life, and my name kept coming up, so he found me on the internet and interviewed me. He was very knowledgeable about the era, and we really hit it off, and after that *BuzzFeed* piece got something over a million views, we discussed doing a book. That was two and a half years ago, and it's taken this long to actually get around to releasing the book. The funny thing is, when I worked for *WWD*, I would go to so many book launches, and people would get up and say, this has been such a long hard process. And I'd think to myself, how hard can it be? But now that I've been in it, I realize that it's a long, difficult process.

*PKM*: Well, especially in your case, when you had such a vast archive of photos. How did you decide what to use?

**STEVE EICHNER:** It was thousands and thousands of photographs, many of them in filing cabinets for years. Choosing was really difficult. I was lucky to have Gabriel, who's a very talented photo editor. He kind of had a vision of what it would be like to walk through each club, where around each corner you'd see either a music performance or a drag queen or somebody making out or a celebrity. Because in Peter Gatien's clubs there was so much going on all the time.

One room might be playing techno with a bunch of ravers, and you'd go into the Limelight chapel and they'd have a punk band and people crowd surfing. So the photos we chose were based on what it was like to be me in the clubs.

*PKM*: And the Gatien clubs weren't the only clubs you were going to. When I first met you, on the Blues Traveler scene, you were constantly shooting everywhere I went, which was a completely different circuit from the Club Kids' scene. How did you manage to pull that off?

**STEVE EICHNER:** Yeah, when I look back at my work now, in the '90s archive, I have one role of film with ten frames of shooting Blues Traveler at Wetlands, and another ten frames at the Roxy shooting Club Kids, and then there's ten frames of shooting random models for a portfolio. Because A, I was poor and had to economize on film and processing cost money. And B, I was going from place to place to place. I'd be at Wetlands and Nightingale and end the night at the Limelight. I was working literally twenty-four hours a day, no sleep, with coffee and stimulants.

*PKM*: And I'm sure all those stimulants helped. But you also managed to segue back and forth between the scenes so effortlessly that it never looked like work.

**STEVE EICHNER:** Well, I'm a chameleon. Whatever I'm photographing, I feel like I can blend into almost any situation. When I was doing all that in the '90s, it was almost like the *Wizard of Oz*. There was the black and white world of the jam bands, and the dirty, gritty downtown scene. And there was this technicolor world of the Club Kids like Really Denise and Richie Rich and James St. James, who dressed up every single night of the week, in the most creative, outrageous, outlandish, upside-down costume-y kind of outfits they could think of, and pranced around the clubs hoping to get photographed.

*PKM*: It was also a lot easier for all of us back then to cross over into different kinds of nightlife. As a fashionista, I appreciated what the Club Kids were doing, but live music venues were always where my heart was. I was always on the dance floor, taking notes in these little notebooks filled with doodles of what the music sounded like, and what I was feeling. Like you were always shoot, shoot, shooting, I was always write, write, writing. But I also went to the clubs, especially Limelight, where I was a regular worshiper at Rock and Roll Church and which was conveniently located near Tramps, one of my favorite live music venues.

**STEVE EICHNER:** In '90s New York, there weren't ghettoes. You weren't just a Wetlands kid or just a Club Kid. You could go see Fishbone at Rock and Roll Church and the next night go see a hippie band at Wetlands. Or Tramps or Mondo Perso. As a '60s hippie child, Wetlands was kind of where my heart was. It wasn't about glitter and glamor. They had their eco saloon and their activism and their petitions. Wetlands were anti-excess. Minimalist. Live with less. Grow your own. And on the other end of the spectrum, I was going to Club USA on Times Square with neon lights and porn booths! And the highest fashion and the most expensive handbags!

*PKM*: Only Psychner could bounce back and forth between those two extremes without getting whiplash!

**STEVE EICHNER:** I was definitely ping-ponging between worlds. But New York was also that kind of place in the '90s. There were so many different cultures and people didn't just stay in one. That was the beauty of it. In the nightclubs you saw Wall St. suits and ties, next to drag queens, next to people from the Bronx, next to hip hop artists. And the Wetlands didn't just have hippie bands, they had their punk Sundays and other types of music every night of the week. I also went to CB's a lot, and that wasn't ghettoized either. I shot Henry Rollins at CB's, but I also shot Dave Matthews Band at CB's. Same with Nightingale. I got some great shots of Patti Smith performing on the Nightingale floor.

***PKM*:** Yeah, those are classic! Tom Hosier, the Nightingale temple guard, was a huge Patti Smith fan. And you never knew who might turn up wherever you went. You shot Madonna dozens of times throughout her career, and yet one of the most famous photos you ever shot of her was actually at Wetlands!

**STEVE EICHNER:** Yeah, I was tipped off that some big shot was coming to the club that night so I was watching the back entrance. And the first person who came out was Liz Rosenberg, her publicist, so now I know it's Madonna coming in. She pokes her head out and I snap a few pictures. And remember in those days, you couldn't really see what you got, it wasn't digital. So I take my film to the lab and drop it off. And the next morning I get my slides back and put them on the light table, and I'm like, she's wearing a nose ring! And I had never seen anyone wearing a nose ring before in like 1993. So I was like OK, these are great for the newspapers. And the *Post* ran it, and the *Daily News* ran it: Madonna seen with her brand-new nose ring! It was a big news story.

**PKM:** I feel like you establish a sense of trust with people, too. You get some kind of intimacy in so many of your shots, even all the supermodels and celebs you shot for *WWD*. And that's hard to achieve. You never turned into a paparazzi.

**STEVE EICHNER:** Well, there are aspects of my work that are paparazzi-esque. But I always try to do it in a respectful way, and an artful way. And in that world, there's a lot of give and take. Celebrities do a lot of things for press and for publicity. But I consider myself more of an event photographer than a paparazzi. I'm not jumping out of a bush, trying to catch someone in the wild. I'm invited to be there, and the celebrities know I'm there, and I'm introduced to the celebrity or the celebrity's publicist as "here's Steve, he's our house photographer." And they know I try to show people in a good light, and make them look good. It's not a gotcha moment.

**PKM:** Like that time Leonardo DiCaprio asked you not to use one of the photos you took of him.

**STEVE EICHNER:** That's a perfect example. I thought it was a cute picture. He was in Club USA, standing by one of the cigarette and candy girls, who were always colorfully dressed. And I just saw him buying something and snapped a photo. And I'm going about my business, and Leonardo DiCaprio taps me on the shoulder and says hey man, would you mind not using that photo or publishing it anywhere? And I was like OK. He said, you can take pictures of me all night, and he was a real sport about it. I got a great shot of him with Dennis Hopper. And at the end of the night, I said can I just ask you why? And he's like well, I was buying cigarettes and I don't want my mom to know I smoke. So I buried that photo for thirty years.

**PKM:** Aw, that's so sweet! And speaking of moms, I'd like to rewind way back to your childhood and talk a little bit about how you ended up becoming a photographer. What was it like growing up with Billy Eichner, who became a pretty famous entertainer himself?

**STEVE EICHNER:** I was born in '65, when my mom was about twenty, and my dad was thirty-five. My mom was a bit of a flower child, who wanted to go out and enjoy life, and my dad was an accountant who wanted to stay home and watch sports. So when I was five, they got divorced. My mom stayed in Long Beach and I grew up there skateboarding and surfing. And my dad moved back to Queens and remarried, to Billy's mother Debby, and started a new family.

**PKM:** So you and Billy have the same father, but didn't grow up in the same nuclear family.

**STEVE EICHNER:** Yeah, we're thirteen years apart. Big age difference. And we didn't grow up in the same household. But Billy was always into entertainment. On Oscar night, he'd dress up in a tuxedo and sit on my dad's floor in the living room in front of the TV. He wasn't at all into what I was into, as far as music goes. I remember I gave him a Led Zeppelin CD, and when I came back a month later it was still wrapped. But he had like Barbra Streisand and Madonna.

**PKM**: When did you first get interested in photography?

**STEVE EICHNER:** In junior high school. My mom was like, you need a job. And there was this little photo and electronics shop in Long Beach that sold vinyl LPs and stereo equipment, and also had a photography department that sold cameras and did film developing. I loved to tinker and I love music, so it was the perfect job for me. I would change all the singles out each week for the Top 40, and I learned how cameras work, how film developing works. The owners encouraged me. You want to borrow a lens, borrow a lens. So I would borrow stuff and try it out. And I'd have my developing all done wholesale. I had some advantages there.

**PKM:** What were you shooting?

**STEVE EICHNER:** I love music, so I would buy tickets to concerts as close as I could to the stage. I'd sneak my camera in. The first shows I remember shooting in New York non-professionally were The Who at Shea Stadium and The Clash at Shea Stadium, and through trial and error I kind of honed my skills. But I never really thought about photography as a profession. So I decided to study accounting, because my dad was an accountant. And just by luck and happenstance, I chose to go to SUNY Freedonia, which had a top music school. So there were a lot of musicians there.

**PKM:** Is that where you became a Deadhead?

**STEVE EICHNER:** Yeah, in like '83 I saw my first Dead show in Buffalo and fell in love. So I started photographing the Dead and the Dead scene. Fast forward about six, ten months. I fail out miserably from Freedonia, because I start to take statistics and business math, so I decide to go on a Dead tour between semesters. And I'm in San Francisco, about to see a Dead show, when I call home on a pay phone and my mom's like you're not going back to college! They just sent me a letter, you're gonna be on academic probation, and I'm not paying for you to party at school!

So I took a semester off and toured with the Dead, just as a fan. And we were coming back toward the East, and we were in Colorado and we'd been up all-night tripping, as you do. And the sun was rising, and I had my camera, and we were in the Rocky Mountains and I was shooting the sunrise and I had this epiphany that I should be a photographer.

**PKM:** Bingo! During this time, you also hooked up with the band Dreamspeak, which eventually brought you to New York City and the Delta Phi frat house at Columbia, which was like the fertile crescent for the jam band scene.

**STEVE EICHNER:** Yeah, Spin Doctors played their first gig ever in the basement of Delta Phi, and the Nightingale/Wetlands scene you and I know all grew out of that. One of the brothers at Delta Phi was David

Graham, the son of Bill Graham, the world-famous concert promoter. So even though I didn't go to college there, I was part of that scene and they said Steve, we'll let you build a darkroom in our house, and gave me gallery space.

**PKM:** When I met you, a couple years later, you were living in your storefront studio on E. 11th St. and Avenue A. That's where we did that big cover shoot for Tangle magazine, with Blues Traveler's John Popper, Spin Doctors' Chris Barron and Trey Anastasio from Phish, right before we went on the first HORDE tour together to promote the magazine.

**STEVE EICHNER:** That was such a fun day! The three lead guys from the biggest jam bands of the time, and somehow, we got them all in my studio. I did a lot of fish-eye shots, and we took them to Tompkins Square Park and shot them goofing around in the playground together. Those photos are really stellar.

**PKM:** Your 11th St. studio also gave you a front row seat for the Tompkins Square Park riots, which you photographed as well. That must have been wild!

**STEVE EICHNER**: Yeah, all the protesters and the squatters had been amassing hundreds of glass bottles for hours. Then the bottles start flying, and there's fires raging in the streets and police in full riot gear start coming in from both sides to crush this riot. And I'm in the middle of this now, it was like holy shit! In that screenshot of me, some poor kid just got bashed with a baton and has blood gushing out of his head. I'm not really a hardcore news photojournalist. But that was what it must be like to cover wars.

**PKM:** There was also a lot of blood years later, when you were still working for Peter Gatien, and Michael Alig and his roommate killed that drug dealer and later dismembered him to get rid of the body. That was a pretty sordid story, which I always thought of as the Altamount of the Club Kids scene.

**STEVE EICHNER:** I think it's an excellent analogy. The Club Kids were constantly pushing the limits of fashion and art and in your faceness and pop cultureness. But they were also pushing the drug use: how high can you get? And Michael Alig, being like the ringleader of the Club Kids, was fully leading the way in drug overuse.

But there were two things going on. The other one was the Giuliani crackdown on the clubs. When Giuliani came in and decided he was gonna clean up New York City, he made Peter Gatien public enemy number one. He tried to infiltrate Gatien's clubs with undercover police officers. They were never able to link Peter to any of the drug dealing, but they started closing his clubs, and that also put a damper on the scene.

**PKM:** What were your impressions of Alig as a photographer?

**STEVE EICHNER:** Well, it's hard to admire a murderer. But in those years before the murder, he was a genius. He came up with the most brilliant ideas for parties and events. He worked directly with Peter, he organized Disco 2000, and if you look at the artwork and the ephemera of those days, and the magazine they started, Project X, Alig was a genius. And like a lot of geniuses, he started getting more attention, and started to push everything he did. He would parade in front of the camera, and he was always someone I focused on because he was constantly there, he was constantly on. And he was constantly moving culture.

**PKM:** You also had a kind of premonition of what might happen that time you stopped by his place in the afternoon to drop off some photos.

**STEVE EICHNER:** Yeah, it was one of those places in the East Village that were basically Club Kid crash pads. So I went in and the place was a wreck. There were like piles of vomit, the floor was sticky and there was a terrible stench. And when I looked into one of the bedrooms, there were blood stains on the pillow, it was soaked in blood. Probably because they were snorting so much heroin and ketamine and everything else, they were having constant nosebleeds. And they never cleaned up after themselves. I mean, I partied, but never like that!

**PKM:** How did you feel about the murder personally?

**STEVE EICHNER:** As a human being, I felt a little dirty about having put Michael on a pedestal and photographed him so much. I didn't know Angel [Menendez] but he was a human being who lost his life. For no reason except drugs. And I thought wow, man, this is getting out of control. In a way it was inevitable. Because when you're pushing limits, like a rock star, everyone's kissing your ass and you're kind of in a bubble. Michael was living in a bubble, but it was still shocking. No one expected it to end in murder. Luckily, I was able to step back from it, and I moved on to a different life.

**PKM:** And before it all collapsed, the creativity of that time was truly magical. Do you think there's any way it could ever be reborn? Or is it just a time set in stone, that we can only long for? That no young people could ever do again now, especially in New York City?

**STEVE EICHNER:** My hope is that real estate really tanks in Manhattan, which it is. Artists always go to where there's cheap rent.

**PKM:** That's true! So there's hope!

**STEVE EICHNER:** Yes! There's hope that these big megaclubs spaces could open again. People are craving to be in crowds again. People are craving to be entertained. People are craving *to* entertain. People are craving to create. So maybe the pieces will fall together and there will be big spaces and people will want to congregate and get back to this circus-y kind of creative atmosphere with all kinds of people mixing together, like it was in the '90s. Because the way it was going [before the pandemic] was little groups, like who could spend the most money on a bottle of vodka, and who could be the most exclusive. So, I do think that something all-inclusive, and fun and entertaining and social that's this Instagrammable, could come back.

# V.

## Declaration of Independents

### *Introduction:*

### *In Praise of Artists Who Dance to Their Own Beats*

If this sounds like a catchall category, that's because it is. Every one of these artists is *sui generis* and doesn't fit neatly into any of the other sections of this book.

Take Bill Hicks, for example. Though his band Marblehead did release an album, and he opened for the metal band Tool on tour, Bill was primarily a comedian, albeit an outrageously dark one. More hipster monologist than stand-up comic, he'd open shows with lines like "come into my twisted fuckin' soul" and proceed to treat us to a Jeffrey Dahmer Tupperware party.

But the epitome of *sui generis* is Roky Erickson, with whom I had the wildest, most idiosyncratic interview of my entire career. On assignment from *High Times* in 1995, I spent several days with the 13th Floor Elevators' godfather of psychedelia in his hometown of Austin, Texas, where The Butthole Surfers' King Coffey had just released Roky's first album in nearly a decade, *All That May Do My Rhyme*, on his Trance Syndicate label. The highlight of that trip was visiting Roky's home, where a white noise cacophony of cartoon shows, Top-40 hits, newscasts, horror-movie soundtracks and just plain static blasted twenty-four hours a day. Wild doesn't even begin to describe it.

When it comes to indie record labels, it doesn't get more independent than SOAR (Sound of America Records), founded by Native American rock star Tom Bee, whose band XIT helped jump-start the emerging Native American political consciousness with their album *Plight of the Redman* back in 1971. While I was riding shotgun with Bee through New Mexico circa 1992, he regaled me with tales about his son, Robbie, who made his stage debut at the Clinton inaugural and performed "powwow hip-hop red house swing" on Lollapalooza's second stage throughout the Southwest.

As a decades-long Nick Cave devotee, I've been following his journey from his 1984 debut as Nick Cave and the Bad Seeds on the Brit indie label Mute to his later releases in various configurations on his own labels. Sadly, I've never had the opportunity to interview Cave (though he remains on my bucket list). But I delved deeply into his artistic vision in my review of *Murder Ballads*, the first Absolutely Essential Cave album since 1987's *Tender Prey*, which was forged in the bitter chamber of re-entry from his heroin addiction and housed his masterful "Mercy Seat," the executioner's song as sung by the executionee.

"The Gospel According to Blind Joe Death: John Fahey in Four Movements" is a collaboration with my late husband and Fahey devotee, the avant-garde guitarist Donald Miller. After releasing *Blind Joe Death* (1959) and several other albums on his own Takoma label, Fahey recorded his later hugely influential *Requia* for Vanguard then disappeared off the radar for years. Byron Coley, editor of *Forced Exposure*, tracked Fahey down in a Salem, Oregon, welfare motel and recounted "The Persecutions and Resurrections of Blind Joe Death" in a 1994 article for *Spin*. That eventually led to *City of Refuge* (Tim/Kerr 1997), Fahey's first new recording in years, and an East Coast mini-tour with Sonic Youth's Thurston Moore in December of 1996. Just before his final Pearl Harbor Day gig at CBGB's, Fahey came to stay with Donald and me in our New York City apartment. That was such a *sui generis* experience it's hard to believe it even happened.

Three of the other Independents pieces are live show reviews, center-pieced by the utter mayhem unleashed in London in 1996 during the epic meltdown of a Prolapse/Descension/Sonic Youth triple bill. So charged was the electronic forcefield of a bill clearly designed by Sonic Youth to implode on impact, you could hear the house crackling by the end of the show. Then dozens of splintering cracks swelled into hundreds, becoming a tsunami of ecstatic static: an ambient ovation from an eighteen-hundred-plus crowd who'd just been spun full cycle from the Prolapse pre-soak through the heavy agitation of Descension (who caused a virtual riot) to the final spin-dry purges of Sonic Youth's *Washing Machine*.

Years later, in 2002, seventy-three-year-old rockabilly icon Link Wray reduced a crowd of New Orleans hipsters at the Shim Sham Club to a quivering mass of flayed neurons. By the time his umpteenth reprise of "Rumble" collided with his other monster riff hog, "Rawhide," for the final denouement, the question "how raw can a hide get?" had long since been rendered moot. Not long afterwards, the Shim Sham hosted the fabled X, which put Los Angeles on the map of the punkabilly avant garde, featuring founders John Doe, Exene Cervenka and original guitarist Billy Zoom. The crowd went so crazy during "In This House That I Call Home" that overly enthusiastic pogo-ers nearly knocked over a P.A. speaker. (Doe saved the day by threatening to sing "warm and fuzzy folk songs.")

Rounding out this section are two highly influential women artists who helped put indie rock on the map in the mid-'90s. Kelley Deal, half of the Deal twins who made a loud *Last Splash* with the Breeders before her heroin bust and subsequent treatment pulled the plug on the band's infamous *Dreamland* sessions, regrouped after she got sober with the Kelley Deal 6000, and later joined forces with Skid Row's Sebastian Bach. And poet/performance artist Nicole Blackman, the reigning diva of "broken word," tongue-lashed Lollapalooza '94, skewered pop culture "Dogma" on KMFDM's acclaimed *CD Xtort*, and collaborated with Anton Fier on the Golden Palominos' *Dead Inside*, their "snuff film soundtrack." Both continue to dance to their own drummers through ever-evolving incarnations.

## Bill Hicks: Comedy for the Head

*High Times*, April 1993

"Come on into my twisted fuckin' soul." Thus, Bill Hicks begins a "giggle tour" of mass murderers, whose highlights include a Jeffrey Dahmer Tupperware party. But what he really lays bare tonight, on the eve on an impending European tour, is the twisted fuckin' soul of Just Say No America.

"My biggest pet peeve," the pallid, black-garbed Texan confides to a hipper-than-usual crowd at Caroline's comedy club is midtown Manhattan, "is the war against drugs. Actually, it's a war against your civil rights." Amidst a loud consensus of claps, Hicks continues. "Marijuana's against the law. Marijuana, a drug that kills no one…Ever."

That single word "ever" elicits more laughter than many comedians' milk from a fist full of one-liners.

A no-bullshit libertarian—he's enthusiastically pro-porn—with an acute sense of the sardonic. Hicks has made his own war against the War on Drugs a comedic *cause celebre*. That he himself is now totally straight following a collision course with booze and cocaine that landed him in recovery, has, if anything, strengthened his stance.

"My honest-to-god belief about drugs?" he asks onstage, not at all rhetorically. "God let certain drugs grow naturally on this planet to help speed up our evolution. Do you think psilocybin mushrooms growing on top of cowshit was an accident? Where do you think the phrase 'that's good shit' comes from?" Amidst hoots and whistles, Hicks demonstrates "god's little accelerator pad for our evolution": the discovery of 'shrooms by Planet of the Ape types, a grunt-and-gobble tour de force which climaxes with his incantation of "The 2001 Theme." "Ommmmmmmm," he chants in blissful elation. "I think we can go to the moon now!" Pause for the organic laugh track then the tagline: "That's exactly how the fuck it happened."

More hipster monologist than stand-up comic, Hicks really believes that's exactly how the fuck it happened. After the show, he greets me warmly. Not once does he plug a career launched by David Letterman and nurtured by HBO. A sponge for quirky detail and useful data, he's as fascinated by my 'shroom experiences (not excerpted here) as his own. Bill Hicks is a dead serious and wickedly funny conversationalist who treats an interviewer just like his audience: as collaborator, not consumer.

**Your management was reluctant for you to do a *HIGH TIMES* interview. Did they think it would spoil your image?**

Well, "Heroin Quarterly" had me first…no. I have no idea what the problem was. I think all drugs should be legal—across the board, effective immediately. Law enforcement doesn't stop anyone from doing drugs. All it does is make criminals out of them.

**Do you think there's any danger that, if drugs are legalized, corporate interests will take over?**

Anything corporate is dangerous and harmful. [Drugs] should all be legal and free. Profit should be against the law. That'll stop those fuckers.

**When you went through recovery to quit drinking and cocaine and clean up your whole act, did pot have to go along with everything else?**

Oh, absolutely. That's part of the deal with the program. Everything goes. There's no middle ground.

**Back in the days when you were still smoking pot, what's the most fun you ever had?**

Well, to be honest with you, I was never a big pot fan. Which is very ironic, because I always espouse the virtues of marijuana. My thing was mushrooms.

**I didn't know there was such a thing as a mushroom abuser.**

There isn't. I went to AA, not MA. It wasn't abuse. It was right on the money. To tell you the truth, the reason I quit doing mushrooms was because I had a UFO experience.

**So that's a true story? That's not just a comic riff?**

No, that's true. What's frustrating is that every time I tell the story, the first thing people ask is were you tripping? And I go, yeah. And they go, oh yeah, right. But it was really profound, and I want to experience it again. Totally straight. So I can tell people I was straight.

**Have you read Terence McKenna's *The Archaic Revival*? Because your routine about apes discovering psilocybin is part of his whole theory of evolution.**

I haven't, but I did read the Esquire article and it sounds incredible. But it's nothing that anyone who's ever experienced it doesn't already know. And we go, yeah, cool, insects—I'm with you! The insect consciousness.

**Tonight's audience really got off on your drug riffs, but I'm sure you get some negative feedback too.**

Oh yeah, What really bugs me is that a lot of people don't even have a tie-in with alcohol as a drug. I've never been attacked by a pothead, but I've had drunks scare the shit out of me. Also, it doesn't always register that people who smoke pot are under arrest in a lot of places and their belongings are taken from them by the government. It's amazing how scared they've made everyone. They can suspend the Bill of Rights and people think it's a good thing. "Just Say No" is the extent of our drug education in this country. All my friends said yes and I'll guarantee you we learned a lot more about drugs. Just say yes, and you'll learn.

**If you were elected President, what's the first thing you'd do?**

I'd make Bush pay for his war against humanity crimes. Same for Reagan.

**What kind of punishment would you mete out?**

I'd make [Reagan] watch his movies.

**What about Bush?**

I'd make him sleep with his wife. Because you know that is not happening.

**And Quayle?**

He's the only guy I'd pardon. I want him. He's the jester of America, man. I'd put him on TV twenty-four hours a day.

**His very own C-Span. Q-Span?**

Exactly!

**What's up for you in 1993?**

I'm going to record a new album with my band, Marblehead—a comedy album but with music all the way through. Totally overboard with music and a spoken-word type poem. A rant. Maybe I'll call it "Bill's Iliad."

**I feel a lot better knowing you're out there in the world. We need more people speaking out about real life.**

Hey, I appreciate that. And I'm sorry about the delay on the *High Times* interview. But those managers who made that little decision? They are no longer! *High Times* will prevail!

## The Eye of Texas: Roky Erickson

*High Times,* April 1995

ROKY ERICKSON PUT THE acid in rock. His Austin-based 13th Floor Elevators influenced Janis Joplin and the whole San Francisco psychedelic scene. But after he was busted for a joint in 1968, Roky was never the same. Cree McCree explores the mind and soul of this living Lone-Star legend.

"This highway goes to Houston, through all these woods, like Muir Woods and Golden Gate Bridge Park," explains Roky Erickson, who's riding shotgun in a black Chevy sports car he's dubbed a "James Bond Maserati" as we cruise through the outskirts of Austin. Looking like an impish, benevolent Charles Manson beneath a tangled mat of hair and beard, the singer/songwriter is in an ebullient mood following two of his favorite activities: going out to eat and browsing the aisles of an HEB superstore, where we've purchased his short-list necessities of stamps, envelopes and candied peanuts.

"Wherever this highway goes, it's really extravagant, so you might not want to go on it," he laughs as we pull up to the XXX adult-video store attached to his federally-subsidized house in Del Valle. "You might not make it, you know."

Indeed, no one but Roky Erickson has made the long, strange trip he's just described: from godfather of psychedelia and the whole San Francisco scene via his band, 13th Floor Elevators, to pot-bust casualty, certified schizophrenic, progenitor of punk, notarized alien and arguably the most influential Texas troubadour since Buddy Holly. Alleged protagonist of the Beatles' "Rocky Raccoon" and acknowledged muse of novelist Thomas Pynchon, Roky's left his mark on everyone from Janis Joplin and ZZ Top to the Jesus and Mary Chain and R.E.M., who contributed tracks to the 1990 Erickson tribute album, *Where the Pyramid Meets the Eye.*

Now two more of his far-flung offspring are honoring their debts. The Butthole Surfers' King Coffey has just released Roky's first album in nearly a decade, on his Trance Syndicate label. *All That May Do My Rhyme*–a classic Roky twist of phrase–features a who's who of Texas musicians, from Charlie Sexton to co-producer Speedy Sparks, backing some of Erickson's most poignant, melodic ballads. Simultaneously, Henry Rollins' book imprint, 2.13.61, has published *Openers II*, a compendium of lyrics from Roky's astonishingly prolific thirty-year career.

"Roky's been more of an inspiration than an influence on me," says longtime fan Rollins. "He's given the world so much he deserves something in return. Revenue from the record and book is what he's basically going to live on for years ahead."

Ever the gentleman, Erickson graciously accepts these offerings and looks forward to his weekly dinners with King Coffey, along with the income that may bolster his $300.00-per-month disability stipend. But he's frankly far more interested in the electromagnetic hum that emanates from his home. Inside, the hum crescendos into a roar. Amidst a pop-culture collage of computer monitors, household appliances, overstuffed bookcases and teetering stacks of videotapes, magazines and unopened junk mail, a cacophony of cartoon shows, Top-40 hits, newscasts, horror-movie soundtracks and just plain static blasts twenty-four hours a day. This disconcerts some visitors, who crank up their voices to be heard above the electronic choir of TVs, radios, stereos and amps Roky's cobbled together with a maze of audio cables and rooftop antennae crammed into corners. But "The Eye of Texas" thrives inside the center of this storm.

"It's a work of art," says King Coffey of Roky's white-noise sound sculpture. "He's fascinated with American culture and sound, and he's trying to receive as much as possible and process it." The effect is through-the-looking-glass trippy and also oddly soothing.

"Roky says, 'My house is my church,'" notes his brother Sumner, principal tuba of the Pittsburgh Symphony Orchestra, who plays on the new album and helped to edit the lyrics book. "I know what he means. Roky's not crazy. His only problem might be that he's *too* connected to the light."

A lightning rod for devotees around the world Roky's spawned a cottage industry of collectors, a la Syd Barrett, and is a perennial cause celebre in Austin, where he's somewhat reluctantly re-emerged after nearly a decade of retirement. Musician friends regularly sponsor benefits for Texas' resident living legend, who, until recently, saw barely a penny of profit from a discography longer than the arm of the law. Roky received his first royalty check from his widely acclaimed work with 13th Floor Elevators only in 1993. But the mythology that enshrouds him—which dates back to his incarceration in Rusk State Hospital for the criminally insane after being busted for a single joint in 1968—sometimes overshadows his genius.

"The whole cult thing has gotten to be like Watergate," observes longtime colleague Doug Sahm, who produced Roky's 1975 seminal punk masterpiece, "Red Temple Prayer (Two-Headed Dog)," witnessed his notarized declaration of alien status shortly thereafter and covered his original

13th Floor Elevators' hit, "You're Gonna Miss Me," on the Roky tribute album. "The madness surrounding Roky is hard to penetrate, and I have mixed emotions about his getting pushed into the spotlight again. But I have no mixed feelings about his music."

A musical prodigy almost from birth, Roger Kynard (thus "Roky") entered the world on July 15, 1947. He was the first of five sons born to Evelyn Kynard Erickson, a classically trained singer who won an Arthur Godfrey talent roundup with a *La Traviata* aria, and her now ex-husband, Roger Erickson, a gifted architect and inveterate alcoholic. Roky made his public debut with Evelyn as a young boy, singing the sentimental standard "Mother Dear" on a local TV show.

"Roky was always a special one," recalls Evelyn amidst the bohemian disarray of his childhood home. Behind us, framed by the defunct swimming pool outside and laden with Evelyn's sheet music, is the piano where Roky wrote his first song. But it was the guitar, which he took up at age twelve and still plays almost daily—as his long, carefully manicured fingernails attest—that really unleashed his voice.

By age fourteen, having soaked up Elvis, Bo Diddley, Buddy Holly and the vocal pyrotechnics of Little Richard, Roky had penned his own ticket to ride: "You're Gonna Miss Me", an instant pop classic that ranks with the best of the early Beatles. Rehearsed in this living room with his original band, the Spades, it became a regional hit just about the time he was ousted from high school in 1964 for daring to let his hair reach his collar.

Enter Tommy Hall, a twenty-three-year-old chemical-engineering student and self-styled philosopher with no musical background, but a bountiful supply of psychoactive drugs. Faster than you could say Owsley Stanley, Roky and Tommy levitated their newly-formed 13th Floor Elevators to the taboo missing floor of the American dream, and shot up the *Billboard* singles chart with a visionary version of "You're Gonna Miss Me" in 1965.

No one had ever heard anything like it. "It's 'Louie Louie' sideways," R.E.M's Peter Buck once said. Dick Clark's genial-host mask slipped to his knees during the Elevators' *American Bandstand* appearance when Roky let loose with banshee screams, while Tommy sucked a roiling glossolalia out of his electrified jug. Attempting small talk afterwards, a dazed Clark asked, "Which one's the head of the band?"

"*We're all heads!*" came the unanimous reply, marking the entry of this hipster password into the mainstream lexicon.

The center of a psychedelic cyclone that swept across central Texas (and was recorded on Lelan Rogers' Houston-based International Artists label), the 13th Floor Elevators dosed San Francisco when the Grateful Dead were still folk-rocking as the Warlocks and the Jefferson Airplane had yet to leave the runway. Their 1966 debut album, *The Psychedelic Sounds of the 13th Floor Elevators*, marked the first use of "psychedelic" as a musical modifier, and heralded the coming revolution in Hall's liner notes: "Recently, it has become possible for man to chemically alter his mental state and thus alter his point of view." True to its title, Psychedelic Sounds took a sonic leap of faith well before the Beatles unveiled "Lucy in the Sky with Diamonds". Surfing the gyroscopic waves of Stacy Sutherland's guitar and the undertow of acid-king Tommy Hall's spittle-infused jug, Roky's keening vocals broke the sound barrier into new dimensions. Fellow Texans, the Moving Sidewalks (featuring Billy Gibbons, later of ZZ Top), took note, riding the elevator to their own "99th Floor"—as did Janis Joplin, who came within a hair's breadth of joining the band shortly before she split for San Francisco with Chet Helms, who then hooked her up with Big Brother and the Holding Company.

"That aspect of Janis, where you thought you were gonna get hit by a flying tonsil at two hundred years, was pretty directly derived from Roky," notes Helms, founder of San Francisco's legendary Avalon Ballroom, where the Elevators became the headline draw on bills featuring such up-and-coming bands as Moby Grape and Quicksilver Messenger Service. "We thought it would go on forever," says Elevators' co-founder Clementine Hall about those heady times. "Not only was the music going to go on forever, the musicians were going to go on forever. We thought the United States had been permanently altered."

But Tary Owens, who originally introduced Hall to Erickson, had intimations of the band's mortality during an all-Texas Avalon show he produced in 1966. "Janis got a standing ovation, and then a whole progression of Texas music led up to the Elevators," recalls Owens, who now helps administer a trust fund established for Roky in 1993 with his long-overdue royalties from International Artists. "They'd just been arrested for the first time and opened with Bo Diddley's 'Before You Accuse Me Take a Look at Yourself'. It became sort of their theme song."

The Elevators learned the hard way that Texas was not Haight-Ashbury East. "They were out to make examples of us—and they did," recalls original drummer John Ike Walton. After cops confiscated his van for seeds found lodged in the floorboards, and following a series of shakedowns and busts, Walton "got tired of being followed around and searched" and quit the band in 1967. "The penalty in Texas for weed back then was two years to life for any amount they considered smokable."

Not long after a blazing sun burst forth on the cover of the Elevators' second album, 1967's *Easter Everywhere*—widely considered their psychoactive masterpiece—a small plastic vial reflected a little too much light," as the *Aus-*

*tin Statesman* coyly reported. Spotted by pursuing cops, the vial contained about a joint's worth of marijuana and was tossed out a car window by one "Roger Erickson". Opting to be institutionalized rather than go to jail, Roky copped an insanity plea and was ultimately remanded to Rusk State.

"Arresting Roky for drugs was a political thing," says Evelyn, who campaigned tirelessly for her son's release. Her pleas fell on deaf ears. And while Evelyn is adamantly opposed to drugs of any kind—she took Roky off all prescription medication a decade ago—Roky's bust and its denouement turned her into a strong advocate of legalization. "None of this would have happened if marijuana were legalized," she notes. "Drugs are a health problem, not a criminal problem. Rusk was a place for killers, not for kids smoking pot."

What went on inside the walls of Rusk, where he was confined for three years as a "certified schizophrenic", only Roky knows for sure. "Supposedly there was a doctor in there experimenting with mind drugs and they used him for a guinea pig," says the Butthole Surfers' Gibby Haynes, echoing popular belief. Certainly, he was subjected to electroshock treatments, then standard procedure; combined with Thorazine, it produced a shuffled-gait numbness he later parodied to perfection in "I Walked with a Zombie". While still confined, he transmuted his daily nightmares into *Openers I*, a slim white volume of quasimystical religious verse. Published shortly before his release in 1972, its very light implied the shadows that would soon unleash a mighty army of demons. As Evelyn notes, "Roky writes two types of songs, black and white—and the black started right after Rusk."

Even if he'd wanted to resurrect the Elevators, the band was now past reviving. Stacy Sutherland had been shot dead in a domestic dispute, and Tommy Hall's daily doses had rendered him incommunicado with the outside world. But Roky was back with a vengeance, producing some of the most profoundly inspired work of his (or anyone's) career. Armed with the slash-and-burn imagery of a horror-movie meister, he disemboweled cultural hypocrisy in rants like "Bloody Hammer":

*The demon is up in the attic to the left*
*My eyes turn to the left to say no*
*He says first I am a special one*
*I never hammered my mind out*
*I never had their bloody hammer!*

Driving the message home was what he called "stand on your amplifier, screamin' feedback, smash-your-guitar kind of rock 'n' roll." What it was

was punk, officially acknowledged in 1977 when *Rolling Stone* cited Roky Erickson and the Aliens' "Red Temple Prayer (Two-Headed Dog)" and the Sex Pistols' "God Save the Queen" as the top two contenders for redeeming rock from terminal irrelevance.

Jinxed by a series of ill-fated deals with various small American and international labels (including CBS UK), the Aliens and their successors (the Explosives, the Resurrectionists and Evil Hook Wildlife) never cashed in like the media-savvy Sex Pistols. But the musicians and underground fans touched directly by Roky's music before he retired from active duty in 1986 invariably describe an almost religious experience.

"I've been higher onstage with that man and his music and the energy that comes off what he plays than any drug I've ever done," marvels bassist Brian Curley, who played in both the Resurrectionists and Evil Hook Wildlife. "We'd all talk about the rush, how the hair on the back of your neck stands up and this big old grin comes over your face. It's a warm, calm feeling, like you've truly hit nirvana."

I'm with Roky and King Coffey at the Austin Record Fair. Roky's spent most of this mid-October weekend trying to avoid the event, where King and I are currently surrounded by thirty years' worth of Roky Erickson records and memorabilia at archivist/collector Jack Ortman's booth. John Ike Walton's doing a brisk trade in 13th Floor Elevator t-shirts with the psychedelic logo off his original drum kit. Roky doesn't fancy being a living collectible. "They have everything here for lots of money and it just gets on your nerves, you know what I mean?"

As long as he doesn't have to sign anything, Roky has agreed to show up. Freed of any burden to endorse his legacy, he ambles through the Record Fair as an interested observer, stopping to greet old friends and peruse a stash of Mexican horror-movie posters that catches his all-seeing eyes. Then we reach the Roky Erickson booth and he visibly recoils. "Have you seen your new forty-five?" Ortman asks eagerly. "No, I haven't," Roky replies, politely adding, "I'm just gonna wait," before beating a hasty retreat to a nearby Coke machine.

"I've given up expecting Roky to do anything," says Texas music archivist Casey Monahan, whose weekly dinners with Roky spawned both the book and the record projects he midwifed into the world as editor and co-producer. "I think the expectation factor for Roky, or for fans of Roky, is a very dangerous thing. Once we expect artists to do specific things, we put our own perceptions of them before who they are."

It's a point well taken. However provocative the subtext of his real-life history, Roky is first and foremost an artist.

Driving home from the Record Fair, it's Roky who sets the agenda with a humorous running commentary on every topic of conversation. My cultural immigration from laid-back New Mexico to New York City is aptly dubbed a "speedball." NORML's pro-legalization lobby is deemed "kind of like the National Rifle Association." And William Burroughs would be pleased to know Roky acknowledges him as "a spy writer."

Once we arrive in Del Valle, Roky surveys the vast and seemingly silent horizon, then asks, "Do you hear that lightning?" No, Roky, I don't. But later tonight the skies will unleash a violent series of flash floods, reminding me of the lesson he taught an unwitting Swedish reporter who asked him about "new directions" in a 1984 video interview.

"Just follow the path, man," Roky advised. "Everything goes in a certain direction each day. I go from a Shangri-La to a learning place every day of my life."

## The Gospel Aaccording to Blind Joe Death: John Fahey in Four Movements

*PleaseKillMe*, October 2019

*John Fahey (1939–2001) was one of the most original composer/guitarists of the late twentieth century and yet he traveled under the radar of anyone but the most intrepid fans of the avant garde. A guitar prodigy out of Takoma Park, Maryland, he went on to fuse old acoustic blues with modern classical soundscapes, producing fascinating montages that attracted the ear of a younger fan base by the time of his death (thanks, partly, to latter day fans like Thurston Moore, Kim Gordon and Byron Coley.) Cree McCree and her husband, the avant-garde guitarist Donald Miller, hosted Fahey at their apartment in the late 1990s and lived to tell the tale.*

### *PRELUDE (Stardate: December 1996)*

In 1959, when "indie" was about three decades shy of entering the pop lexicon, a young guitar player named John Fahey from Takoma Park, Maryland, released one-hundred copies of his debut vinyl album on his own Takoma label. *Blind Joe Death,* which the enterprising college kid hustled (with scant success) to customers at his moonlighting job as an Esso station attendant, announced a radical intention: to fuse the jarring dissonance of modern classical composers like Bela Bartók with old blues 78s. Fahey had cut his teeth on the classics, but had started collecting the 78s after Blind Willie Johnson's "Praise God I'm Satisfied" deflected him from the hillbilly music he'd initially been tracking.

One of the most original composer/guitarists of the late twentieth century was about to hit the streets, and more than a few back roads.

Some twenty-five years later, in the mid-'80s, when Fahey was battling the chronic fatigue of Epstein-Barr virus, Thurston Moore and Lee Renaldo stumbled upon two matching copies of Fahey's 1967 album *Requia* in a ninety-nine-cent bin while on tour with Sonic Youth. Fahey then lived in near obscurity after having dragged his eccentricities (and a variety of vintage instruments) halfway around the world and into guitar legend.

"We were in a period of consciously trying to expand our musical references," recalls Moore, who knew only Fahey's reputation prior to the bargain-bin score. "Lee called me a couple days later and said, 'Have you listened to the John Fahey!!??'"

What they'd unearthed was a revelation: the "Requia for Molly" suite, which dominated the album's second side, juxtaposes Fahey's minimally laconic and maximally manic acoustic guitar stylings against a tape collage combining Charles Ives, Nazi rallies, and zoo and barnyard animals at various speeds. The whole reflects the nervous disintegration of a female friend--and, by extension, California of the late '60s and all of Western Civilization. The climax pits a solo quote of "California Dreamin'" against oinking pigs and performing seals; this would be Berkeley in 1967, where Fahey then lived.

Fast forward to 1996. Byron Coley, editor of *Forced Exposure* and friend of Thurston Moore's, tracked Fahey down in a Salem, Oregon, welfare motel and recounted "The Persecutions and Resurrections of Blind Joe Death" in a 1994 article for *Spin*. That eventually led to *City of Refuge* (Tim/Kerr 1997), Fahey's first new recording in years, and an East Coast mini-tour with Moore in December of 1996.

"I had no idea what to expect," says Moore. Neither did Fahey. When he showed up for soundcheck in Boston with a cheap Epiphone he'd picked up en route at one of numerous Salvation Army stops he made during a $200.00 cab ride from Providence, RI, Fahey initially mistook Moore for a guitar tech. After that got sorted out, Fahey invited him up to his hotel room.

"He answered the door stark naked," Moore recalls, laughing. "And said, 'You want to come in and listen to some Stravinsky?'"

Later, during the road trip, stretched out on Moore's backseat with his trusty boombox, Fahey made tape collages of his own music, birdcalls, Balinese dance tracks, and whatever else struck his immediate fancy.

"He was in a zone between wakingness and sleep, emitting some kind of sound that wasn't really a snore, more of a roaring hum," recounts Moore. "And the whirr of the tape machine between the stuff he was recording became part of the collage. I still have a bunch of the tapes he made scattered on the floor of my car."

The final date of this tour was Pearl Harbor Day at New York's CBGB, where the line for the sold-out show went around the block in New York rain. Throughout the trip, Moore had peppered the bill with a number of "out" guitar players, all reverential fans of Fahey.

Tonight, while Fahey co-opted the CB's ladies' room to restring, practice and deal with a dreaded photo shoot, a *sine qua non* of America's young guitar avant garde--Davey Williams, Jim O'Rourke, Michael J. Schumacher and Donald Miller--nervously cavorted in another of CB's glamorous back rooms where Williams summed up the mood of the assembled acolytes: "It's always cool to share a bill with a genius."

Then Thurston popped in with an announcement that silenced all further conversation: "Fahey just crawled out on stage."

You could hear pins drop at CBGB. Anyone daring to discuss their roommate problems was curtly sshh'ed with looks recalling those of an old South lynch mob.

Fahey had mentioned beforehand that he needed to start his shows with aggression to accommodate his medically defined levels of energy. (He beat Epstein-Barr but was still contending daily with diabetes and Parkinson's). And he opened with a vengeance.

With his steel laptop seriously detuned (by an octave, two-fifths and whatevers per string) and a 250w floodlamp bulb for a slide, Fahey blithely set his sizable sneakers in the door of the post-Derek Bailey avant garde with an "are you kidding, I've been doin' this shit for years" glee.

He labored with well-calloused virtuosity on that shitwad hardstring Epiphone through "City of Refuge," the new CD's centerpiece and the only composed track on an otherwise improvised album. No quotes from Blind Willie, only from Skip James, whom Fahey "rediscovered" and once carted around. They snarled at each other at the time with the combined hatred of the obscured, but both won, as they did once again for the ghosts tonight.

Fahey encored out the CBGB set with "Oh Holy Night." Kids who had no idea it first appeared on his best-selling album *ever*, 1968's *The New Possibility: John Fahey's Guitar Solo Christmas Album*, thanked him afterwards for playing a song they loved long before they were born. "A hymn, as always, to the end."

"I couldn't have gotten away with this even ten years ago," Fahey observed after the show. "Nowadays, kids are a lot more intelligent, rebellious, and interested in experimental music. They stand out there and listen. Very carefully. And it's a real release for me. Because this is the kind of stuff I've wanted to play for years but was afraid to."

## *PRELUDE PREQUEL*
## *(Stardate: October, 2019. Entry by Donald Miller)*

Flashback to John Fahey's 1996 overnight stay at Donald & Cree's New York City apartment on E. 38th St. before and after his CBGB Pearl Harbor Day show.

Prior to Fahey's arrival, a great deal of data came pouring in. Drawing on Thurston's fresh-from-the-road-with-Fahey tour experience, Kim Gordon gave Cree the dietary gross-out preamble: As a diabetic, Fahey was dedicated to the mass consumption of artificial sweeteners. Diet Coke on demand, to be augmented by ultra dumpage of Sweet' N' Lows into every delivery system. Ice coffee, same, but worse. We got, and pre-bought, the drill.

The previous night in Manhattan, Fahey had been booked into a West Village (pre-Air) BnB, but for one night only. Then he was unceremoniously evicted, unwashed and somewhat eternally dazed, before noon this momentous Saturday. After some concerned phone interaction with the "Get JF From Point A to B" HQs, I managed to get him to our midtown address. I assume someone from the BnB went "above & beyond" to funnel Fahey and his musical flotsam-cum-ballast into a paid vehicle.

I should hereby do full disclosure: I met (and befriended many) of my music and art heroes in my late teens and early twenties (Evan Parker, Peter Brœtzmann, Derek Bailey, Steve Lacy, La Monte Young, Henry Flynt, Rashied Ali, Jack Smith, Harry Smith, etc.). But though Fahey had left our identical home ground in DC/Maryland a decade-plus before I did, this was our first encounter. I was actually nervous, and it showed.

And then he showed.

When Fahey buzzed our apartment on the third floor, I ran down to assist him. He had made it up to our first-floor landing, where he was slumped against the wall in his sweaty, unchangeable tee, with his objets d'art collected in an elegant pile next to him. And I realized immediately that the collected objects--his "clothes" army surplus sack, two (two!) boomboxes for his endless Fahey-isms with Tibetan Malagasy gamelan collaged cassettes, a cheap Epiphone six-string in a case, and an uncased beautiful old eight-string lap-sized laptop--were now MY duty. We were all playing that night.

Once he had assumed his settled-in position in our bedroom, which he'd been given for reasons of girth, and set his booms up with electrical outlets, I suggested a visit to The Academy, an unusually wonderful used book and record shop not far downtown.

Fahey was eager to do this in a serious old addict way, as obsessed as ever with searching, searching, searching for used recordings of old music. But as we prepared to descend and grab a cab, I dithered to leave, as I am wont. Fahey, having none of it, bellowed "MOVE!" at a volume that reverberated in the stairwell like a supersonic boom. (It remains one of Cree's favorite admonitions, which she invokes to this day whenever I dither.) And by the time we arrived at the Academy, he was chomping at the bit.

Driven by a delusion planted by a wealthy fan pretending to be a broker for a fictional market in Japan so he could keep Fahey solvent by giving him a mission, he was hot on the trail of important classical LPs as a hunter/gatherer/spy. Which Academy has in abundance. And I made the mistake of telling my amigos there that John Fahey, big gig later that night, super genius, was in da house, blowing his cover as what HE thought was a secret agent man for Japan. As we exited to grab dinner before the onerous duty of getting him (and me, separate cab) to CBs, he snarked at me: "Don't ever let me ask you to do a crime!"

After Fahey's performance at CB's, where I was a performing seal closing the night, Cree took charge of transporting the star of the show in and out of a cab with all his gear and helping him schlep it up the two flights to our apartment. Later, after lugging my own gear up said flight, we curled up with the cats on the foldout couch on the living room floor and drifted off to sleep on waves of ambient sound. Behind the closed door of our bedroom, Fahey was still intoning into one of the two boomboxes, using a stash of blank cassettes I had on hand and threw to him. Judging from what he left behind, he was likely fiddling with them all night.

Next morning, while I committed to bloody marys, Kim phoned Cree and made her commit to the Fahey airport drill:

"Make sure you take him to the fucking gate for his flight home or he will take the cab you call to Connecticut to look for used records!"

Cree did as instructed and got him to the gate at JFK, where Fahey went on loudly about terrorism/ists in the security line (pre 9/11, but still).

And That Was The Weekend That Was, much of which was captured in three hours' worth of taped conversations with our house guest.

## *CONVERSATIONS WITH JOHN FAHEY: 10 DISTILLATIONS*

### *Notes on the Boombox Sound of the Bi-Millennium*

**CM:** What I love about the opening track [on *City of Refuge*] is it's really an invocation. This is not like any John Fahey record you've ever heard before.

**John Fahey:** Right. "Fanfare." This is an entirely new guitar sound, as far as I know. An acoustic guitar, miked and distorted in a cheap little mixer, recorded in my motel room. The background noise Thurston likes so much is a Champion juicer. And the clanking sound comes from holding a bar against that metal fret. Brang, brang, brang.

**DM:** What about the tape collages you play the guitar against? The obvious precedent would seem to be the "Requia for Molly."

**John Fahey:** That took a big studio, with all kinds of speakers. Now I can do it in my own room, with my DAT and four or five boomboxes.

And some kids I hired to turn them on and off. Little JD's eight, ten, eleven years old, who've been kicked out of school and don't have any money and come around asking for work. Sometimes they're hard to control, but you get a great sound. I haven't heard anyone complain about the fidelity of six boom boxes and a guitar.

There's no mixing. In fact, I would consider it kind of unethical to use a mixer. I just want blips. Or a long drone for background things that I play over my hi-fi or over the boomboxes. And I record the guitar over the DAT.

So that's all new. I started doing it because I was lonely and didn't have anything to do.

**DM:** That's always a good inspiration.

**John Fahey:** Yeah, for a lot. But for me, the boombox has become a musical instrument. I sleep with one. I bet in my room I could make a better sounding record utilizing noise, melody, distortion, echo and on and on than anyone has ever made. Including Sonic Youth, including everybody I've heard, better than Bang on a Can, better than Einsturzende Neubauten. Who I like very much. And I could do it for less than $300.00. Right in my own little room.

That's why I'm so excited about this record. I got a new sound out of the guitar. And it's violent and questioning and forward looking.

**DM:** You're gonna scare the shit out of some people.

**John Fahey:** Well, "Fanfare" is also about the bi-millennium. I'm sort of announcing it. First, it's incredible that the human race hasn't blown itself up. Second, the world is quite different from the way we looked at it even thirty years ago. Fractured…To me, the bi-millennium is a big mystery. What's it gonna be? I'm cautiously optimistic. That last one was horrible. Here it comes: Bang de bang bang!

## *NOTES ON THE PROVENANCE OF JOHN FAHEY'S GUITAR*

**CM:** The eight string is electric? Where did you find it?

**John Fahey:** Guy brought it by the studio in Rhode Island. He paid $40.00 for it and I paid him $50.00. He wanted to sell it to someone who would use it. It's quite a rare and valuable instrument. It sounds even more monstrous and horrible and crazy and frightening and ghostly than it looks. It's like guitar Auschwitz. And I turn the echo up to at least ten.

**CM:** Do you work much with effects boxes?

**John Fahey:** No, I don't really have to. I try to get most of the effects or unusual sounds out of the instrument. Like putting the steel on the steel guitar and playing it on the wrong side. You'll see while I'm playing. And I'm not doing that to show off. You'll hear very strange sounds. Every once in a while, an angelic sound comes out. I don't know how, but it does.

## NOTES ON SKIP JAMES, MONTGOMERY COUNTY & THE BERKELEY INVASION

**John Fahey:** The third part of "City of Refuge" is a circumlocution of a Skip James blues song, played over and over again. I don't think too many people remember or care that I was the one who rediscovered Skip James.

**DM:** Everybody here cares. Our cat's care.

**John Fahey:** He was a jerk and I didn't like him and he didn't like me. But I spent a lot of time taking him around, getting him Social Security, that kind of thing. And he'd get into those long things that just went over and over and over for like an hour. He'd go into some trance or something. He played a lot of stuff that he didn't record. So I know a lot of licks.

**DM:** Even the way you invoke Skip James isn't the typical tribute to the bluesman whatsoever. It's the distinctive Fahey run-through, you can recognize what it is. You actually know your music very well, just like Bartók did with his folk songs.

**John Fahey:** Bartók. I love Bartók.

**DM:** You're very similar figures, really.

**John Fahey:** Well, he could read music.

**DM:** Actually, John, I stopped taking formal training after I began listening to you when I was seventeen. I'd heard *Requia* several times because it was part of the Montgomery County Library system.

**John Fahey:** How I hate that county! [laughs uproariously]

**DM:** I left it too; I live here now. When I was seventeen, I was still taking classical guitar lessons and had already been listening to Xenakis and Schoenberg and Bartók. Then I listened to *Requia,* and listened to it again and it sort of shattered my life. And the old-timers I used to buy guitar strings from in downtown DC were like, 'hey, you know John Fahey?'

'Yeah.' 'You as good as him?' 'Uh, no.' 'You ain't worth spit if you come out of this town and you ain't as good as Fahey.'

**John Fahey:** Oh yeah? That happened a long time ago. The DC scene was so awful. Especially the folk music scene. That's why a lot of us left there. There were about forty of us who left there specifically to invade Berkeley, California, and take over the folk music scene. And we did. We vanquished them very quickly and I'm glad we did.

## *NOTES ON MODES & FANBOY DEFERENCE*

**CM:** Do you ever feel like you've stumbled on an undiscovered mode?

**John Fahey:** No. Most of the modes I learned are major and minor. I learned from Vaughn Williams symphonies. He'll play stacked minor chords up the neck at certain intervals. I'd forgotten it was Vaugh Williams. British composer. I got *Pastoral Symphony* the other day. Gee, I thought I wrote that…I do weird things with modes. Like use them incorrectly on purpose.

**DM**: Yeah, I've noticed.

**John Fahey**: Sometimes. Not all the time? What are you laughing at? Where do I do that? C'mon Mr. Brain.

**DM:** I'm not gonna perjure myself.

**John Fahey:** You're probably right. I'm just curious what you noticed.

**DM:** I've been doing a paltry imitation of you since I was a kid, as a regular practice idiom.

**John Fahey:** Boy, you sure like to put yourself down. You don't need to.

**DM:** I'm very good at what I do.

**John Fahey:** I bet you are.

**DM:** I'm just giving that idiotic sense of deference. How often do you get that?

**John Fahey:** All the time…I appreciate the polite deference at first but you can drop it.

## *NOTES ON CHORDS & INSTRUCTIONAL VIDEOS*

**DM:** I've been going over your chords for a long time, and my very favorites…the only thing I can refer to here is the stupid instructional videos Stefan Grossman got you to do. Oh yeah, this is one of those chords. I don't know what it is. And those are the chords I've been working entire pieces around. I stopped formal lessons after I began listening to you seriously. I forgot how to read.

**John Fahey:** Good.

**DM:** I can't sight read for shit.

**John Fahey:** You could probably learn again in five minutes.

**DM:** I just sort of play intuitively and I usually do all right because: I'm terribly good.

**John Fahey:** I believe you. There's a couple places on the tape where I'll say 'what is this, Stefan, a major seventh'? And he said 'yeah'. Oh OK. It's a major seventh. I'm not sure that it was, to tell you the truth.

**DM:** You're just being polite?

**John Fahey:** No, trying to get it over with.

**DM:** Yeah, it looked like it was an ordeal.

**John Fahey:** Yeah, I thought it would be. I haven't seen any of them.

## *NOTES ON THE KIDS & OLD FARTS IN FAHEY'S AUDIENCE*

**CM:** What's this tour been like, the shows with Thurston? Are the audiences mostly kids?

**John Fahey:** Yeah. And they seem to love it. And that's who I'm trying to appeal to.

**CM:** Plus they're not carrying the baggage of the old farts who remember John Fahey from thirty years ago.

**John Fahey:** Oh, they come. They come. But when they ask me to play "Sunflower River Blues," I say no. I don't play that shit anymore. If you want to live in the past, go ahead. But don't try to drag me with you. At which point, several people usually get up and leave. And I love it. Cause I don't like to be forced back into that.

## *NOTES ON THE NAZI ENCLAVE OF LAKE WOBEGON*

**John Fahey:** "On the Death and Disembowelment of the New Age" is a good attack on that horrible period. My next objective is the Lake Wobegon show.

**CM:** You're going after Garrison Keillor?

**John Fahey:** Yeah, man, I've already started it.

**CM:** Good old folksy Garrison?

**John Fahey:** He's a Nazi, man. That program is racist and a lie. Cause there's no Jews on his show. No Chinese. No Catholics, even. And I've been in those little towns and those little towns have Jews. I mean, what's he trying to pull? Underneath it all, it's a Nazi show. I'm trying to think of a piece of classical music I'd like to evoke for Lake Wobegon.

**DM:** How about Bartók's solo sonata for violin? That's pretty shrieky.

**John Fahey:** I know that piece. Not bad. But it's too emotional. I want something dry, suggesting death and strangeness. The music's always been terrible on Lake Wobegon. Eventually, Leo Kottke and Chet Atkins ended up on there. Too cute. They're part of the schtick. They're both WASPs. It's a show about WASPs. Nobody exists except WASPs.

**CM:** I never realized Lake Wobegon had such a hidden agenda. I just thought Keillor was annoying because he's terminally folksy.

**John Fahey:** He sure is. It's like that book *Nazi Art* that shows how the Nazis took over all the cultural, artistic and architectural aesthetics.

**CM:** And there's a direct link between Nazi art and Lake Wobegon?

**DM:** It is terminally kitschy.

**CM:** So that's where kitsch came from, Nazi art? Actually, kitsch is a Yiddish term.

**John Fahey:** Yeah, it's a lot older. Stuff that was always terminally folksy is kitsch.

## *NOTES ON CANNIBALISM IN THE CITY OF REFUGE*

**John Fahey:** Here's the story of "City of Refuge." When I was thirteen or fourteen, I found Blind Willie Johnson's record "I'm Gonna Run to the City of Refuge," and the title was in my head when my mother and father were traveling north on vacation along the ocean. We were hungry and running out of gas when we saw this city we hoped would be a city of refuge. But when we got to this city, there were no human beings. Just a factory with a big conveyor belt that takes stuff out to the ocean and drops it in.

Before we took that trip, I had a dream. So before we got there, the factory started sending me messages to warn me that when we got to that city, my parents were gonna chop me up and eat me. So when we actually got to the City of Refuge, I had become the factory. The factory and I were one. And instead of them chopping me up and putting me on the conveyor belt, I chopped them up. And consumed them.

## *NOTES ON HOAXES*

**John Fahey:** I actually had a whole album ghostwritten by a friend of mine. And handed it into Shanachie, but they never issued it. I don't know why.

**CM:** Actually ghosted? You don't play on it at all?

**John Fahey:** Yeah, it's this guitarist Charlie Schmidt. I love hoaxes. But it didn't get issued. After two or three years, I would have told people about it. It probably would have been valuable. He can play me note for note. The only things he does different from me, when he accelerates, he accelerates faster. Always. I mean, I listen to it sometimes and forget that it's not me.

## *NOTES ON THE BIBLE OF STYLE*

**CM:** How long have you had that particular pair of Blind Joe Death shades?

**John Fahey:** I bought 'em in a thrift store about a year ago.

**CM:** Really? They look like they've seen some wear.

**John Fahey:** They have. I sat on 'em a couple of times. They're prescription.

**CM:** You're wearing random thrift store prescription shades?

**John Fahey:** They're not random. There's boxes of 'em. You just go through 'em until you find one that works. I've had plenty. Glasses cost a fortune these days.

**CM:** They're stylish. You'd pay $250 at an LA-designer optician. Easy.

**John Fahey:** Oh yeah? They're pretty intimidating. That's why I bought them. If I take them off, the world will explode.

## *CODA (Stardate: October 2019. Entry by Donald Miller)*

The aftermath of John Fahey's New York City visit until his death in 2001: The year of the true start of the pseudo-bi-millennium

Shortly after the CBGB show and the release of *City of Refuge*, Fahey began being booked and recorded by a number of decently-heeled indie labels. He also streamlined his touring by requiring venues to rent a backline for him with a Fender Strat and Twin Reverb--and once at Tramps, back in New York City, a battery-dying pedal that sounded like crackling 78s.

The reaction to Fahey 2.0 amongst the faithful was hardly Dylan-goes-electric, and he enjoyed an artistic and financial renaissance until his health once again became a terminal albatross.

Before that tragedy, we personally enjoyed the comedy of an out-of-the-blue phone call to Cree, which I grokked quickly was his idea of an "obscene phone call": he formally requested her assistance to ghostwrite sexual adventures into his anthology of his best writing, *How Bluegrass Music Destroyed My Life* (And he definitely did not want to speak with me; when Cree insisted, the withering "Oh. Hello, DONALD" was semi-precious.)

The albatross put on more weight. He post-mortem morphed into one with his doppelcritter Blind Joe Death on a not-leap-year day two months into the actual Gregorian bi-millennium, after being an obese and extremely ill man undergoing very serious surgeries. He was six days shy of his sixty-third birthday.

His legacy? Between Fahey and Andres Segovia, the solo guitar, not just a guitar solo, is an official *idiom in musica*. The gorgeous grotesque of his playing haunts anyone who hears and gets it ad hoc diem, ad infinitum, ad astra.

[*This first section of this piece (Prelude) was resurrected from an article that appeared in RayGun magazine (March 1997), which butchered the original text with a fractured, unreadable design.*]

# Nick Cave: Murder Ballads (Mute)

*huH*, February 1996

Nick Cave, known as St. Nick around my household, wields his bloody hammer in a work-space hung with his own household saints: Jesus, James and John Lee. As in Christ; Ellroy ('The Demon Dog' of neo-noir crime writing); and Hooker (ascended master of the blues of no remorse.) Framing the Big Three are scarlet women torn from soft-porn stroke zines; a B&W photo of a bruise-lipped, smeary-eyed Deanna, who inspired the proto murder-rocker 'Deanna'; and Paul Celan's 'Death Fugue,' which opens with a trope of pure obsession: "Black milk of daybreak we drink it at sundown/we drink it at noon in the morning we drink it at night..."

I know all this because he told me. Well, me and a few thousand other devotees who accessed 'A Letter From Nick' after it was posted on the Internet last spring. At the time, he was "hammering away at this collection of murder ballads," originally conceived as a kind of bastard side-project that would fill in the gap before the next 'real' record.

Not surprisingly, 'Murder Ballads' turned out to be it. Nick's ninth studio release with Bad Seeds is the first Absolutely Essential Cave album since 1987's 'Tender Prey,' which was forged in the bitter chamber of re-entry from his heroin addiction and housed his masterful 'Mercy Seat,' the executioner's song as sung by the executionee.

The new disk owes more to James and John Lee than Jesus (though He is ever with us), and returns to the scene of the crimes Cave's been publicly committing since 1979, when he spat "deep red is the color of murder" on 'The Hair Shirt' with Boys Next Door before escalating the violence with the deeply demented Birthday Party in such swinging funeral classics as 'Deep In The Woods.'

During his twelve-year tenure with Bad Seeds, even disposable Cave efforts have always had brilliant tracks—which tend to be the blood-and-goriest. (The jolly punk snuff-film 'Jangling Jack' and the gorgeously sinister 'Red Right Hand' redeemed 1994's otherwise underwhelming 'Let Love In.')

What makes 'Murder Ballads' such a (duh) killer album is that Cave dispenses with all the major variations on his theme—the byzantine biblical epics, the suicidal love songs—in favor of the theme itself, distilled into Essence of Nick.

Re-working the killed/killer dialogue, over and over again, from multiple points of view and musical angles—with the help of Babylon sisters PJ Harvey and Kylie Minogue and his brother Bad Seeds, whose dogs are let loose upon him most serendipitously--he explicates his basic text. Which is illuminated by the "groovy quote" from Hannah Arendt that closes his 'Letter From Nick' to fans: "The sad truth is most evil is done by people who never make up their minds to be either good or evil."

There are, to be sure, a couple bona fide evil-doers who get their due here. In Bad Seeds' way-nasty spin on 'Staggerlee,' the original bad muthafucka struts in amidst gun-blazing rimshots, snarls lines that would scare the bejesus out of hardcore gangstas—"I'd crawl over fifty good pussies just to get to one fat boy's asshole"—and struts out over two warm corpses to the screams of Nellie Brown on Blixa Bargeld's guitar. And the deliciously deranged Loretta, who gleefully details dozens of grisly crimes to the tune of a foot-stompin' beer-barrel polka, looks back on her long career as 'The Curse Of Millhaven' with only one regret: "They ask me if I feel remorse/and I answer well of course/there's so much more I could have done to 'em if they'd let me!" But mostly the murders just happen with their own impartial logic, proving Arendt's "sad truth" by taking the murderer as much by surprise as the victim.

The most cogent case-in-point is the dark comedic set piece 'O'Malley's Bar,' an epic, serpentine vamp wrought in gorefest technicolor that offs a dozen friends and neighbors of the self-appointed assassin by final count. Our boy hasn't quite made his mind up when he sits in his usual barstool and there's a long split second when it could go either way: "a hand decided the time was nigh/and for a moment it slipped from view." But whoever that hand belongs to—God? Fate? The Devil? Or just the Random Factor?—"when it returned it was fairly burned/with confidence anew." Cave crawls right inside the hide of this born-again psychopath, observing every detail of his bar mates' messy demise with journalistic detachment, naming them one by one, delivering painfully precise personal eulogies while punctuating their deaths with orgasmic spasms and groans. Killing them not because he must—"I bear you no grudge!" he cries in all sincerity midway through the carnage—but because in one heady, fleeting instant he realizes that he can.

While 'O'Malley's Bar' directly confronts the complex equation of murder, from the killer's free will (or lack thereof) to the passive-aggressive complicity of his victims, it's the more oblique 'Ballads' that are ultimately most disturbing. I can hardly bear to listen to the muffled sobs of Mary

Bellows, who dies "cuffed to the bed with a rag in her mouth and a bullet in her head" to the strains of a beautiful Tennessee waltz in "The Company Of Strangers." And the terrible beauty of the two love duets has been haunting me for days.

"Where The Wild Roses Grow," which alternates accounts of a courtship and murder from both points of view, is Cave's valentine to fellow Australian chanteuse Kylie Minogue, who sings from beyond the grave in a voice tender as the rose that petals her blood-red lips after her lover bludgeons her, whispering "all beauty must die." The roles flip-flop in the traditional English ballad "Henry Lee," in which Cave's stabbed and tossed in a well to a lilting chorus of la-la-la-lis by his Jungian anima PJ Harvey, who croons "lie there till the flesh drops from your bones" in a voice fresh and clear as spring water.

What's most striking about "Murder Ballads"—which opens with a drifter's chilling account of an all-in-the-family murder of his wife and three young daughters—is their intimacy. This is a real personal album about real personal deaths which, even when the settings are contemporary, evoke a bygone Golden Age when murder actually meant something. And there's something oddly comforting about that in a world of drive-by shootings and TV serial-rights killers.

Lest we wax too nostalgic about good old-fashioned murder, Cave exits the corpse-strewn "O'Malley's Bar" with a knockout punchline. His entire supporting cast, along with pub pal Shane McGowan, give the redemptive Dylan hymn "Death Is Not The End" a lurching "We Are The World"-at-closing-time treatment. By the time McGowan rasps the last verse—"when the cities are on fire with the burning flesh of men"—it's eminently clear that the tagline "just remember that death is not the end" offers scant comfort.

Welcome to eternal suffering, sucker.

## Native Son: Tom Bee

*Spin, December 1993*

THE ROCK 'N' ROLL dreams of Native American youth conjure images of Tom Bee, a rock legend on reservations and founder of the first Indian indie label. Cree McCree cruises with the electric warrior.

"I am a rock 'n' roll star," Tom Bee says, as we drive through the surreal landscape of western New Mexico. Billboards touting "Indian Curios" loom against the vast crystalline sky. "In Native America I am a rock 'n' roll star," he clarifies, "and that's what counts. In my own community, I'm a legend. Or so they tell me." Bee is casually clad in a t-shirt and Redskins cap. ("What happens at games is a mockery" he says, "but the actual logo has class.") A six-footer with hair flecked gray and with long-lobed ears of his Dakota Sioux tribe, Bee sneaks in the measured tones of a former stutterer. It's the ghost of an obstacle overcome, and for Bee, life has been loaded with such phantoms; most strikingly, the painful story of his beginnings, abandoned at birth in a garbage can in Gallup, New Mexico. From there, Bee fought his way into reservation rock stardom, onto the Motown label, and onto stages in front of his fans. In 1989, he made history when he founded the first Native American label: Sound of America Records, or SOAR.

In 1971, Tom Bee and his band XIT (pronounced "exit") helped jump-start the emerging Native American political consciousness with their album Plight of the Redman. The American Indian Movement (AIM) was just coming together then, urging native peoples to stand up to the perceived pressures.

XIT show, circa 1973: In darkness, the laconic voice of John Wayne drawls the Pledge of Allegiance. Then, a spotlight on Bee's back, draped with an upside-down, rhinestone-encrusted American flag as a signal of distress. Bee recites a litany of bloody battles and broken treaties. The band kicks in, and traditional chants and drums Infuse the raw energy of rock.

"It was incredibly inspiring to have our own big time rock band," remembers Haney Gelogamah, now the director of American Indian Dance Theater. "It was a sophisticated musical realization of emotions that had been collecting for years in the Native American Psyche."

SOAR was launched out of Bee's Albuquerque garage, the solo project at first just old XIT albums. After four years in business, the label's annual sales are over a half million units of some fifty titles–a figure expected to double this year, thanks to a recent mainstream international distribution deal. "It's been a long time coming," observes SOAR artist Roger Cultee, leader of the adobe-grunge band, Mud Ponies, whose recent release includes "Perestroika for the BIA," a send-up of the long-despised Bureau of Indian Affairs. "We're the last people to get involved in the recording community. The white man's been doing rock. The black man's been putting out blues, soul, R&B, and hip hop. And gee, the yellow man—he's been making the equipment! Where's the red man been? Standing there watching," says Cultee.

Bee guns his Blazer into Gallup, where he was born forty-nine years ago. He was just four pounds and already turning blue when his cries alerted a woman who rescued him from the trash can and later adopted him. Bee's boyhood home was on the wrong side of the tracks but on the right side of the action -adjacent to the Indian Ceremonial Grounds, site of mega-powwows, and the Armory, where Bee odd-jobbed to see such greats as Fats Domino, Ike and Tina Turner, and Buddy Holly.

In his teens, Bee traveled to Los Angeles whenever he could afford bus fare, and pounded on record company doors until he finally won the attention of Motown. When it came time to hammer out their contract, Bee sang his way through negotiations, lest he lapse into stammering. XIT was born there, and Bee collaborated with such house acts as Smokey Robinson and the Jackson Five, writing and producing.

As we cruise the streets of Gallup, the Cathedral Lake Singers—a top-selling SOAR act—whoop it up on the Blazer's tape deck. Today's young Indians are rediscovering their roots in the heartbeat of tribal drums, and traditional music is in heavy rotation. Though SOAR's biggest numbers to date have come from new-age crossover artists, such as flutist Spotted Eagle-who sold more than fifty-thousand records in '92-sales to Native Americans remain the backbone of the company that Bee built from the back of his truck.

Despite its success, the company is still virtually a one-man operation. There's Bee in dark shades and pearl-gray Stetson, working LA, taking meetings with execs. There's the storyteller and archivist who spins riveting tales involving talismans of power, such as the turquoise ring he bequeathed to a young, wide-eyed Michael Jackson, for whom he wrote and produced a swan song Motown single, "Joyful Jukebox Music." And then there's President Tom Bee who rules the record company flanked by a portrait of Sitting Bull, monitoring everything from studio sessions to cover art.

Later that day in Window Rock, capital of the half-million-strong Navajo Nation, Bee invokes the spirit of the vision quest: "Entering this world the way I did, for years, I felt betrayed. Not having been raised truly in the Dakota way of life, *Plight of the Redman* was something that was buried in my heart."

Woodstock was the lens that focused his inner vision and gave birth to XIT. "Seeing how the hippie movement wanted to relate to the Indian way of life, I realized music was a powerful means to create unity among my people. *Plight* was meant to be, and I was chosen. The lyrics all flowed out in a big rush, like a message that had to be heard."

That message is now being carried by such SOAR artists as Guy & Allen. With more than ten-thousand copies of *Peyote Canyon* already in circulation on the reservation, reports filter back about semi-miraculous cures attributed to the music's healing powers. "It's like a dream when you're singing," Paul Guy, Jr., tells me. "You sit there and imagine what it was like before, and what it would be like."

In the last year, SOAR artists have expanded their audience with projects including the soundtrack for *Paha Sapa: The Struggle for the Black Hills*, an HBO documentary about the long-standing battle by the Sioux to reclaim their land. And Tom's son Robby Bee-who made his stage debut at the Clinton inaugural-performed "powwow hip-hop red house swing" on Lollapalooza's second stage throughout the Southwest this year.

Robby Bee and his posse are not just XIT revisited, though they are a direct descendant. Tom Bee and most of his '70s AIM peers-primarily dislocated urban Indians needed to search their hearts for a spiritual link to their ancestry. Young people such as Robby already know precisely who they are and can observe, without irony, as he does in "Powwow Girls" that "going to a powwow is like going to the mall" because, well, that's where the babes are.

They rap, as a beatbox cuts a path through thumping tribal drums, lusty whoops, and a wildcat wail of guitar: "We're not just a myth, let's set the record straight / We're alive and well today so let's not discriminate... / We're out to ln-di-an-ize the world."

"Back in the '70s, for us to make any political statements with music was the kiss of death," says Tom Bee, watching his son with a mix of parental pride and bemusement. "We were blackballed from tours because we were labeled as militant activists. Now, through the rap medium, you can make political statements and still make a living. That's the key difference."

Later that night, Robby Bee considers his group's "mission" as he stands under a shimmering burst of New Mexico stars. "You can do more in a three-minute song than in three years on Capitol Hill," he says. "All I need is a classroom. I'm ready."

## Link Wray: Shim Sham Club, New Orleans

*No Depression*, September-October 2002

Looking like an ancient Hopi trickster, his eyes gleaming with malevolent glee, Link Wray took the stage like a primal force of nature with the elemental power chords that announced he was ready to "Rumble"—the murderous instrumental that caused thousands of 1950s mothers to lock up their daughters, and countless latter-day guitar heroes to plug in.

Over the course of the next two hours, the seventy-three-year-old rockabilly icon reduced a crowd of New Orleans hipsters to a quivering mass of flayed neurons. By the time his umpteenth reprise of "Rumble" collided with his other monster riff hog, "Rawhide," for the final denouement, the question "how raw can a hide get?" had long since been rendered moot.

Half a century after Wray first punched holes in his amp and forever fuzzed up rock 'n' roll, his sound remains as vital as the muscular sinews of his arms. Flanked by his own band of gypsies—bassist Atom Ellis and drummer Doug Heifetz, both of Dieselhed—Wray spewed roiling distortions like Dick Dale's evil twin. Punctuating his performance with Cheshire cat grins, he stalked the stage in all-black Ninja garb, dragging Ellis by the neck of his bass into ad hoc duos and pumping Heifetz into overdrive. Beating her own sense of time on tambourine was Wray's zaftig Danish wife, Olive, who stepped in frequently to free his flailing ponytail from the strap of his black Fender Strat.

Bookended by his trademark sonic tsunamis, the emotional heart of Wray's performance came midway through the set, when a few strangulated yelps heralded a song cycle. Though powered by just one lung (the other was lost to tuberculosis during the Korean War), his voice, once loose, was a real crooner's instrument: buttery, rich and warm. He used it to great effect to amplify the bone-chilling lyrics of "Fallin' Rain": "I see a man cryin', lyin' on the cold, cold ground." Memorably covered by the Neville Brothers—"I cry every time I listen to them sing it," Wray confided—it resonated strongly in the Nevilles' hometown.

In a perfect piece of theater, Wray would have left us gasping for more after a jaw-dropping ninety minutes. Instead, like the Energizer Bunny, he kept going and going and going, almost past the point of no return. Then again, he may still be years ahead of his time and we're all just a bunch of wimps.

## X: Shim Sham Club, New Orleans

*No Depression*, January—February 2002

THE SHIM SHAM'S GOLD lame curtains sometimes open to reveal the club's risqué revue of old-timey burlesque. But on this particular night, before an oversold crowd in the heart of the French Quarter, the glitzy drapes framed another kind of revival: vintage X in all its glory, complete with founding guitarist Billy Zoom.

Kicking off with "Soul Kitchen", the band visibly shed two decades as they devoured the lion's share of their first four albums (recently reissued on Rhino), hitting all the classics from "White Girl" to "Nausea." And though most of the material was around twenty years old, it sounded as fresh as the day it first was minted and put Los Angeles on the map of the punkabilly avant garde.

Make that Zoomabilly. Though X owes its literate lyrics to John Doe and Exene Cervenka, whose off-center harmonizing can cut as close as a Bowie knife, it was Zoom's channeling of Carl Perkins via Johnny Ramone that gave the group its musical edge. (Neither Dave Alvin nor Tony Gilkyson ever quite filled Billy's blue suede shoes when he hung them up).

And the fifty something Zoom has grown even cooler with age. Beaming beatifically beneath his trademark bleached-blonde pompadour, Zoom didn't once break a sweat in biker leathers as he cranked out blistering riffs on his Gretsch Silver Jet. Just like the old days, he left the histrionics to his bandmates: Exene snaked her black-laced arms around the mike while DJ Bonebrake beat the drums into submission and John Doe drenched his shirt pumping the bass into overdrive.

Needless to say, the crowd went wild—so wild that at one point during "In This House That I Call Home," overly enthusiastic pogo-ers nearly knocked over a P.A. speaker. (Doe saved the day by threatening to sing "warm and fuzzy folk songs.") Throughout the nearly two-hour show, the mood remained so exuberant it almost felt like deja vu all over again: LA circa 1980, right in the midst of a bona fide people's revolution.

Zoom shot photos of the cheering throng at the end of the set while we loudly demanded an encore. The band made us wait until our voices grew hoarse, then aimed its best shot directly at the White House. "This song keeps coming back 'cause history repeats itself," Doe announced as they launched into "The New World." Written during the depths of their disenchantment with Reagan's America, it remains as relevant as ever in W's America: "This was supposed to be the New World!" Hundreds of voices were raised in collective indignation as house lights illuminated the mosh pit.

X made us work even harder for the second encore, which they delivered in spades, tearing into "Hungry Wolf" like they were eating Dick Cheney alive. "We love you guys!" Doe shouted while Exene blew kisses and Billy Zoom blessed the fans by handing out guitar picks. Second that emotion. And thanks for keeping the faith.

## Sonic Youth/Descension/Prolapse

*The Forum, London*

*huH*, **Summer 1996**

Live Rounds: Sonic Youth/Descension/Prolapse, The Forum, London England, April 19th, 1996

So charged was the electronic forcefield of a bill clearly designed by Sonic Youth to implode on impact, you could hear the house crackling by the end of the show. First it was just an isolated boot or two stomping on the Forum's industrial strength plastic pint glasses (which I'd been shamelessly scavenging off the floor to take home to the land of wimpy Coors cups). Then dozens of splintering cracks swelled into hundreds, becoming a tsunami of ecstatic static: an ambient ovation from an eighteen-hundred-plus crowd who'd just been spun full cycle from the Prolapse pre-soak through the heavy agitation of Descension (who caused a virtual riot) to the final spin-dry purges of Sonic Youth's *Washing Machine*.

But I'm getting ahead of myself.

Prolapse set the tone for the evening, and refused to pander to expectations. Instead of referencing their US debut disc *Back Saturday*—a savvy conjunction of blitzkrieg noise, pub-fueled rants, and pure, poisonous pop that's received considerable UK airplay—the six-piece kamikaze unit cut-and-pasted obscure old material with new works-in-progress. With equal audacity, ex-lovers/front persons Scotch Mick Derrick and Linda Steelyard ignored cameras poised to document their now-legendary physical fights and didn't lay a glove on each other. But during the brief half hour they commanded the stage in front of several hundred young fans who'd come early to see them, Prolapse killed.

Petite, pigtailed Linda (cute as a button in a vintage Mod mini) paced tiny circles on the stage, sprinting catlike to the mic to confront gangling, ale-swilling Mick, who stalked back and forth like a lumbering cartoon triangle, elbow jutting into space from an arm flung repeatedly across his face. Countering Mick's thrash-speed rants with a honeyed voice dipped in rat poison, Linda played prim school Marm in "Tungusta" (during which she deconstructed a paperback text of *The World's Biggest Mistakes*);

let loose some banshee screams on "Headless in a Beach Motel"; and deftly sidestepped Mick's motormouth spews on "Flash Stroke Oblique."

Cocooning this geometry of obsession were figure-like spirals of hyperactive guitars, a thunderous melodic bass and percussion that seemed to emanate from inside a kettle drum. All of which peaked on the set closer, "Flex"—the band's sole nod to *Back Saturday,* and its epic magnus opus—which rained down on the hopped-up crowd like radioactive manna from heaven.

Then Descension took the stage and all hell broke loose. "The real irony is that this 'riot' was caused by four middle-aged farts playin' 'free music!'" guitarist Stefan Jaworzyn later observed about an instantly historic scene Thurston Moore likened to a Sex Pistols show.

I was actually backstage querying Prolapse's Mick and Linda about tonight's ceasefire on their own violent confrontations—to which they respectively replied "we're on a one-day liking spree" and "we don't want to be that predictable"—when Descension drummer Tony Irving charged into a catcalling crowd of glass-hurling alternarockers and tackled a particularly obnoxious female heckler. But I caught the full force of the aftermath and honey, it was wild.

Descension soldiered on with grinding guitar feedback, screeching saxophone and formless double bass & drums, playing to a house as noisily divided as opposing team supported at a violent UK football match. Upstairs in the balcony, old Sonic Youth fans dating back to their early Glenn Branca experiments cheered lustily and loudly; down on the dancefloor, kids whose only links to SY were Nirvana and Lollapalooza escalated their chorus of boos. Only Sonic Youth, with feet planted firmly in both camps, could have bridged this cacophonous rift. Which is, of course, exactly what they proceeded to do.

Opening with a slow, majestic descension into distortion, strobe lights flashed on Kin Gordon centerstage while Thurston and Lee Renaldo staked out the periphery under asymmetrically suspended globes that pulsed with the hypnotic colors of Steve Shelley's drums. SY wove a deliciously sticky, multitextured web that lured old farts and newbies alike. Again and again, during an hour-and-a-half long set that segued into an expansive encore, they resolved the thesis/antithesis explicitly stated in "Skip Tracer"—"song forms and freedom"—with Hegelian synthesis.

That you can rock much harder when you roll deep and wide has always been Sonic Youth's subtext, but only with *Washing Machine* did they elevate it to text. And as their most consistently brilliant album since 1988's landmark *Daydream Nation,* that text warranted the explication which (amid numerous looping detours) it received tonight—an event as unpredictable as Prolapse's truce and Descension's call-to-arms, since Sonic Youth's usual m.o. Is to eschew current product.

Thus we actually got to witness Kim's paranoic freefall into "Becuz" and to pogo along with the blonde topknot thrashing above her demure baby blue dress on "Washing Machine." To revel in Thurston and Lee's parallel translations of "Skip Tracer's" "twister/dust buster/hospital bed." And to marvel at the impeccable choice of "Diamond Sea" as Thurston's personal dedication to "our good friends Prolapse and the group that will not be denied: Descension!"

Amidst enthusiastic cheers from young naysayers who shortly before had so vociferously decried Descension, Sonic Youth reminded the now solidly-united house that "your mirror's gonna crack when he breaks into it"—and proved the point with an odyssey worthy of Homer that was even more epic than the album's studio version. "The Diamond Sea" swelled up in angry waves, lashing us to the mast and taunting us with beautiful siren calls that dashed us against the rocks. Then slowly the storm subsided and we were eased to a distant shore where the keening cries of fledgling birds harmonized—however improbably—with the ponderous sound of ancient hippos sludging through the mud.

There wasn't much you could say after that except exactly what Thurston said: "Thank you, my beautiful friends."

## Kelley Deal 6000: Deal Stories of the Highway Patrol

*huH*, August 1996

"I LOVE THAT SONG 'Bag Of Nails'!"

Sebastian Bach, Skid Row's proudly unreformed head headbanger and a staunch Kelley Deal 6000 fan is screaming in my ear at the end of a crowded bar in New York's Brownies. Onstage, the Kelley Deal 6000 is oom-pah-pahing through the loopy metronomics of "Tick Tock" from their self-released album *Go to the Sugar Altar*, a cogent compilation of eleven wildly divergent tracks. The tune Bach's touting was nailed earlier tonight, and is the hardcore core of a three-song suite that begins with the Prince-like seduction of "Sugar," self-immolates in "A Hundred Trees," then Phoenix-rises from burning rubber to the ethereal aethyr of "Head of the Cult."

"'A Hundred Tires," I screamed back at my bar mate. "That's what it's called."

"Fuckin' heavy song, man," enthuses Bach, who's been adding back-of-the bar harmonies to Deal's shapeshifting vocals as an ad hoc preview of their upcoming duet project. "'A Hundred Bags of Tires" fuckin' rocks."

Hello? What's up with this "bags" fixation?

"It's a Freudian slip!" he shouts while the band gets all blurry around the edges with the languid "Nice." "That heavy riff is like a bag of nails being dragged across my forehead till blood runs into my fuckin' eyes and I cannot see. And if you've ever felt that sensation, that's what 'A Hundred Bags of Nails'...what's it called again?"

"'A Hundred Tires.'"

"Well, 'Bag of Nails' is what it sounds like!"

He's right. Of course, if you land elsewhere on *Sugar Altar*, it might sound like a dog show on Oz when Deal hollers "Trixie! Trixie!" to the sound of four hands clapping on "Trixie Delicious." Or like closing time at the Terminal Cafe if you lay down with "Mr. Goodnight" (Which the band literally does onstage tonight.) Or even vaguely like the Breeders if you hike into "Canyon," which wraps lines like "success fit me like a shroud (oh you fox)" in perfect pop-punk hooks—and which Deal did, in fact, write for the Breeders before her heroin bust and subsequent treatment pulled the plug on the band's infamous *Dreamland* sessions.

What it does not sound even vaguely like is a recovery album. Deal's clean & sober record (casually produced by Grifter Dave Shouse) is deliciously dirty & drunk and works like a voodou altar: seemingly random juxtapositions of objects all signify if you know how to read them. To these ears, it's a thirty-one-minute double album made out of silly putty that stretches and bounces and takes cartoon impressions.

"Cool! Well said. Like like that," Deal grins, taking a sip from her Mountain Dew. Her lanky hair still damp from stage sweat, she's sitting cross-legged on the floor of Brownies' cramped, graffiti's band room in comfy old jeans and a bright red blouse that picks up the piercing spark in the eyes of this one time technical analyst.

Though another band laid claim to Deal's original name Solid State—making way for Kelley Deal 6000's far cooler acronym of KD6K—the solidity of her state since swearing off drugs and booze is evidenced by her ease with a post-gig milieu that's hardly a Steven Tyler-style sobriety scene. Sebastian Bach's stretched out on an instrument shelf toking killer "stealth weed," drummer Nick Hook's downing whiskey-and-cranberry's and I'm on a stealth weed beer buzz.

None of which phases Deal, whose bond with her band—Hook, guitarist Marty Nedrich, and bassist Steve Salett—goes beyond camaraderie to KD6K mind meld. I mean, when Kelley Deal said *Go to the Sugar Altar*, these guys actually *built* one.

Our guided tour of Mystery Science Theater KD6K begins at that very altar. We'll be making stopovers in the Twin Cities (talk about Freudian slips!), where the Dayton, Ohio-bred Deal recovered in a St. Paul halfway house and is now based, as is her new indie label Nice Records. If you haven't been keeping track, Kelley's former fellow Breeder and still twin sister Kim—who spun the Breeders out of the Pixies—released her own sort-of-solo album, the lovely *Pacer*, with her new band, the Amps, earlier this year.

The way the sugar altar happened was, Nick and Marty were up really late. And they were naked. Well, Nick was clothed but Marty was naked. "Nobody was naked," clarifies Deal, who wasn't an eyewitness but as Head of the Cult knows all. Even the little statue of Buddha which inspired the altar builders wasn't naked. He was wearing a kind of loincloth and he didn't have a penis—"just like a Ken doll," we girls interject—which they noticed because they lifted his loincloth to check.

"Anyways, for some reason I went out and got more stuff and started making these weird symmetrical shapes," continues Marty, who put the sound of his peeing on tape tonight when he hijacked my recorder into the john. (Came out loud & clear, Marty!) "Then Nick joined me and Steve came in, and the next thing we knew we had this huge shrine of laundry detergent and pencils and potato chips and statues and straws."

The sugar itself was implied.

"And it was really well thought out," adds Nick, who knows this guy who shoplifted a $700.00 parrot, took it into a bar, put it in a drink, and replaced the eyeball with a maraschino cherry. ("True story," Deal confirms.) "There was a light bulb hanging above the altar, he continues," and we hung this carpenter's level that cast a shadow that landed perfectly on this card with a little king on it. And the shadow that was cast by the level made a perfect triangle."

Whoa! The eye in the pyramid strikes again! A clear sign from the unseen forces who govern *The Illuminati*, Robert Anton Wilson's proto-'60s take on the Ultimate Conspiracy Theory.

When Kelley Deal first entered Hazeldon clinic in April of '95 she brought along "a little light reading." You guessed it. She did not, however, plow her way through the whole *Illiminati Trilogy*. "In the very beginning, there's all this pot smoking and wild sex and I'm like, I do *not* need to be reading this in treatment," she recalls. "But I really like the phrase, 'the head of the cult flies westward.' I thought that was so cool. The head...of the cult...flies eastward."

Which she herself had literally just done. After signing for the delivery of the infamous Emory package of heroin in Dayton, Ohio and plea bargaining for treatment—a process jumpstarted by an intervention by Kim and her family—she flew westward to Minnesota. Well, northwestward.

"You're right," she laughs. "So I'm in the treatment place with all this stuff about God, and like my dad is a physicist and my mom is Pentecostal Holiness." Talk about a house divided. "No kidding."

To keep her sense of humor amidst the pieties of rehab, she cobbled together a kind of Pentecostal physics with an enlightenment system lifted from a hippie era cult called Arica. "I don't give a shit about this cult, except that it made for an interesting story," she notes. And so it does. Arica's achievable levels go beyond a mere twelve steps all the way into the hundreds, two-thousand being the highest. The fact that such states are achieved through meditation and pot smoking—which Deal, of course, had given up—just made the punchline better when she anointed herself State 6000 in the gorgeously orchestrated spaciness of "Head of the Cult."

Deal has variously described State 6000 as "like nirvana" and "really unserene, a state of ultimate pettiness." (Another Freudian slip?) But when it comes right down to it, she just thought it sounded cool. "It sounds like a Motocross race: Kelley Deal 6000, vroom, vroom, vroom!"

## Golden Palominos: They Shoot Horses, Don't They?

*huH*, October 1996

LATE SUNDAY NIGHT, SUMMER of '95. The only light in a New York apartment glows from a computer screen, framing the burning-coal eyes of a stunning young woman with bone white skin and jet-black hair. Her fingers dance feverishly across the keyboard, fast, faster, fastest, she types one-hundred words a minute and still she can barely keep up with the Voice inside her head, the Voice speaking from beyond the grave, the Voice recounting the hours and minutes before her death at the hands of a serial killer in exquisite, painful detail, from the moment she wakes up in a trunk where "the air is blue-black, brown-black, black-black" through the last rites she administers to herself before a shotgun presses between her eyes. "The last thing I hear is a click," the Voice concludes.

"And then what?" asks Nicole Blackman, turning to face the unseen presence that's haunted her ever since she saw the Voice's face flashed on the local news and knew in her guts the missing woman was already dead. "And then what?" Dead silence.

"It was like the radio was turned off," says Blackman, who's been describing her channeling of "Victim"—the first cut off the Golden Palominos' *Dead Inside*, her "snuff film soundtrack" collaboration with Anton Fier—quite matter-of-factly over a glass of red wine and an endive salad at her midtown neighborhood bar. "Like they say about ghosts, here was a spirit who was caught between worlds," adds the reigning diva of "broken word." who tongue-lashed Lollapalooza '94 and skewers pop culture "Dogma" on KMFDM's acclaimed new *CD Xtort*. "She didn't get a chance to say what she wanted to say before this happened to her, and once she'd accomplished that, she moved on."

The same could be said of Anton Fier, who's been reinventing the Golden Palominos in successive incarnations since its inception thirteen years ago. ("At some point, every musician in America has been in the Golden Palominos," Blackman quips about an ever-mutating lineup whose alumni include Michael Stipe, Matthew Sweet and Syd Straw.) This time out, Fier's goal was "to make something that doesn't exist in any other format" by sculpting a soundscape with spoken words as a primary instrument, and he originally intended to use several vocal collaborators. But when he heard Blackman's invocation of prophet-of-doom "Cassandra" on the *Myth: Dream of the World* compilation, produced by longtime Fier collaborator Bill Laswell—which features an eclectic roster of artists from Iggy Pop and Lady Kier to George Clinton—he was hooked.

"What first attracted me to Nicole was the sound of her voice," says Fier, speaking by phone from the studio where he spent the past year digitally mixing live instrumentalists and computer audio bites with the sound Blackman created during an intense, month-long writing-and-recording marathon. "Once I got past the sound of her voice and heard what she was actually saying," he adds, "I knew I could finally make a record that pushed as far as the imagination will take you."

A record that subverts the mind by enticing the body with densely textured ambient grooves that "taste like hot candy" in "Ride," smell like "a perfume too heavy for summer" in "Drown," feel like "teeth-scraped knuckles in "The Ambitious Are." sound like the "frozen chrome" of "Metal Eye" and "burn" and "bleed" like the "red, red howling" of "Curses."

"It was enormously liberating working with Anton," says Blackman, whose imagination unleashed an entire pantheon of "corrupted Goddesses," from the cloistered anorexic starving herself into sainthood in "Holy" to the future-sex android of "Metal Eye," while listening to Fier's tracks-in-progress on headphones. "I knew nothing I wrote was gonna be too violent, too dark, too sexual. He was constantly encouraging me to go deeper, go darker, get to the core. Everything was written in a fever. I'd stay up for twenty-four, forty-eight-hour periods and start to hallucinate, which was a very surreal experience. All these endlessly intriguing characters spoke to me, and I trusted them to tell me the truth. I just had to ask them the right questions and let them talk."

What they say is pretty disturbing. Disconnected from an earth debased by the concrete jungle of postmodern futureshock, these superheroic X-women take to the sky, live under water, and inhabit "other people's machines" while parrying violence, sexual abuse and their own obsessions. "None of them is weak, and virtually every woman is poised on the brink of transformation," says Blackman, "'Victim' is probably the most self-realized, because she's gone through a doorway and realized she's not coming back, which gives her a sense of peace." It's also Fier's favorite track, which is why he put it first—despite Blackman's initial misgivings about opening the album with the very darkest of very dark cuts. "As a clarion call of 'the Golden Palominos are dead, long live the Golden Palominos,' it really works," she notes now. Fier, a man of few words, says simply "this album is the best work I've ever done. Everything I have to say is on that record."

The titular "Dead Inside" (from "Metal Eye") is another Fier favorite, and hardly your typical club house mantra. But the album's super-seductive grooves—out of which the vocals alternately leap in boldface and bury themselves in dissenting, polyphrenic footnotes—make it eminently danceable. "Which is like the most subversive thing you can do," Blackman points out with a sly grin. "That pop dance element draws people in, gets you in its grip, everyone's enjoying it, they're like 'I'm dead inside' on the dance floor—and then they realize what they're listening to. Which is great. People should be thinking on the dance floor."

# Afterword

Back in the late summer of 2024, after I'd finally finished this book and gotten lots of positive feedback, I was chomping at the bit to start sending it to agents and publishers. But then two things happened that threw me completely off course, and ushered in what I later dubbed "my terrible, horrible, awful year."

In mid-August, shortly before my should-have-been-lucky seventy-seventh birthday, a real estate agent showed up on our porch asking to see our house, which she said had just been put up for auction. Say what!? My husband Donald Miller and I had lived in the home we bought in New Orleans for twenty-three years, and always made our mortgage payments on time. Or at least I thought we did. Every month, I'd faithfully send him my share of the mortgage, but because we had separate checking accounts, I had no idea that he'd stopped paying our bill nearly three years ago. But it got worse.

Upstairs in his studio, I discovered a crate of unpaid mortgage bills, along with two notices from the sheriff's department saying the property was going up for auction, which Donald took off our door and hid from me. We were about to be evicted, and I only found out by chance.

I immediately began scrambling for lawyers who could help us, and eventually found an excellent legal aid attorney, who was able to stave off eviction for a couple months. Donald watched from the sidelines while I did all the work until he finally fully checked out. Literally. He died on October 22nd, 2024, after his kidneys and liver completely failed, which was no big surprise. A former junkie, he'd also abused alcohol for years…

I was filled with rage and grief simultaneously, since we'd been together for over thirty years as, in my humble opinion, one of the world's coolest couples. Amidst all this, I had to stage a couple of eviction/estate sales, find a new place to live and move what I could from a big house where I had my own studio into a small one-bedroom apartment. It was brutal.

I couldn't have done any of this without a lot of help from my friends, and the music that helped me power through it all. Shortly after I moved to my new apartment, I got a Wonderboom remote speaker that lets me stream and blast my favorite artists, many of whom appear in the pages of this book. And despite the fact that I'm recovering from a broken femur and have to hobble around with a cane, I still go out to see live music whenever I can.

Armed with my trusty Rollator (a walker with wheels), I went to both weekends of the New Orleans Jazz & Heritage Festival, which is spread out over the entire New Orleans Fair Grounds. I also wrote about it, natch. The final piece in this collection is a live-show review of Jazz Fest that I wrote for *DownBeat*, which was published in late May.

A fortuitous connection with an old friend led me to Rare Bird, which turned out to be a great fit. And for that I'm eternally grateful.

**—New Orleans, Louisiana, June 2025**

# Acknowledgements

I'M FOREVER GRATEFUL TO my dear friend and partner in crime, Linda Kelly, without whom this book literally would not exist. After I was diagnosed with stage 4 terminal cancer, and decided I wanted to leave behind a legacy of my best music writing, Linda flew out from San Francisco to help me achieve that goal. For two weeks, she sat at my laptop and diligently digitized a slew of old print newspapers and magazines where my work originally appeared in the early '90s, and made quick work of it, too. She's a lightning fast typist.

Though he could care less about most of the music I covered, my late husband, the avant garde guitarist Donald Miller, was always supportive of my writing and quick to praise my pieces on his own heroes like the great jazz improviser Kidd Jordan. He also thought My Life Under Deadline was a great idea for a book, and would be thrilled to know it got published.

Special thanks to Donald's frequent musical collaborator, John Coogan, aka 99 Hooker, who gave me lots of positive feedback over the past few years and personally connected me with Rare Bird.

I also got great support and editorial advice from my old friends and fellow writers Larry Smith (Six-Word Memoir Project) and Piper Kerman (Orange Is the New Black), who helped me keep this project on track.

My dear friend Pamela Des Barres, author of several of her own books, helped me hone my chops in her "Let It Bleed" writing workshops, encouraged me to pursue my dream of compiling this book, and remains a guiding star.

*My Life Under Deadline* might never have been written without the wisdom I gleaned from my mentor and editor, the late Eve Muir, who edited my first book Flea Market America. Though Eve died long before I began compiling this book, she helped set me on my path as a writer decades ago, and I know she'd be pleased with the results.

Shoutout to Steve Bloom, my High Times editor in the '90s, who assigned me a cover story on the late Janis Joplin and gave me the opportunity (and travel budget) to fly to Texas and spend several days with the 13th Floor Elevators' father of psychedelia, Roky Erickson.

Countless other friends, editors and fellow writers also helped keep me on track, but if I try to list all of them, I'm sure to leave somebody out.

Last, but by no means least, kudos to my fellow New Orleanian Rickie Lee Jones, who encouraged me to write my own memoir while we were discussing her compulsively readable *Last Chance Texaco*, and graciously consented to write the Foreward to this book.

www.ingramcontent.com/pod-product-compliance
Lightning Source LLC
Chambersburg PA
CBHW020840120726
47946CB00005B/5/J

* 9 7 8 1 6 4 4 2 8 5 3 7 4 *